UNIVERSITY DYNAMICS
AND
EUROPEAN INTEGRATION

HIGHER EDUCATION DYNAMICS

VOLUME 19

SCOPE OF THE SERIES

Higher Education Dynamics is a bookseries intending to study adaptation processes and their outcomes in higher education at all relevant levels. In addition it wants to examine the way interactions between these levels affect adaptation processes. It aims at applying general social science concepts and theories as well as testing theories in the field of higher education research. It wants to do so in a manner that is of relevance to all those professionally involved in higher education, be it as ministers, policy-makers, politicians, institutional leaders or administrators, higher education researchers, members of the academic staff of universities and colleges, or students. It will include both mature and developing systems of higher education, covering public as well as private institutions.

The titles published in the series are listed at the end of this volume.

University Dynamics
and
European Integration

Edited by

Peter Maassen
University of Oslo, Norway

and

Johan P. Olsen
University of Oslo, Norway

 Springer

A C.I.P. Catalogue record for this book is available from the Library of Congress.

ISBN-13 978-1-4020-5970-4 (HB)
ISBN-13 978-1-4020-5971-1 (e-book)

Published by Springer,
P.O. Box 17, 3300 AA Dordrecht, The Netherlands.

www.springer.com

Printed on acid-free paper

TABLE OF CONTENTS

HARRY F. DE BOER is senior researcher at the Center for Higher Education Policy Studies, University of Twente, Enschede, the Netherlands. His research topics in the field of higher education concern governance and steering models at macro level, institutional governance, management en leadership styles in professional organizations, strategic planning en decision making. He frequently contributed to higher educations studies in these areas, including articles in Higher Education Policy, Public Administration, the European Journal of Education and Tertiary Education and Management. Moreover, he has conducted several reports for the Dutch ministry and is lecturing and tutoring in courses in higher education management.

ÅSE GORNITZKA is senior researcher at ARENA – Centre for European Studies, University of Oslo. Building on previous comparative research on policy and governance in higher education and research, her current research focus is on European integration in the field of education and research policy and institutionalization of a European dimension in these policy areas. She holds a doctoral degree from the Faculty of Public Administration, University of Twente, the Netherlands, and a masters' degree from University of Oslo, department of Political Science. She has been senior researcher at the Norwegian Institute for Studies in Research and Higher Education (NIFU) and at the Centre for Higher Education Policy Studies (CHEPS) at the University of Twente. She has been a visiting scholar at SCANCOR, Stanford University and at the department of sociology, Michigan State University.

PETER MAASSEN is professor in higher education studies at the Faculty of Education, University of Oslo, where he is also the director of *Hedda*, a consortium of European centres and institutes in the area of higher education studies. His academic areas of specialization are "the public governance of higher education," and "higher education and development." Previously he was working at the Center for Higher Education Policy Studies (CHEPS), University of Twente, the Netherlands, where he was the director from 1997 to 2000. He is the editor of the book series Higher Education Dynamics (Springer Publishers), and has written and (co-) edited numerous books, book chapters and articles (in 6 languages) in journals of higher education, political science, management studies, and policy analysis.

GUY NEAVE is professor of comparative higher education policy at the Center for Higher Education Policy Studies (CHEPS), University of Twente, Enschede, the Netherlands, and has been (until recently) director of research at the International

Association of Universities (IAU). He has published over 150 articles in scientific journals, written more than 60 chapters in multi-authored books, (co-) authored 15 books and (co-) edited a similar number, produced more than 40 consultant and technical reports and given over 100 key-note and paper presentations at conferences. He has served for a decade as joint editor of the European Journal of Education, as editor of Higher Education Policy since 1988, Joint Editor-in-Chief (with Burton R. Clark) of the Encyclopaedia of Higher Education (Pergamon Press), and general series editor of "Issues in Higher Education" (Elsevier Science). In 1999 he became member of the National Academy of Education of the USA.

THORSTEN NYBOM is since 2001 professor of history and director of International Relations at Örebro University, Sweden. He has a PhD in History from the University of Stockholm, 1978. Previously he has held positions as associate Professor at Uppsala University 1980–1989; Director of the Swedish Council for Studies of Higher Education, 1989–1998; Professor at the Graduate School of Interdisciplinary Studies, University of Linköping, 1994–1998; Visiting Professor, Center for Studies in Higher Education, UC Berkeley, 1991 and 1996; and Stiftungs-Professor at the Humboldt-Universität zu Berlin, 1998–2001. Nybom has published numerous articles and books in the fields of higher education and science studies, most recently (with Neave and Blückert) *The European Research University – An Historical Parenthesis?* (2006).

JOHAN P. OLSEN is professor in political science at ARENA – Centre for European Studies, University of Oslo. Either alone or in collaboration with colleagues, he has written or edited 20 books and written more than 100 book chapters and articles, many of them in leading international journals. Together with James G. March and Michael D. Cohen he developed the "garbage can"-model of organizational decision making, and together with March he launched the concept of "new institutionalism" in the mid 1980s. He holds an honorary doctorate at Åbo Academy, Finland, Copenhagen University, Denmark, the Erasmus University, Rotterdam, the Netherlands, and the University of Tromsø, Norway. He is a Fellow at the Center for Advanced Studies in the Behavioral Sciences at Stanford University, California and he has received the American Political Science Association's John Gaus Award for his lifelong contribution to public administration and political science in 2003 and the The Aaron Wildavsky Enduring Contribution Award (with James G. March) in 2004.

CARLO SALERNO currently works as a Senior Analyst with the United States Government Accountability Office (GAO). From 2001 until the summer of 2006 he was a Senior Research Associate with the Center for Higher Education Policy Studies (CHEPS) at the University of Twente in the Netherlands. His research focuses on the economics of higher education with special attention to issues surrounding universities' behavior as nonprofit organizations as well as their productive and cost efficiency. Since completing his PhD in the Higher Education program at the Pennsylvania State University in 2002, he has authored or co-authored a number of monographs, journal articles and book chapters in the areas of higher education privatization, financing, per-student cost estimation.

BJØRN STENSAKER is working at NIFU STEP in Oslo as programme director for studies on higher education. He holds a doctoral degree from the School of Business, Technology and Public Administration at the University of Twente in the Netherlands, and has a special interest in studies of quality, leadership and organisational change in higher education. Stensaker is the Editor-in-chief of *Tertiary Education and Management (TEAM)*, one of the editors of *Quality* in *Higher Education*, and a former member of the Executive Board of EAIR – The European Higher Education Society.

PREFACE

The subject of this book is the institutional dynamics of the European University. We are interested in how this institution is affected by ongoing processes of European integration. What attempts are undertaken at the European level to build up institutional capacity in the areas of higher education and research policy? How do these emerging European capacities relate to the traditional national policy making responsibilities and arrangements in these areas? How is the organization and functioning of the European University influenced by the adding of a new governance layer with respect to higher education and research? How do the developments with respect to European higher education and research policy compare to the situation in other, federal systems, such as the USA? This book explores the visions underlying the attempts to reform the European University as well as two European integration processes affecting University dynamics. Above all, the book presents a frame of analysis and a long-term research agenda addressing the above questions.

At the beginning of the twenty first century there is a clear political "momentum" for the University in Europe. The Lisbon summit of 2000 has (re-)confirmed the role of the University as a central institution in the "Europe of Knowledge." Consequently, we can observe that since 2000 the Commission has become highly interested in the University as an object of European level policy-making. This is clearly inspired by the interpretation of the University's central role in connecting education, research, and innovation, and the assumption that the effectiveness of this connection is considered to be of major importance for the competitiveness of Europe's economies, and the level of social cohesion of its societies. In the Commission's communications and other policy papers the University has either directly or indirectly become a central concern, and as support to the Commission's views on the University's role in the European knowledge economy, various background reports have been produced by the Commission's bureaucracy analyzing specific features of the European University especially in comparison to universities in non-EU OECD countries.

Nonetheless, as is argued throughout this book, the evidence used as a basis for European level reform proposals with respect to the University is very "thin." There are important gaps between the problems identified and the solutions advocated in the European level policy debates, and the quality of the analyses and evidence reformers have forwarded. The University as an object of policy at the European level can be argued to be over-debated and under-investigated. This presents the main rationale for this book: contributing to the improvement of the theoretical and empirical basis for understanding ongoing reform- and change processes in higher education in Europe.

Our view is that the specific nature and history of the European University as a social institution are widely neglected in the current reform efforts. In addition, research on higher education is of a strongly "sector-isolatedness," nature that is the image is presented that the University and its reforms are disconnected from developments and reforms in other sectors. Further solid comparative higher education studies on the effects of European integration on University changes are rare. This can be attributed, amongst other things, to a lack of funding, a lack of research capacity, and a dominant national focus in higher education studies. This is all the more an unfortunate situation since the University is one of the few European institutions where European integration efforts can be argued to affect the institutions' basic activities directly. The authors contributing to this book operate on the basis that combining general conceptualisations and knowledge on European integration processes with specific empirical knowledge on higher education forms a prime way for breaking through this stalemate situation.

The origins of this book go back to a seminar organized in Oslo, Norway, 27 and 28 April 2006 by ARENA, Centre for European Studies, with the Faculty of Education (both University of Oslo), and NIFU STEP, an independent research institute in Oslo. A small group of researchers from these organizations came together with colleagues from Sweden and the Netherlands for discussing possibilities for cooperation and strategies for improving the knowledge basis with respect to changes in the European University. The agenda presented at the end of the book indicates the research areas where we feel our joint research efforts should be focused on the next 5 to 10 years. We hope that the route for further research set out in this volume will show that research on the institutional dynamics of the European University is not only necessary for strengthening the knowledge basis under the European level reforms proposals and efforts in this area, but will also contribute to a better overall understanding of European integration processes at large and their effects.

At various stages in writing University Dynamics and European Integration the authors received critical comments of a number of colleagues: we want to thank Voldemar Tomusk, as well as Simon Schwartzman, Romulo Pinheiro, Stig Slipersæter, and Monika Nerland, for their input into the April 2006 seminar in Oslo, and the participants to the Douro6 seminar, October 2006 in Pinhão, Portugal, for their comments on two of the chapters of this volume. We are especially indebted to Anne Corbett and Jürgen Enders who provided us with valuable feedback after the seminar. Our thanks also go to Øivind Bratberg, Sverker Gustavsson, Ragnvald Kalleberg, James M. March, Nils Roll-Hansen and Ulf Sverdrup for their comments on the ARENA working paper (No. 15, March 2005) that forms the basis for chapter 2 in this volume. Finally we want to thank Jennifer Olson for her support in the processing of the manuscript.

Peter Maassen
Johan P. Olsen

Oslo, October 2006

PART 1

INTRODUCTION

EUROPEAN DEBATES ON THE KNOWLEDGE INSTITUTION: THE MODERNIZATION OF THE UNIVERSITY AT THE EUROPEAN LEVEL

Johan P. Olsen and Peter Maassen

DEMANDS FOR RADICAL REFORM

European universities[1] face demands for urgent and radical reform. A standard claim is that environments are changing rapidly and that universities are not able or willing to respond adequately. It is necessary to rethink and reshape their internal order and role in society simply because European universities do not learn, adapt and reform themselves fast enough. Reform plans comprise the purposes of universities, that is, definitions of what the University is, can be and should be, criteria for quality and success, the kinds of research, education and services to be produced, and for whom. Reform plans also include the universities' organization and financial basis, their governance structures, who should influence the future dynamics of universities, and according to what principles.

The reform rhetoric is both problem driven and solution driven. On the one hand, reform demands are raised in an atmosphere of a perceived performance crisis, or even an identity crisis. In particular, Europe's capacity to compete in the global "knowledge economy" is seen to be affected negatively by the perceived incapability of her universities to meet the fast growing demand for higher-level skills and competencies, and research-based commercial technologies. Europe has to prioritize university modernization because her universities are lagging behind the best universities in the USA and because upcoming China and India will make competition among universities and economies even stiffer. On the other hand, reform proposals are launched in an atmosphere of high hopes and expectations. Reformers do not despair. They claim to know what has to be done: "The challenge for Europe is clear. But so is the solution" (Schleicher 2006: 2).

The solution prescribes a new organizational paradigm, rebalancing external and internal relations of authority and power in university governance. It presents the kind of University that is deemed to be necessary for the "Europe of knowledge"

---

[1] In this book the term University refers to the traditional European research University as well as other types of higher education institution. European universities have currently more than 17 million students and some 1.5 million staff members working within 4000 institutions (Commission 2006b). The World Higher Education Data base identifies over 16,500 higher education institutions, of which 9760 university level institutions, from 184 countries and territories (IAU 2005).

3

P. Maassen and J. P. Olsen (eds.), University Dynamics and European Integration, 3–22.
© 2007 *Springer.*

as envisioned by the European Commission (Commission 2003a, 2004b; Corbett 2005). The claim is that the solution, if implemented successfully, has a potential for improving performance by changing university practices and structures developed over long historical periods, as well as conceptions of the proper role of government in the economy and society. The basic ideas are well known from the New Public Management and from neo-liberal public sector reforms (Hood et al. 2004). The remedies offered are celebrating private enterprises and competitive markets and they can be seen as "a solution looking for problems" (Cyert and March 1963; Cohen et al. 1972), and usually finding them, in all sectors of society.

The "solution" is to a large extent based upon causal and normative beliefs that are taken as givens, that is, it is in general not necessary to argue for them. The main assumption, in simplified form, is that more complex and competitive economic and technological global environments require rapid adaptation to shifting opportunities and constraints.[2] This, in turn, requires more determined university strategies and a strong, unitary and professional leadership and management capacity that matches those of modern private enterprises. University management needs to control available financial and human resources and the power of the executive and the central administration of the University has to be strengthened. Collegial, disciplinary and democratic internal organization and individual academic freedom are viewed as hindrances to well-timed decisions and good performance.

Furthermore, it is argued that because government interference tends to reduce adaptability, performance and competitiveness, government and politics should have a less prominent role in the governance of universities as well as in society at large. Universities should have more autonomy and greater distance to government. Intervention by public authorities should be at arms length and not go beyond providing a "leveled playing field," clear mission statements and accountability mechanisms for the results achieved. Universities should, however, be better integrated into society, in particular into industry and the business community, and should be governed by bodies that reflect a wide range of stakeholders. Third party evaluation and quality assurance should be organized through a variety of university-external bodies, such as research councils and accreditation agencies.

Reformers argue that the proposed changes will advance knowledge, produce functional improvement, and benefit society in general. The dominant language is emphasizing "modernization," the economic functions of the University, necessary adaptations to economic and technological change, and economy and efficiency. The vision is a University that is dynamic and adaptive to consumers and that gives priority to innovation, entrepreneurship and market orientation.

In contrast, it can be argued that the currently dominant reform rhetoric is only one among several competing visions and understandings of the University and its dynamics. What is at stake is "what kind of University for what kind of society" and

---

[2] As will be documented later, this stylized version of reform plans can be found in a number of reform documents as well as in the writing of advisors, commentators and lobbyists such as Soete (2005) and Schleicher (2006).

which, and whose values, interests and beliefs should be given priority in University governance and reforms? These are basic political questions that are unlikely to be completely free of legitimate tensions and conflicts.[3] Attention to the political dynamics of University reform is also required by historical realities. Throughout history there have been colliding visions and power struggles over the autonomy, content, organization, governance and financing of universities. Academic autonomy and freedom have been challenged by political, economic, social, military, and religious power-centers with competing concepts of the good society, university and performance, and with shifting trust in the University's ability to settle its own affairs and its relations with society without external intervention. Furthermore, attention to the political dynamics of reform is required because the rebalancing of power within and over the University is part of a general rebalancing of Europe's political and economic institutional order (Olsen 2007).

THE EUROPEAN DIMENSION

While reform demands are currently raised, and reforms are taking place, at the local, regional and national level, this section of the paper primarily explores the significance of the emerging *European* layer of cooperation and policy making for University dynamics. A key question is: How do European processes of cooperation, integration and policy making affect the institutional dynamics of the University?

In Europe, universities have historically played an important role in nation- and state-building, that is, in supplying states with educated manpower, building a national consciousness and identity, integrating national elites, and providing a national research capacity for economic and social development. As a result, research and even more so education has turned out to be politically sensitive, making it difficult to achieve institutionalized European-level cooperation and integration in these policy areas.[4] The idea of a European University was, for example, presented at the Messina Conference in 1955 and one argument was that integration should not be limited to the economic domain but should also include some form of cultural integration (Corbett 2005: 26). Yet member states did not want Commission control and university rectors preferred a federation of universities and freedom from intervention (Corbett 2005: 36, 40, 48).

---

[3] Democracy involves the belief that human destiny can (and should) be influenced decisively by human will, reason, and experience. Different conceptions of democracy, however, suggest different roles for institutions of higher education, for example, according to whether democracy is seen as the aggregation of pre-existing individual preferences, or as also forming human beings into democratic citizens and members of a political community (March and Olsen 2000).

[4] Nevertheless, in 2006 the European Union celebrated 30 years of European cooperation in education (IP/06/212). For the history of research cooperation, see Guzzetti (1995). Corbett observes that in 1971 eight DGs were undertaking education-related services and there was rivalry about which DG and Commissioner should be responsible for higher education. Corbett also traces the establishing of some common principles, a rudimentary bureaucracy, an organized action capacity, and a line in the budget (Corbett 2005: 63, 68, 102, 110, 174).

However, recently it has become more common to emphasize the need for a European perspective on universities and university governance has become embedded in a variety of organized settings beyond the territorial state. There are trans-national, intergovernmental and supranational processes of cooperation and policy making and new actors, issues, solutions, resources and modes of governance have been introduced. The Commission, in particular, has claimed that a dynamic knowledge-based economy (and society) requires modernization of the European University. The president of the Commission and the Commissioners responsible for higher education and for research observe that universities have never featured so high on the Commission's agenda, that the political interest in universities is growing, and that reforms are urgently needed (Barroso 2005; Figel 2006; Potočnik 2006b).[5] The vision of the European Research Area (ERA) was launched by the Commission (2000a, b) and formally decided by the Lisbon European Council in March 2000 (European Council 2000; Commission 2002a). The intergovernmental Bologna Declaration and the subsequent process, aiming to establish a European Higher Education Area (EHEA) without borders in 2010, have also aroused high expectations.[6]

While the Commission sometimes plays down its own role, it has also produced a steady stream of documents promoting reforms of a radical nature.[7] Common institutions have been established and *The Charter for Researchers* and *The Code of Conduct for the Recruitment of Researchers*, specifying roles and responsibilities have been developed (Commission 2005b). The European Research Council is presented as a revolutionary institutional innovation and an autonomous entity under independent scientific leadership (Potočnik 2006b). The European Institute of Technology is portrayed as Europe's 'knowledge flagship' bringing together research, education and innovation. One of its missions is also supposed to be "to disseminate new organizational and governance models." Its governing board is to consist of academics and business people who are imagined to be able to select the best areas for long-term investment in research 10–15 years ahead (Commission 2006a: 7; also Figel 2006: 11).

The launching of the ERA was supposed to provide member states with a framework for voluntary coordination within an internal knowledge market and for "strengthening and opening up new perspectives" (Commission 2002a). However, the demand for radical change and the mistrust of university traditions are clearly expressed:

"We need a new model – we need something which can demonstrate to countries where university models still hark back to the days of Humboldt, that today there are additional ways of doing things" (Figel 2006: 12).

---

[5] Ján Figel is Commissioner in charge of Education and Training and Janez Potočnik is Commissioner in charge of Science and Research.

[6] For examples, Corbett claims that: "The European Higher Education Area may be set to transform the European states' higher education institutions as fundamentally as the nation state changed the medieval universities" (Corbett 2005: 192).

[7] For example: "The Commission is not a direct actor in the modernization of universities, but it can play a catalytic role, providing political impetus and targeted funding in support of reform and modernization" (Commission 2006b: 11). See, however, (Commission 2000a, b, 2002a, c, 2003a, 2005a, b, 2006a, b, and c).

The "new model" proposed by the Commission comes close to the stylized, dominant reform model sketched above. It questions the Humboldtian ideal of a community of autonomous professors (chapter 3) and doubts that self-governing scholars will produce the best results for society at large. It emphasizes leadership, management and entrepreneurship more than individual academic freedom, internal democracy and the organizing role of academic disciplines. Universities should have more autonomy and also be more accountable and this requires new internal governance systems based on strategic priorities and on professional management of human resources, investment and administrative procedures. There is a mismatch between, on the one hand, the traditional disciplinary structures and the institutional set-up for research in most European countries and, on the other hand, the requirements of new leading sciences, such as biotechnology and nano-technology (Potočnik 2006b: 5; also Aho et al. 2006). Universities must overcome their fragmentation into faculties, departments, laboratories and administrative units and target their efforts collectively on institutional priorities for research, teaching and services (Commission 2006b: 5–6). All this "necessitates new institutional and organizational approaches to staff management, evaluation and funding criteria, teaching and curricula and, above all, to research and research training." There should be multilateral consortia, joint courses, joint degree arrangements, networks and cooperation (Commission 2006b: 8–9). The Commission also opens for a further separation of teaching from research and for more differentiation and stratification among universities, so that not all research and higher education will be of equal excellence, yet with fewer differences between countries and more differences within each country.

The reform program lacks an institution and sector specific view taking into account the specific properties of the University as an academic institution and higher education as a policy sector. It is argued that the EU has already supported the conversion process of sectors such as the steel industry or agriculture; it now faces the imperative to modernize its "knowledge industry" and in particular its universities (Commission 2005a: 10). According to the Commission the "knowledge industry," like other industries, urgently needs reform and the goals and remedies are basically the same as for other sectors.[8]

Indicators of reform success are primarily economic. The ERA is a key component of the Lisbon process and the proposed University reforms reflect the aspirations to make Europe the most competitive economy within 2010. Research and higher education are identified as key instruments for economic performance and growth and for mastering global competition. The guiding philosophy for research policy is to create a single market for research – the creation, diffusion, and exploitation of scientific and technical knowledge (Potočnik 2006b), a vision that dovetails nicely with the general

---

[8] The urgency aspect is found in several documents from the Commission and also in reports from expert groups, such as the Aho-group on "Creating an Innovative Europe": "A final word – The opportunity to implement the proposed actions will not be available for much longer. Europe and its citizens should realize that their way of life is under threat but also that the path to prosperity through research and innovation is open if large scale action is taken now by their leaders **before it is too late**" (Aho et al. 2006: 30).

8

CHAPTER 1

market-building ideology of the EU. Strengthening the triangle between research, higher education and innovation is supposed to make Europe more successful in converting its research achievements into commercial technologies (Potočnik 2006a). While the Commission claims that there is a reform consensus,[9] it also observes that there is a general need to build trust in science and technology among ordinary citizens. The general public in Europe is seen to become more concerned about the social and economic impact of scientific and technological advances, as well as about how decisions relating to these developments are taken.[10]

International competitiveness and the University's ability to do good for society are seen to be "held back" by the role historically played by governments (Figel 2006: 7).[11] The state is supposed to have a less dominant role as funder, receiver of graduates, and user of knowledge. There should be governance by standardization, dialogue, benchmarking, and exchange of "good practice." "Soft" methods, such as the Open Method of Coordination (OMC), are presented as an alternative to the "hard" laws that cannot easily be used in European coordination of the sector. The accountability of the University to society also requires an external system of quality assurance and accreditation, and a move from state control to being accountable to society and customers (Commission 2005a). There should be external controls through increased competition, externally defined standards and goals, demands for results that can be documented in numbers, and external monitoring units.

Reforms are driven both by the fear of falling behind and by promises of new resources. There is a funding deficit and investments in European universities need to be increased and diversified. The average gap in resources compared to the USA is, according to the Commission, some €10,000 per student (Commission 2006b: 4). As is argued by European Commission President Barroso (2006) "Europe's economic future depends on having the best educated and trained people, with the full range of skills and the adaptability required in a 'knowledge economy.' That is why we must boost investment in higher education significantly. The Commission is suggesting a target of 2% of GDP by 2010." Obviously, this proposal for a 2% of GDP investment target for higher education has to be distinguished from the 3% of GDP investment target with respect to R&D as agreed upon by the Barcelona European Council in 2002 (Commission 2002b).

Of course, the reform rhetoric is multi-vocal and evolving over time and the Commission is not blind to other aspects than the economic ones. Nevertheless, when a

---

[9] The Commission, for example, writes that "discussions at European level show an increasing willingness to modernize [university] systems, and the agenda mapped out below is not, in essence contested" (Commission 2006b: 4).

[10] This is also a theme found in many documents from the Commission and, again, it is a view that is supported by an expert group appointed by the Commission (Ormala et al. 2004: 3).

[11] Here, too, the Commission can find support in the Aho-group: "Alongside the operation of sufficient markets, one significant constraint to the efficient exploitation of research and knowledge lies in the surrounding framework conditions and structures, which today limit mobility and adaptability" (Aho et al. 2006: 22).

Commissioner sees it as necessary to claim that "I don't want to give the impression today that I see universities as a purely economic instrument" (Figel 2006: 10), the statement suggests that many observers perceive a dominance of the "knowledge economy" over the "knowledge society." The statement also acts as a foil to the lack of a systematic discussion of the democratic purposes of higher education (McDonnell et al. 2000) and how university reforms may affect the civic and democratic quality of Europe. That is, reform documents give little attention to the possible role of universities in developing democratic citizens, a humanistic culture, social cohesion and solidarity, and a vivid public sphere. Neither is university reform linked to the Union's "Democratic deficit" and the limited citizens' commitment to the Union as a political community. Furthermore, there is no serious discussion of how a commitment to economic (as well as democratic or social) goals can be squared with academic values and the potential dangers of subordinating the academic curiosity for knowledge and the pursuit of truth to some external agenda. In sum, the role of Academia and Democracy is primarily defined as serving economic purposes and the growth of competitive markets.

The Bologna Process

The Bologna process focuses on structural convergence of, and a common architecture for, higher education systems in Europe. To some extent the Bologna process can be seen as, at least initially, an attempt to recover a national and educational sector initiative as a countermove to the power of the Commission and to reforms giving priority to economic concerns. The process also represents an attempt to define a European role in higher education and to give premises from the educational sector a more important place in European policy making (chapter 7).

In general, ministers responsible for education tend to define European cooperation as a cultural project and they emphasize that the need to increase global economic competitiveness must be balanced with the objective of improving the social characteristics of the EHEA. Europe's cultural richness, national identities, and linguistic diversity have to be preserved, and educational reforms should take an interest in the region's social cohesion and cultural development (European Ministers Responsible for Education 2003, 2005).

The Bologna process has seen an expansion of both the substantive agenda and the patterns of participation and representation. While starting out as an intergovernmental process, "Bologna" has gradually attracted an increasing number of participants and issues. From the start, academia and social partners were not formally participating. University and student associations have, however, become represented. Likewise, the attitude towards the Commission has changed and the Commission has achieved an increasingly strong role.[12] Brussels is now interacting directly with

---

[12] According to Uniforum, the newspaper of the University of Oslo, at the 2005 Bergen meeting of Ministers, the Norwegian Minister of Education rejected a proposal to give the EU control over the Bologna process. The newspaper quotes Minister Clemet as having stated that "A proposal came up to make the Bologna process an EU process, but I made it clear that this proposal was not acceptable. That

universities and a new type of coordination and collaboration has been launched (chapters 7 and 8).

There has, however, been a gap between intention and the organized capacity to get things done in a coordinated and consistent way, making the road from political declarations to implementation uncertain. For example, there was an "utter absence of any prior assessment into the capacity of national systems to adapt to the Bologna principles and even less whether the dateline set was itself set on any basis other than hunch and ad-hocracy" (Neave 2006a), and the lack of a permanent secretariat, an institutionalized administrative executive support structure, and independent resources has opened for Commission influence based upon relatively modest support in terms of money and staff. Therefore, while the Bologna process was initiated as a countermove to EU and external sectors, it has increasingly become dependent upon the Commission and its definitions of problems and solutions. The Commission from its side links the Bologna process to its own actions in the field of education and training by stating that the Bologna process "contributes actively to the achievement of the Lisbon objectives and is therefore closely linked to the 'Education and Training 2010' work programme" (Commission 2006d) (chapter 7).

The Magna Charta Universitatum

The Magna Charta of European universities (1988), together with institutionalized rector-conferences and cooperation between individual universities, research groups and professional associations, are examples of ongoing trans-national processes (chapter 2). In the *Magna Charta*-process University rectors have been the main participants, and rather than seeing the University as a tool for economic and social goals it has been conceptualized as a specialized, rule-governed institution with a constitutive academic identity, purposes, and principles of its own. The University is a trustee of the European humanist tradition. "The Humboldtian model" and its embeddings in the *Kulturnation* (chapter 3), more than the economy, are celebrated and not scorned. While the term is used in different ways in different contexts it is often advocated as a bastion against a new order based upon commercial capitalism and the commercialization and commodification of research and higher education.[13]

The European University is mainly seen as a public institution, rooted in the Enlightenment, and serving the common good. Teaching and research are inseparable and an important task is to encourage individual intellectual and moral development. The aim is to form individuals in academic-humanist attitudes and make them informed and

---

marked the end of the rivalry that has existed between the European Commission and the Bologna process. The continuation of the Bologna process after 2010 will also not become an EU project" (Uniforum 20 May 2005: http://wo.uio.no/as/WebObjects/avis.woa/wa/visArtikkel?id=22304&del=uniforum).

[13] See Observatory for Fundamental University Values and Rights (2002) and Chapter 2 in this Volume. For a more general comparison between market values and educational values, see McMurtry (1991: 216).

responsible citizens. Consequently, academic autonomy, freedom and authority must be protected against all arbitrary external interference. The search for truth is based upon the belief that knowledge is most likely to be advanced through free inquiry, validation through peer review, independent expertise, and organized public skepticism. To be "useful" in generating and disseminating objective knowledge, there must be academic freedom of inquiry – the right to fearlessly question the received wisdom and publish the result even if it is controversial and may harm political, economic, religious, military, and other, power groups.

In one important respect the Magna Charta-process goes beyond the European perspective found in the other reform processes. The Commission, for example, takes it as given that there is a shared European identity. In this perspective researchers' mobility out of the EU is assessed as brain-drain to be counteracted, while mobility within the EU is seen as positive and to be encouraged (Potočnik 2005). In the Charta-process, in contrast, the main tendency is to see knowledge as global, to be searched wherever it is to be found. Increased cooperation and mobility between universities are encouraged in particular, but not only in Europe. Many non-European universities have also joined the Charter and an objective is to increase mobility and exchange of knowledge across *all* geographical, political, cultural, religious, economic, and social borders.

The conclusion is that while one view has a dominant position in reform documents and speeches, there are competing views. This impression is also documented when the Commission asks stakeholders to comment upon policy documents and ideas, for example, with respect to its vision of a "Europe of knowledge" (Commission 2004a, b). As will be documented in the following chapters, attitudes, perceptions and reform rhetoric usually reflect the actors' different institutional belongings and positions. They also tend to be differently colored by different organized contexts in which processes take place. Therefore, actors are not necessarily consistent. For example, it cannot be taken as given that professors and universities will always be carriers of academic principles and values, when both researchers and universities increasingly have commercial interests in their research and teaching (Nelson 2005). University rectors may say different things in the context of the Magna Charta and in fierce competitions for funds, and so may other actors.[14] As a consequence, coalitions across levels of governance, institutional spheres and groups of actors can be hypothesized.

---

[14] For example, the European University Association (EUA) combines elements of the Commission rhetoric and the Magna Charta rhetoric: "Mission diversity, strategic capability, and accountability can only be developed if universities have the freedom to do this. The higher education system must therefore be based on autonomous institutions, with freedom to control and manage their own resources and to compete as well as collaborate, accepting the responsibility to make the most efficient use possible of the resources they command; this require that universities are trusted to act responsibly. Old state bureaucratic systems which prefer control over trust must be swept away so that universities can respond rapidly and efficiently to the needs of society and the economy" (European University Association 2006: 3).

A PARADOX

The book addresses both the reform debate and the actual university dynamics. It asks: Why has half a century of unprecedented growth and change in European universities not eliminated, or at least reduced, the claim that new radical reforms are urgently needed? The phenomenon – that reforms tend to create a demand for new reforms rather than eliminating the felt need for them – is well known in the general reform literature (Brunsson and Olsen 1993). The observation, therefore, invites the questions: if the earlier reforms have been unsuccessful, why is this so and what can be learnt from the fate of earlier reforms? Do they illustrate another case of the triumph of hope, conviction and passion over reason and experience? We explore to what degree the weakness of the knowledge base of university reforms may provide a partial explanation of the lack of success, and we start out from an apparent paradox.

Reform plans aim at making universities better instruments for the "knowledge economy" or in the words of the Commission the "Europe of knowledge" (Commission 2003a). The role of research-based knowledge in policy making and implementation processes in general is also emphasized (Commission 2000a: 6). Nevertheless, there are large gaps between the claims made and the solutions advocated by reformers, and the quality of the evidence they have forwarded. University reform policies are to a considerable extent based on belief systems and a set of commitments where key assumptions are problematic and unverified by theoretically oriented, empirical research. Performance, for example, is usually attributed to organizational properties of European universities, rather than being documented, based on a systematic analysis of the widely varying organizational configurations called "universities" or "institutions of higher education."

The book addresses this paradox and aspires to contribute to a better theoretical and empirical basis for understanding the institutional dynamics of the European University. Contra the determinism of the TINA-syndrome ("There Is No Alternative"),[15] it is argued that the dynamics of European universities cannot be understood solely in terms of environmental necessities and functional improvement. Contra the European focus, it is assumed that there may be local, regional, and global identifications, as well as European ones. Contra the idea of widespread consensus and the avoidance of references to conflicting priorities and political struggles over what is the problem and what is the best remedy, attention is called to the politics of university reform and the fact that reformers usually have to encounter and overcome opposition.

A politics of University reform is relevant because processes of change impact the distribution of benefits, burdens and life chances and create losers as well as winners. There are competing legitimate interests and several lines of conflict when it comes to what universities should do and how they should be organized and governed

---

[15] "Confronted by fundamental challenges in our external environment with the entrance on the world scene of major new emerging economies, and in our internal environment by ageing populations and new technologies that change our way of life, we have no other choice but to embrace modernization" (Soete 2005: 2).

(chapter 2). University dynamics may include struggles over competing concepts of the university and its role in society, for example, university autonomy, differentiation and stratification within the system of universities, the relative priority of "world class" aspirations and massification, the balancing of economic, cultural and critical aspects of universities and of what research and education should be for sale and what should be freely available to all.

Likewise, there may be conflicts over the relative importance (or even survival) of higher education and research as policy sectors of their own versus these sectors becoming a net recipient of premises from other sectors, and consequently the relative power of ministries/ministers/Commissioners responsible for education and research compared to other ministries/ministers/Commissioners. Furthermore, there may be conflicts over the use of different instruments of steering, the role of the territorial state compared to other levels of governance and to different types of societal actors, and over what should be paid by general taxes, families, buyers of research and education, and external stakeholders.

STRONG CONVICTIONS, WEAK EVIDENCE

In reform documents and debates there is an abundance of fashionable assumptions, terms and doctrines about how the internal and external organization and system of governance affect university performance. These assumptions have come to be widely believed, yet they have rarely been examined in a systematic manner. Popular conceptions of how a good University or good University governance is supposed to operate are loosely coupled to theoretically informed, empirical studies of how universities are actually organized and governed, how they function, and how they change.

Rather than being driven by the ideal of clear goals, solid causal knowledge, and control over processes and outcomes, the European reforms are haunted by two ghosts: "the American Ivy-League University" and (the American) successful private enterprise and its assumed style of organization and governance. The first defines the crisis of the European University and is organized around the question: Why is there no Euro-Ivy League (Science 2004: 951)? The second presents the solution: European universities have to become more like private enterprises operating in competitive markets, or rather, more like how markets and private enterprises are portrayed in economic and managerial text-books.

In spite of the strong convictions among (many) reformers that problems and solutions are clear and agreed-upon, reform debates and actual reforms are to a limited degree founded on clear, consistent, stable and agreed-upon success criteria. There are many, shifting and not necessarily operational and consistent goals. While the "European knowledge economy" is often used as a frame of reference, this is usually done without a discussion in some detail of what role the University (or higher education as a whole) is expected to play in the knowledge economy. There is no specification of what, from that perspective, the main problems of University functioning are that the reforms need to address. Aspiration levels often seem unrealistic and there are only vague ideas about how reform plans can be implemented. Examples are the goal to make the EU the most competitive and dynamic knowledge based economy in the world by 2010 and the idea that two thirds of the stipulated 3% of EU GDP investment in research will come from the private sector. Absent is an analysis of whether the European pattern reflects political priorities and a model of society that includes other success criteria than economic utility, competitiveness and growth, rather than some defect to be remedied through radical reform.[16]

The general worry about "global competitiveness" is primarily focused upon the European research-intensive University. Based on indicators and statistics, especially international rankings, but also on statistics such as the number of international students in Europe, the number of European students in Australia and the USA, and the number of European academics in US universities, the view dominates that the European University is lagging behind. The arguments related to the perception of lagging behind are expressed by European level actors as well as rectors and national politicians and bureaucrats. Reform is promoted as the means through which European universities can compete (again) with their US counterparts. What is lacking is a thorough analysis of the "lagging behind situation." The arguments for reform are presented towards the higher education sector as a whole, while the research-intensive universities only make up a small part of the some 4,000 institutions in the sector. It is seldom explained how the "lagging behind situation" and reform arguments refer to the other institutions. Which groups of European universities are "underperforming"; what are the nature of and the reasons for their bad performance?

Weak and ambiguous data are in general often used for strong conclusions. Yet there is little research-based causal knowledge and empirical evidence concerning how university organization and systems of governance actually contribute to performance. Evaluation and impact studies are generally conducted too early for major

---

[16] For example, *Science* argues that the goal to create American-style research universities goes "against the grain of European egalitarianism" (Science 2004: 951). It is also argued that "European society with its high level of social welfare has undoubtedly more difficulties in managing change" (Soete 2005: 13). However, the Commission also argues that "Europeans are attached to a model of society based on a combination of a market economy, a high level of social protection and quality of life, and a number of principles, such as free access to knowledge. They are also aware of the richness of their cultural diversity and sensitive to the need to preserve it" (Commission 2000a: 20).

Like many other actors, the Aho-group argues that competitive markets and economic performance is a precondition for welfare and social security and cohesion. Yet, different from many other actors, these factors are not seen as a sufficient means: "A marked-led vision does not mean an abandonment of what is distinctive about European values but rather the use of the force of the market to preserve them, both by harnessing innovation to engage with public services and by creating the wealth necessary to finance the equality, health, social cohesion and common security that our citizens desire. Investment in education, science, research and innovation should not be seen as alternatives to investments in the welfare society in Europe, but as necessary though not sufficient means to ensure its sustainability, albeit through a reformed social model conducive to innovation." (Aho et al. 2006: 6). For the view that it is social cohesion that contributes to economic success, see Chapter 7.

impacts to be evident (Ormala et al. 2004: 5) and lacking is a serious discussion of the methodological difficulties of widely trusted ranking exercises and quality assessments (Cavallin and Lindblad 2006). There are also unclear concepts and problematic methods. As is indicated by Teichler (2000: 4) "Paradoxically, many politicians and administrators in this field as well as the academic profession itself, while trying to persuade society that systematic scholarship is superior to practitioners' experience, are most skeptical about the value of scholarship and research if it comes to their practical turf, that is, higher education."

Furthermore, while no single group of reformers has the authority or power necessary to control reform processes and outcomes, the power-relations relevant for successful reform, are rarely analyzed. The myth of an existing, or previously existing, government command and control system is taken for granted without a careful documentation of what the historical and existing order was like and how different it is from an emerging new settlement (chapter 4). However, the unsuccessful attempt to found a European University (Corbett 2005) indicates the complexity of power distributions in this policy field and so do the Bologna process and the Lisbon strategy. The use of the OMC indicates the current limits of supranationalism and suggests that vagueness about what OMC means and what the method is assumed to, and can in fact, accomplish in different contexts, may be a necessary condition for agreement (chapter 8). Likewise, the uneven implementation of the Bologna process (Tomusk 2006) and the uncertainties of the Lisbon strategy illustrate that actors without authority can rarely rely on (coercive) power. The causal chain from political intention and declarations to implementation can easily be broken or weakened and building support and mobilizing partners is a key process in University reform.

In conclusion, rather than being based on firm evidence, the discussion of remedies to a considerable degree reflects the world-wide dominance of elite US universities. Many governments and universities have pronounced that they want to emulate the top ranked US universities, thus opening up for the possibility that "Europeanization" in practice comes to mean "Americanization." The possibility is real enough to make it necessary for the Commission to explicitly deny that the EU is just importing the American model and to claim that proposed reforms means adapting to the particular circumstances of Europe (Commission 2006c: 7).

Instead of making a careful analysis of how American elite universities are differently organized and governed, proponents of European university reform usually refer to an imagined US business model, as carried around the world by a multitude of consulting firms and international organizations.[17] Often this recipe advocates a "one

---

[17] Nevertheless, also in the USA there is a perceived need for reforms. It is, for example, argued that: "Many university presidents believe that the greatest challenge and threat to their institutions arises from the manner in which their institution are governed both from within and from without" (Duderstadt 2002: 10). There is a perceived need for "Stronger Leadership for Tougher Times" (Association of Governing Boards of Universities and Colleges 1996). "The View from the Bridge" is that strong visionary leadership is desperately needed and that leaders currently have more responsibilities than authority and power

size fits all" reform approach – general remedies that ignore variations in history, cultures, experiences, and institutions. For example, the Search for Excellence-reform rhetoric, developed in the context of American enterprises and now also popular in EU rhetoric, suggests a standard recipe across a variety of different contexts, without an analysis of what are the problems, how the different systems to be reformed actually work, and the wider political, economic, social, and cultural conditions in which reforms are to take place.

In this literature, the key to success is to respond to perceived performance failure by imitating more successful peers. The method is to isolate the characteristics of organization and management that are believed to make an organization successful. For example, in their "*In Search of Excellence,*" Peters and Waterman (1982) presented eight lessons from the successful and presumably best run US companies. The book became a bible for American business managers and a great sales success. Nevertheless, its lack of an adequate methodology was also heavily criticized. The book was "distilling experience into platitudes." Myths were held to be truth and assumptions were untested (Barabba et al. 2002: 6, 7).

Time has also proved it difficult to identify a single and endurable organizational panacea to complex tasks across a variety of political, economic, social and cultural contexts. It has also been shown that quick fixes based on contemporary success turn out to be problematic in the long, and even in the not-so-long, run. A growing literature on benchmarking, that is, normative emulation (compare oneself to others with whom one has contact) and competitive mimicry (adaptive emulation to successful peers where causal relations are not well understood), has documented the centrality of the success-story. Success stories dominate business discourse to the virtual exclusion of close theoretical and empirical analysis of the many potentially spurious interrelations between performance and specific organizational properties (Strang and Macy 2001: 155). Novel success stories routinely arise, yet often a recipe rises to prominence rapidly, maintains support for a modest period of time, and then disappears (Strang and Macy 2001: 162).

While simple solutions to complex problems tend to be popular also among reformers of European universities, there is little hard evidence showing that New Public Management reforms have successfully contributed to academic success (Amaral et al. 2003: 292–293). The conditions for perfectly functioning markets assumed by economic text-books are difficult to achieve in higher education (Geiger 2004) and there are a number of flaws in the interpretation of this vision in the current reform debates. For example, the ideal of the "private service enterprise in competitive markets view" held up for the European University has come primarily from American economists' studies of American universities. Even if Europe increasingly embraces market-driven, consumer-oriented practices, it is far from obvious that this recipe fits European conditions, with a history of public

---

(Duderstadt 2002). In addition, issues such as the affordability of higher education, and the disparities between social groups in access to higher education have become major policy issues in the US promoting a different reform agenda than in Europe (see, for example: Kelly 2005).

responsibility, social agenda, equity concerns, and socio-cultural commitments (chapters 5 and 6).

MAKING SENSE OF "THE MOST MAGNIFICENT FORM OF CULTURAL INSTITUTION CREATED BY THE EUROPEAN MIND"

These observations suggest that there is neither a generally accepted analytical framework nor a solid data-basis for thinking about and explaining the processes, determinants and consequences of change in the European University. There is relative little research-based evidence when it comes to how university performance and development may depend upon how the University is organized and governed, including the factors that affect the likelihood that deliberate design and reform will be a dominant process of change. Much remains to be known about the types of change that have taken place in European universities, the processes through which change has occurred, and the determinants and consequences of change for university performance.

First, how much, and what kinds of, change have there actually been in university organization and governance and in the authority and power over the European University? For example, what changes have occurred in the relations between individual academic freedom, elected leadership and professional management, and in the relative importance of disciplinary versus task-oriented organization? What has happened to inter-university relations? Have there been more differentiation and stratification and more hierarchy, so that universities must develop highly diversified profiles before "taking their place in a system of higher education institutions" (European University Association 2006: 2)? What changes have taken place in the external organization of universities? Has university autonomy increased or decreased? Have there been significant changes in the (power) relationships between the University, government and society and who can legitimately act on behalf of the University and society? Has there been a disintegration of the relationship between the state and the University – have public authorities been abdicating, retreating, or simply regrouping and inventing new methods of intervention? Have specific social and economic interest groups increased their influence? Has the autonomy of the educational sector, as a sector with the responsibility to organize, store and transfer knowledge, declined or increased, making it a net receiver of premises from (and an instrument for) other sectors, or a net exporter of premises to other policy sectors? Has there been a development from higher education policy to a knowledge policy governed by economic goals? Have the boundaries between policy sectors been more blurred, or have they collapsed? Has the relative importance of different instruments of governance changed – have legally enforceable decisions become less important compared to financial and budgetary policies, different "soft" instruments of coordination and voluntary pooling of resources, benchmarking, monitoring, and shaming? Finally, to what degree has there been a "Europeanization" of the universities, and if so, in what meaning (Olsen 2002)? Have, for example, changes in the ways European universities are organized and governed implied an "Americanization"?

Second, compared to other processes of change, what has been the relative importance of deliberate institutional design and reform? Whose definitions of problems
and solutions have been accepted as a basis for collective decisions? How has support been mobilized and around which lines of conflicts have coalitions been built?
Compared to other determinants of change, how much change can be accounted for
by European-level policy making and to what degree is European university dynamics still primarily taking place within the traditional territorial, nation state context?
How much is European-specific and how much is more global, reflecting general
institutional ideologies imported from other sectors?

Third, is there a performance crisis and, if so, according to what success standards?
What have been the impacts upon university performance of change in university
organization and systems of governance, in particular upon the quality, amount, and
type of research and education taking place, and for its development patterns in
general? In retrospect there has, for example, been little evidence showing that the
democratization of European universities during the 1960s and 1970s made them
more adaptive and responsive to social needs (chapter 5). To what degree, then,
is there any evidence that more recent reforms driven by economic concerns have
had any positive effects in terms of improved scholarly or economic results? How
have the democratic and social purposes of education been taken care of, and how
have reforms affected the confidence citizens have in the University? What kinds of
mentalities and characters have the reforms selected or formed? What have been the
implications for the University's ability to learn from own and others experiences and
adapt to new circumstances?

Finding answers to such questions requires "independent" voices in the current
reform debates that are able and willing to challenge the dominant reform rhetoric
and the assumptions upon which it is build. From this perspective it may be asked
whether the universities, through their representative body, the European University
Association have developed a too close relationship to the Commission. It may be
asked why the academic representative bodies have been mainly silent at the European
level, and why most researchers on higher education have until now not taken the
challenges with respect to the need for a better theoretical and empirical basis for
understanding University dynamics seriously?

There are many unanswered questions, yet the aspiration of this Volume is modest.
The aim is to suggest elements of a possible analytical framework and a way to think
about the institutional dynamics of change of the European University, to provide
some empirical observations relevant for this framework, and to suggest a research
agenda (chapter 9). Our theoretical approach to institutions and institutional change
starts out from the assumption that governance and reform of the European University
mean intervention in, and through, complex institutional structures and evolving
patterns of behavior, meaning and resources, and that the organization and history
of these institutions make a difference for both policy making and the institutional
dynamics of change (March and Olsen 1989).

Modern European societies can be described as configurations of partly
autonomous institutional spheres, founded on different principles and logics of

appropriate behavior which are sometimes in balance and sometimes invading each other or colliding (Weber 1978; Olsen 2007). This perspective suggests that actors' institutional belonging, positions and roles are significant factors explaining the modes of thought and behavior (March and Olsen 2006a, b). For example, faculty, students, university leaders, and administrators are likely to hold different views. Presidents, prime ministers and economic ministers and Commissioners are expected to be carriers of different definitions of problems and solutions than are ministers and Commissioners responsible for education and research. Acting and thinking about universities, university reforms, and the role of higher education, is furthermore likely to take color of at which level of governance and in what institutional context it is taking place. Supranational, intergovernmental and transnational processes are expected to provide different settings and to prioritize different definitions of problems and solutions, and so are higher education and research as policy sectors compared to other policy sectors.

An institutional perspective also hypothesizes that institutional change will be path dependent and that history is "inefficient" in the meaning that well-entrenched institutions do not easily and costlessly adapt to changes in their environments or deliberate reform efforts that are inconsistent with existing institutional identities. This perspective stands in opposition to attempts to modernize the European University by assuming that an organizational recipe can be exported across political, economic, social and cultural contexts and downplaying the importance of history and institutional traditions.[18]

Making sense of the institutional dynamics of the European University, therefore, has to take into account that the University is strongly embedded in history. The long history is one of more than 900 years of developing the University as an academic institution with foundational principles and rules of its own, yet in cooperation, collisions and struggles with other institutional spheres and powerful groups. The specific postwar history in the European Community/Union context is characterized by the priority given to economic recovery after the war and the European Union as primarily a market-building project. For example, when Walter Hallstein proposed a European University and a "common market of intelligence" and argued that such a "market" would accord with the concept and tradition of a university, "the most magnificent form of cultural institution created by the European mind," he did so in a section on "Industrial policy" (Hallstein 1972: 200).[19]

In an attempt to get beyond the currently dominant reform rhetoric and possibly capture alternative prescriptions and descriptions of the European University

---

[18] For example: "The world is indifferent to traditional and past reputations, unforgiving of frailty and ignorant of custom and practice. Success will go to those individuals and countries which are swift to adapt, slow to complain and open to change" (Schleicher 2006: 16).

[19] The original German text is: *"Wir brauchen den 'gemeinsahmen Markt der Intelligenzen'. Was enspricht mehr der Idee und der Tradition der Universität, die doch die grossartigste Schöpfung des europäischen Geistes auf dem Gebiet der kulturellen Institutionen ist"* (Hallstein 1969: 258–259)?

and its dynamics, the Volume starts out from four visions, or models, of university organization and governance that assume different constitutive logics, criteria of assessment, reasons for university autonomy, and dynamics of change. The four are the University as:

- A rule-governed community of scholars.
- An instrument for national political agendas.
- An internal representative democracy.
- A service enterprise embedded in competitive markets.

The four visions are introduced in chapter 2 and then elaborated in the four subsequent chapters (3–6). Each vision can be imagined to describe how the University operates, reform decisions are made, and change happens, or they can be used to justify or criticize processes of decision-making and change. Advocates usually claim that their favorite model generates superior performance, while the critics usually foresee a performance crisis following from the same model.

Together, the four models allow us to explore the relative importance of authority based on scholarly merit, representative democracy, work place democracy and internal power resources, and market performance. They also allow us to inquire the relative role in reform behavior and change of academic rules and principles, governmental hierarchies, bargaining among interested parties, and competitive markets. Rather than assuming a single trend and institutional convergence, driven by global competition and strategic choice, evoking university dynamics as a relation between some "forerunners" and others "catching up," an institutional perspective invites the question, whether there are any general trends and whether there is convergence at all. Or whether variations in state- and university traditions, identity, and resources matter for trajectories, responses and outcomes, creating heterogeneity and variation affected by different historical starting points, institutional identities, and path dependencies (Hood et al. 2004).

From an institutional perspective, then, a challenge is to explore to what extent each model can help explain important aspects of the ongoing reforms and changes in European universities, including variations between different types of universities, disciplines or departments, specific activities (research, education) or issue-areas (budgets, faculty recruitment, student enrollment), developments in specific countries or regions, and in specific historic periods. In particular, if there has been a trend towards the service enterprise embedded in a competitive markets-model and away from the three other models (the University as a rule-governed community of scholars, an instrument for national political agendas, and an internal representative democracy) what are the main conditions favoring such a development?

In a situation where the European University finds itself in an ecology of competing and not easily reconcilable expectations, demands and constituencies across levels of governance and institutional spheres, university dynamics can be hypothesized to include several different processes of change, more or less loosely coupled. Processes such as deliberate design and reform, competitive selection, experiential learning, rule driven change systems, and political processes of argumentation and bargaining can be expected to have shifted in relative significance over time, sometimes reinforcing, sometimes counteracting each other. The Bologna and Lisbon reform processes also document that two processes with different starting points over time have become blended (chapters 7 and 8). While these two reform processes have been dealt with in two separate chapters, the *Magna Charta Universitatum* is not treated in the same way simply because there has not been a similar European political follow-up of this initiative. Arguably, the recommendation from the Parliamentary Assembly of the Council of Europe on academic freedom and university autonomy (30 June 2006) is the first significant political support at the European level for the Magna Charta.[20] In the recommendation it is referred to the role universities have played in the European humanist tradition and the importance of university autonomy and individual academic freedom for fulfilling this role. It is also argued that "The social and cultural responsibilities of the universities mean more than mere responsiveness to immediate demands of societies, to the needs of the market, however important it may be to take these demands and needs into account" (Council of Europe 2006).

Rather than purifying each model and pitting them against each other; rather than assuming that University dynamics can best be explained either with reference to changing environments or to internal processes; and rather than taking as given that explanatory frameworks must assume either consensus or conflict, the research challenge is to improve our understanding of how such processes interact, sometimes with unexpected consequences for both participants and on-lookers (Moen 1998; Olsen 1998; Ugland 2002; Witte 2006). In the end, the question of whether and how the European University is changing, has to be supplemented by the question whether the way in which the University changes is also changing – whether increased complexity, confluence of processes of change at different levels of government and in different sectors possibly are creating a new type of dynamic.

From an institutional perspective, one possibility is to view each of the four visions as part of a set of independent constraints that viable reform proposals have to meet (Cyert and March 1963). In one period one vision may generate new solutions, while the others act as constraints (Simon 1964). In other periods the roles may be changed. For example, during the late 1960s and early 1970s the traditional balance between government authority and professorial autonomy (chapters 3 and 4) were challenged. Democratic models giving formal representation to all involved groups were the main generators of change, while the others provided constraints on what reforms were actually implemented (chapter 5). More recently, the service enterprise in competitive markets-model has been the prime reform generating force, while the three others have provided the constraints (chapter 6). One hypothesis, furthermore, is

---

[20] The Assembly resolves to cooperate with the Observatory of the Magna Charta Universitatum in monitoring the observance of the principles of academic freedom and university autonomy in Europe. The Assembly also recommends that the Committee of Ministers should strengthen its work on academic freedom and university autonomy as a fundamental requirement of any democratic society and invites the ministers to require recognition of academic freedom and university autonomy as a condition for membership of the Council of Europe (Council of Europe 2006).

that the more consensus and common understanding, the more willingness there may be to leave decisions to universities and to higher education as a policy sector. The more conflict there is, the more likely that there will be competing demands for representation and participation in reform processes and in University governance in general.

Stylized visions as those presented in chapter 2 will under some conditions and in some historical periods capture important aspects of how universities are organized and governed and how they change. Under other conditions and in other periods things are more complex. As is argued in chapter 3 institutional change is not an instant shift from one stylized form to another – a historical development that can be characterized as a "revolution." There are many actors and driving forces and uncertain consequences and complex mixes of principles and organizational forms.

An institutionalist credo is that there are no universal and permanent answers to how to best organize and govern formally organized institutions. Given the well-known difference between the ability to change formal structures and the ability to achieve desired substantive results (performance), there is a need for detailed studies of how far into the University's core activities – its work organization, practices of research and teaching, and the knowledge produced and transmitted – have European reforms penetrated. Possibly, there has been more convergence in reform rhetoric than in actual reforms and (even more so) in University practices, inviting questions about the consequences of possible tensions between University reform rhetoric and University practices? Then, what are the consequences, in terms of different and competing success criteria, of using each model of organization and governance under different conditions, and in particular under conditions that deviate strongly from the ideal conditions assumed by each model?

A hypothesis is that reform strategies that reduce the complex set of roles the University has performed historically in the national context to solely an economic role in the European context is unlikely to be successful. Most likely any attempt to purify a single model will mobilize countervailing forces in defense of the other visions and increase the level of conflict. That is, we are likely – again – to experience that reforms create demands for new reforms, rather than eliminating such demands.

Finally, studies of how European integration and cooperation impact the dynamics of the University and higher education as a policy sector are important in themselves. In addition such studies can also contribute to an improved understanding of the conditions for European cooperation and integration in general. First, because these studies explicitly focus upon (also) the institutional level, while mainstream integration literature is concerned with the relationship between the European and the national level. Second, because the mainstream literature focuses on economic integration, while studies of the European University will illuminate how cultural integration may be more politically sensitive, follow different trajectories, and lead to different results, and therefore may provide a basis for more interesting theoretical ideas about the prerequisites for and constraints upon European cooperation and integration.

PART 2

PERSPECTIVES ON UNIVERSITY DYNAMICS

CHAPTER 2

THE INSTITUTIONAL DYNAMICS
OF THE EUROPEAN UNIVERSITY

Johan P. Olsen

WHAT KIND OF UNIVERSITY FOR WHAT KIND OF SOCIETY?

The University, in Europe and elsewhere, is currently involved in changes that have a potential for transforming its institutional identity and constitutive logic. At stake are the University's purpose, work processes, organization, system of governance and financial basis, as well as its role in the political system, the economy and society at large.

The rethinking, reorganizing and refunding of the University are part of processes of change in the larger configuration of institutions in which the University is embedded. These processes link change in the University to change in the role of democratic government, in public-private relations, and in the relationship between the local, national, European and international level.

The current dynamics raise questions about the University's long-term pact with society: What kind of University for what kind of society? What do the University and society expect from each other? How is the University assumed to fit into a democratic polity and society? To what extent and how, are the University, government and society supposed to influence each other? What is the extent and direction of change?[21]

Observed or predicted transformations suggest that the time of the self-governing Republic of Science has passed. A revolution is underway (Marginson and Considine 2000: 3).[22] There is a reshaping of institutional purposes and the University jeopardizes its legitimacy by losing sight of its identity and its distinctive features, functions and achievements as an academic institution. Prevailing trends include fundamental change in the autonomy of the University and in the academic freedom of individual faculty members, in the University's collegial and disciplinary organization, the unity of research and teaching, who controls specific bodies of knowledge and who defines criteria of excellence and social needs, the structure of departments, degree programs and courses, the relations between those who do research and teach and academic and

---

[21] An earlier version of this chapter was published as: Olsen, J.P. 2005, The Institutional Dynamics of the (European) University. ARENA Working Paper 15/2005. (http://www.arena.uio.no/publications/working-papers2005/papers/05_15.xml)

[22] Marginson and Considine refer to Australian universities, based on a three year study of 17 Australian higher education institutions, covering about half of the Australian system (Marginson and Considine 2000: 12).

P. Maassen and J. P. Olsen (eds.), University Dynamics and European Integration, 25–54.

administrative leaders, and in governments' commitment to funding universities.[23] Research is increasingly de-nationalized and less constrained by national borders (Crawford et al. 1993) and European and international developments make the continued existence or current roles of the University and the nation state less certain (Wittrock 1993: 361).

As often before, a period with a potential for radical change also invites speculations about what kind of organized system the University is and how it works, how the University ought to be organized and governed, what consequences different arrangements are likely to have, and how external demands for radical reform may depend on the University's capacity for self-governance and adaptation. There are different accounts. The University has been described as obsolete and mediocre. It has also been described as "a phenomenal success" (Veysey 1970: ix).

The aim of the chapter is to contribute to an improved understanding of the institutional dynamics of the University, in particular in the European context. Instead of starting with a definition of what a University is in terms of its purposes and functions or its organizational characteristics, *first*, a distinction is made between seeing the University as an instrument and an institution. *Second*, four visions, or stylized models, of university organization are outlined and it is asked to what degree these abstract visions are of any help in understanding universities as practices. *Third*, since University dynamics usually are seen as externally driven, we attend to one important environmental change: the emergence of European-level debates and policy making processes that take University dynamics beyond the frame of single universities and single nation states. How coercive are environmental actors and forces? Do they generate imperatives or clear behavioral guidance for universities; or, is there a multitude of environmental expectations, demands and success criteria pointing universities in different directions? *Fourth*, we attend to the significance of University actors, structures, legacies and dynamics – the ways in which the University responds to and acts upon the environment, how it protects its institutional identity and integrity, and how it explains and justifies itself to society at large. How much discretion is there, what are the dilemmas facing the University, and does the ideal of the University as a fiduciary arrangement dedicated to academic values and excellence have a future? *Fifth*, it is suggested that an improved comprehension of University dynamics may depend on a better understanding of how institutional success, confusion and crisis can be related.

THE UNIVERSITY AS AN INSTRUMENT AND INSTITUTION

The University can be seen as an organizational instrument for achieving predetermined preferences and interests. Then the issue is how the University can be organized and governed in order to achieve tasks and objectives in the most efficient way. In an

---

[23] See: Gibbons et al. 1994; Gumport 2000; Kogan et al. 2000; Novotny et al. 2001; Amaral et al. 2003; Currie et al. 2003; Neave 2003; Lay 2004; Neave et al. 2006.

instrumental perspective, the University is involved in a set of contracts. Support, economic and otherwise, depends on contributions. Change reflects a continuous calculation of relative performance and costs, and the University, or some of its parts, will be replaced if there are more efficient ways to achieve shifting objectives. Key questions are, for whom and for what is the University an instrument: for shifting national purposes and governments, "stakeholders" and "customers," or individuals and organized groups within the University? For whom and for what ought the University to be an instrument?

While an instrumental view dominates most reform programs and debates, the University can also be seen as an institution. An institution is a relatively enduring collection of rules and organized practices, embedded in structures of meaning and resources that are relatively invariant in the face of turnover of individuals and relatively resilient to the idiosyncratic preferences and expectations of individuals and changing external circumstances. Constitutive rules and practices prescribe appropriate behavior for specific actors in specific situations – for example, codes a scientist/scholar or student cannot violate without ceasing to be a scientist/scholar or student. Structures of meaning, embedded in identities and belongings explain, justify and legitimate behavioral codes; they provide common purposes and give direction and meaning to behavior. Structures of resources create capabilities for acting; they empower and constrain actors differently and make them more or less capable of acting according to prescriptive rules (March and Olsen 1984, 1989, 1995, 2006a, b).

The degree and form of institutionalization impact both *motivation* and *capacity* to follow institutionalized rules and codes of behavior. In contrast to an instrumental perspective, an institutional perspective assumes that constitutive rules and practices have a value in themselves and that their immediate substantive effects can be uncertain or imprecise. For example, the benefits of the University are not easily planned or predicted. To a large extent the University is a set of activities whose benefits have to be enjoyed after they are accomplished – in Maddox's words, as ripe fruit can be picket from a tree (Maddox 1964: 159). In contrast to an instrumental perspective, an institutional perspective also assumes that well-entrenched institutions reflect the historical experience of a community, that they take time to root and that they are difficult to change rapidly and radically, except under special circumstances such as widely agreed-upon performance crises.

As an institution the University is involved in a pact based on long-term cultural commitments. The University is a fiduciary system. Those belonging to the University are supposed to be the guardians of its constitutive purposes, principles, rules, and processes. They are supposed to defend its institutional identity and integrity whether the threat comes from outside or inside. Third parties are also supposed to enforce rules and sanction non-compliance of institutionalized codes. In an institutional perspective, key questions are, to what degree is the University a strong institution, well-entrenched in contemporary society? What kind of institution, based on what kind of principles, is the University? Do reformers try to enforce existing characteristics or do they try to impose alternative values and principles on the University?

Are there attempts to change structures of meaning and causal and normative beliefs, organization and systems of governance, or to reallocate resources?

Historically, the development of the University as a specialized institution dedicated to specific purposes and principles was part of the large-scale transformation from pre-modern to modern societies in Europe. Institutional differentiation created interdependent but partly autonomous institutional spheres of thought and action based on different logics, norms and values, principles of organization and governance, resources, and dynamics, such as democratic politics, market economy, religion, science, art, and civil society. In some periods institutional spheres are in balance, but historical dynamics can be understood in terms of tensions between them. In different time periods the economy, politics, organized religion, science, etc. can all lead or be lead and one can not be completely reduced to another. At transformative points in history institutions can also come in direct competition (Weber 1970, 1978).

In constitutional democracies the University is functionally dependent on, but partially autonomous from other institutions. Contemporary political-administrative orders, nevertheless, routinely face institutional imbalances. Collisions between key institutions are an important source of change and radical transformation of one institution is usually linked to changes in other institutions (Orren and Skowronek 2004; Olsen 2007). As a consequence, there is a need to clarify the conditions under which institutional reform is a fairly autonomous (internal) process, and the conditions under which internal processes are overwhelmed by wider political processes and societal mobilization. We need to distinguish between, on the one hand, incremental change and reforms within fairly stable organizational and normative frames and, on the other hand, change and reforms where the legitimacy of an institution's mission, organization, functioning, moral foundation, ways of thought and resources are thrown into doubt and challenged (Olsen 2004a, 2006).

Institutional imperialism, with intrusions and attempts to achieve ideological hegemony and control over other institutional spheres, may threaten to destroy what is distinct about other institutional spheres. There is, however, also institutional defense against invasion of alien norms. Typically, an institution under serious attack reexamines its pact with society and its rationale, identity and foundations, its ethos, codes of behavior and primary allegiances and loyalties (Merton 1937, 1942). Likewise, there may be public debates about what different institutions are supposed to accomplish for society, how each is to be justified and made accountable, what is to be core institutions and auxiliary institutions, and what kind of relationship government is supposed to have to different types of institutions. A possible outcome is the fall and rise of institutional structures and their associated systems of normative and causal beliefs and resources. Arguably, the University now faces this kind of situation.

VISIONS OF THE UNIVERSITY

What kind of organized system is the University? Students of formal organizations provide a set of theoretical ideas about how we might view the University as an organization (Hayes and March 1970; Cohen and March 1974; Olsen 1988); and inspired by these efforts four stylized visions, based on different assumptions about what the University is for and the circumstances under which it will work well, are presented (Table 1). The first portrays the University as a rule-governed community of scholars and an institution constituted upon academic values. The three other portray the University as a tool for different groups: an instrument for shifting national political agendas and governments, an instrument for a variety of internal individuals and groups constituting a representative democracy, and an instrument for external "stakeholders" and "customers" treating the University as a service enterprise embedded in competitive markets. The organizing principles are respectively constitutive rules, hierarchy and command, bargaining and majority voting, and market prices and competitive selection.

The University is a Rule-governed Community of Scholars

This vision portrays the University as an institution with a *raison d'être* and constitutive normative and organizational principles of its own. The University is a Republic of Science and an association of *die Gelehrten*. There is *Lern- und Lehrfreiheit* and the University's corporate identity and integrating self-understanding is founded on a shared commitment to scholarship and learning, basic research and search for the truth, irrespective of immediate utility and applicability, political convenience or economic benefit. The advancement, validation and dissemination of knowledge are founded on cognitive categories such as free inquiry and intellectual freedom, rationality, intelligence, learning, academic competence and expertise, fidelity to data and knowledge, theoretical simplicity, explanatory power, conceptual elegance and logical coherence. These are universal criteria, independent of the particularities of a specific geographical, national, cultural or religious context or sacred text. The University is supposed to benefit society as a whole and not specific "stakeholders" or those able and willing to pay, and education is to be open and accessible to all formally qualified.[24]

The holistic nature of knowledge and the unity of research, humanistic scholarship as well as natural science, are emphasized. Science and scholarship provide not only technologies but also codes of conduct and concepts, ideas and beliefs by which humans understand themselves, others and society. The University has a key role in shaping individuals with character and integrity and in developing and transmitting a culture distinguished by humanistic *Bildung*, rationality and "disenchantment of the world," enlightenment and emancipation.

The organization and governance of the University reflect its institutional identity and its special role and responsibilities in society. There is individual autonomy – *Einsamkeit und Freiheit*, yet the shared vision of the University provides integration and keeps together functionally specialized sub-systems (Schelsky 1971; Habermas 1987). The only legitimate authority is based on neutral competence. There is collegial

---

[24] See: Merton 1937; Schelsky 1971; Searle 1972; Habermas 1987; Wittrock 1993; Nybom 2003.

Table 1. **Four visions of university organization and governance**

Autonomy: / Conflict:	University operations and dynamics are governed by *internal* factors	University operations and dynamics are governed by *environmental* factors
Actors have *shared* norms and objectives	**The University is a rule-governed community of scholars** *Constitutive logic*: Identity based on free inquiry, truth finding, rationality and expertise. *Criteria of assessment*: Scientific quality. *Reasons for autonomy*: Constitutive principle of the University as an institution: authority to the best qualified. *Change*: Driven by the internal dynamics of science. Slow reinterpretation of institutional identity. Rapid and radical change only with performance crises.	**The University is an instrument for national political agendas** *Constitutive logic*: Administrative: Implementing predetermined political objectives. *Criteria of assessment*: Effective and efficient achievement of national purposes. *Reasons for autonomy*: Delegated and based on relative efficiency. *Change*: Political decisions, priorities, designs as a function of elections, coalition formation and breakdowns and changing political leadership.
Actors have *conflicting* norms and objectives	**The University is a representative democracy** *Constitutive logic*: Interest representation, elections, bargaining and majority decisions. *Criteria of assessment*: Who gets what: Accommodating internal interests. *Reasons for autonomy*: Mixed (work-place democracy, functional competence, *realpolitik*). *Change*: Depends on bargaining and conflict resolution and changes in power, interests, and alliances.	**The University is a service enterprise embedded in competitive markets** *Constitutive logic*: Community service. Part of a system of market exchange and price systems. *Criteria of assessment*: Meeting community demands. Economy, efficiency, flexibility, survival. *Reasons for autonomy*: Responsiveness to "stakeholders" and external exigencies, survival. *Change*: Competitive selection or rational learning. Entrepreneurship and adaptation to changing circumstances and sovereign customers.

organization, elected leaders and disciplinary organization. All activities and results are assessed by the internal norm of scholarship (peer review) and truth is an end in itself. The basic mechanisms of change are found in the internal dynamics of science and scholarship in general and in specific disciplines. The system evolves through more or less internal, organic processes rather than by external design.

Protection and funding from the state, together with autonomy from government and powerful economic and social groups, is justified by the assumptions that society values objective knowledge, that knowledge is most likely to be advanced through free inquiry, and that "claims of knowledge can only be validated as knowledge – as opposed to dogma and speculation – by being subjected to the tests of free inquiry" (Searle 1972: 171). Free inquiry is also a key feature of an open society and science can aspire to be culture-shaping and provide models for problem solving, conflict resolution and social integration for a democratic society and civilization, based on communicative rationality and the power of the better argument (Habermas 1987; Kalleberg 2000).

The University is an Instrument for Shifting National Political Agendas

Within this perspective, the University is a rational tool for implementing the purposes and policies of democratically elected leaders. It is an instrument for achieving national priorities, as defined by the government of the day. The University cannot base its activity on a long-term pact based on constitutive academic values and principles and a commitment to a vision of civilized society and cultural development. Instead research and education is a factor of production and a source of wealth or welfare. The University's purposes and direction of growth depend on shifting political priorities and funds more than scholarly dynamics. A key issue is the applicability and utility of research for practical problem-solving, such as defense, industrial-technological competition, health and education. The University is a multiversity, and "the multiversity serves society almost slavishly" (Kerr 1966: 19), as defined by shifting governments. In other words, the University is "for hire" (Wolff 1969: 40).

Expansion and fragmentation come together. Serving national objectives makes the University richer, at the price of reduced internal unity and coherence. The assumption that the University could explore independently the unity of knowledge is replaced with the need to specialize in order to maintain excellence (Parsons and Platt 1973; Perkins 1966). Due to the changing nature of science, some types of research require large-scale facilities and huge budgets. Individual research is replaced by team-work and the disciplinary organization of knowledge is supplemented with or replaced by cross-disciplinary, application-oriented research and institutes. The University is a series of communities and activities held together by a common name, governing board, and related purposes (Kerr 1966). Leaders are appointed, not elected. The administration, with its hierarchies, rules and performance statistics, becomes the core of the University. Autonomy is delegated and support and funding depend on how the University is assessed on the basis of its effectiveness and efficiency in achieving political purposes, relative to other available instruments. Change in the University is closely linked to political decisions and change.

The University is a Representative Democracy

This vision sees the University as an instrument for internal, not external individuals and groups. The University is an interest group democracy allowing representation on governing boards and councils to all categories of employees as well as students.[25] The unions of employees and students are also significant participants in University governance. Focus is upon formal arrangements of organization and governance, more than on the special characteristics of work processes in the University. Decision-making is organized around elections, bargaining, voting and coalition-building among the organized groups with the aim of accommodating their interests. The groups' relative success in building and maintaining support decides how the University works and develops.

Democratization of the University is linked to enhancing democracy in society at large (Habermas 1967; de Boer, Maassen and de Weert 1999) but internal democracy and external autonomy are justified by reference to a mix of principles and concerns. Workplace democracy and co-decision are seen as improvements compared to antiquated formal hierarchies. Giving more power to younger faculty and reducing the sovereignty of senior professors are assumed to improve the scholarly competence of the University. Giving power to administrative and technical staff is justified by their contributions to the performance of the University. Student power is related both to the significant impact Universities have on their lives and to *realpolitik*, the students' ability to cause difficulties for the operation of universities and societies. The basic mechanism of University change is internal bargaining and shifting coalitions.

The University is a Service Enterprise Embedded in Competitive Markets

Within this perspective the University is an economic enterprise or a service station operating in regional or global markets (Marginson and Considine 2000). The University is governed and changed by its sovereign customers. Research and higher education are commodities, bundles of goods to be sold in a free market. Competition and achieving profit and other individual gains are key processes. Students, faculty, donors and communities select from alternative universities in terms of how well they meet individual preferences. Information and knowledge are private strategic resources for competitiveness and survival, not a public good. The University provides any research and teaching that can be sold for profit, and quantity, quality and price are determined in competitive markets (Hayes and March 1970; Cohen and March 1974).

Market competition requires rapid adaptation to changing opportunities and constraints, which again requires strong, unitary and professional internal leadership. Leaders have a responsibility for the University as a whole; therefore they need to control its human and material resources. The University has more freedom from

---

[25] "Assembly of the academic estates" may be a more correct label since different organized groups are represented but not based on the principle of one-person-one-vote. Models of direct participation played a role at some universities in relatively brief periods during the 1960s and 1970s but are not attended to here.

the state and political authorities. Government involvement is at arm's length and there are regulation and incentives rather than governmental dictates. Simultaneously, the University is more dependent on "stakeholders," donors, buyers, student fees, competitors and society at large and University leaders are market entrepreneurs.

Autonomy from government is turned into a management tool for changing universities and New Public Management ideas and techniques from private enterprises are celebrated (Marginson and Considine 2000; Amaral et al. 2003; Felt 2004). Collegial, disciplinary and democratic organization and individual autonomy are viewed as hindrances to timely decisions and good performance, to be replaced by strong management and inter-disciplinary organization. The new role model for researchers is the entrepreneur-innovator, rather than the Nobel laureate (Westerheijden et al. 2006: 97). There are appointed academic leaders and external representation on the governing boards of the University. There are also external accreditation and mechanisms to oversee and evaluate the quality and quantity of university performance (Brennan and Shah 2000). As part of improving fiscal balances, there is appropriation of intellectual property rights (a principle alien to science) and pressure towards "patent or perish" rather than "publish or perish" (Amaral et al. 2003: 291). In the market-vision, change is governed by competitive selection and the survival of the fittest, that is, those best able and willing to adapt to market imperatives and incentives.

ABSTRACTIONS AND PRACTICES

As less than perfect approximations to the abstract visions, universities as practices show "a shocking diversity" (Neave 2003: 151). While the historic development of science and universities in Europe have distinct characteristics compared to developments in other civilizations (Huff 1993), talking about "the European university," characteristics that apply to more or less all European universities and institutions of higher education, and only to European ones, refers at best to a normative vision and not an achievement. The relations among universities, public authorities and society are characterized by a great variety of forms of interaction, intervention and control (Hood et al. 2004: Part III). The market vision (Teixeira et al. 2004), as well as other visions, can be rhetoric or reality, different scenarios may be plausible under different circumstances (Enders et al. 2005).

The four stylized visions are not mutually exclusive. Each is based on assumptions which make it unlikely that any of them alone can capture current university practices. In practice, university dynamics are likely to be affected by the external setting (government, markets, demographics, the overall development of European cooperation and integration), as well as by internal properties and dynamics (academic values and rules, management, power relations) of the University. Do, then, the four visions give a rough approximation to *stages* in the European historical development, or is each vision an *aspect* of university organization and governance throughout history?

The University is an old institution; the University of Bologna, regarded as the oldest in Europe, was established more than 900 years ago and thus long before Italy was founded as a nation-state. The University also shows traces of medieval and eccle-siastical ways of thought, organization and governance, as well as sediments from historical encounters with governments and powerful groups (Huff 1993; Wittrock 2004).[26] Still, the modern research university and the conduct of scientific research in large-scale formal organizations is relatively new – a phenomenon of the late nine-teenth century. In this period, two university systems of special importance have been the German in the late nineteenth and early twentieth century and the American research university in the twentieth century (Wittrock 1993: 328–329).

The vision of the University as a rule-governed academic community of scholars is usually linked to the legacy of "The Humboldt University" (1810), an arrangement where institutional autonomy and individual freedom are protected by the Constitution and sponsored by the state in order to prevent the University from being corrupted by powerful actors and forces in politics, the economy, or organized religion. Self-governance, however, took place within constraints, and not only the constraints from academic values, principles and rules. Universities were part of the state apparatus and professors were civil servants (*Beamten*). The state kept the right to appoint professors and academic autonomy was linked to abstention from politics. While the University was a cultural core institution of modernity, Humboldt was well aware of science as a significant productive force. He used economic and utilitarian arguments and saw the University and science as important in nation- and state-building processes (Habermas 1987; Nybom 2003).

The successful American research university, the multiversity, was in many ways a new type of institution (Kerr 1966) and increasingly it became dependent on fed-eral support and its contributions to defense, industrial-technological competition and other national purposes (Reagan 1969). World War II experiences of the appli-cability of research for practical problem-solving, together with the Sputnik shock strengthened the link between basic research and national goals in many countries. In 1963, for example, Congress asked the National Academy of Sciences what level of federal support was "needed to maintain for the United States a position of leader-ship through basic research in the advancement of science and technology and their economic, cultural, and military applications" (The National Academy of Sciences 1965: 1)? Humboldt's philosophical-humanistic vocabulary and the idea of unity of purpose and homogeneity of constitution were gradually replaced with functionalism as the justification for the diversity of the American educational institutions (Parsons and Platt 1973; Wittrock 1993).

---

[26] The historical struggle with the Church is, for example, revoked when (then) Rector Linda Nielsen, Copenhagen University says that business is the new "Church" challenging the autonomy of the University (Nielsen 2002). The historical importance of the church is also visible when it is argued, "A university is only incidentally a market. It is more essentially a temple – a temple dedicated to knowledge and a human spirit of inquiry. It is a place where learning and scholarship are revered, not primarily for what they contribute to personal or social well-being but for the vision of humanity that they symbolize, sustain, and pass on" (March 1999: 378).

The idea that science can, and ought to be, planned at the service of national objectives and social needs spread throughout the OECD area during the 1960s (OECD 1963, 1965, 1968). Still, the ideas were not completely new. They had roots in Marxist thinking (Bernal 1939; Gustavsson 1971: 81–132) and arguably the myth of the Ivory Tower tends to conceal that combining basic and applied research, and being both a Republic of Science and a national instrument for coping with economic and social needs, have a long history (Roll-Hansen 1985).

During the 1960s and 1970s the vision of the University as a representative democracy was boosted by student revolts and their criticism of overcrowded universities with very limited access to professors and the repressive authority of universities and government, the younger faculty's struggle against senior professor dominance, and democratic developments in society at large, emphasizing work-place democracy and co-determination. Students and faculty organizing to protect intellectual and material self-interests were, however, key elements when the University of Bologna was founded, with the students as the key "entrepreneurs" (Lay 2004). The modern implementation of the vision has also been complicated because the key ideas were never fully reconciled with the commitment to intellectual excellence: that the distribution of authority in the University should be in rough conformity with demonstrated competence and expertise, and that science was the affair of "an intellectual aristocracy" (Weber 1970: 134; Wolff 1969: 132; Searle 1972: 203). Neither were the ideas easily reconciled with the observation that faculty historically has shown little enthusiasm for using their participatory rights. Non-participation has often reflected a choice rather than exclusion (Olsen 1976a) and this tendency is also observed after the democratic reforms of the 1960s and 1970s (de Boer et al. 1998).

Finally, the main trend during the last decades has been that the dominant legitimating idea of the University has changed towards the vision of a service enterprise embedded in competitive markets.[27] While the reforms during the 1960s and 1970s were inspired by models of political democracy, the normative climate, the reform rhetoric and the standards of assessment have more recently been dominated by the ideologies of neo-liberal economics and business, in higher education as well as in the public sector in general.[28] The conception of the University as a competitive enterprise, open towards society and protected against the state is newer and more contested on the European continent and in the Scandinavian countries than in Anglo-American countries, even if the criticism of the enterprise-ideology has long roots also in the United States (Veysey 1970; Currie et al. 2003; Neave 2003).[29]

---

[27] See: Gumport 2000; Kogan et al. 2000; Marginson and Considine 2000; Amaral et al. 2003; Currie et al. 2003.

[28] Sometimes the two are also directly related. For example, the Japanese government was eager to turn universities into agencies because they by doing so could nominally remove many employees of national universities from the total of state employees – an indicator of reform success (Suleiman 2003: 167).

[29] For example, Veysey observed that:

"Loosing a clear sense of purpose, spokesmen for the American university around the turn of the century ran the danger of casually, even unconsciously, accepting the dominant codes of action of their more numerous and influential peers, the leaders of business and industry" (Veysey 1970: 346).

In sum, the historic stages-perspective gets modest support. There are trends but also variation and countertendencies that make it more plausible to treat the four visions as enduring aspects of university organization and governance. The mix of visions varies over time and across political and cultural systems and invites questions about the scope conditions of each vision. Under what conditions are professors, other university employees, students and governments likely to be fully committed to the vision of a rule-governed community devoted to academic values, excellence and freedom? Under what conditions are governments able and willing to provide well defined and fairly stable objectives for the University and forecast what it takes to reach these objectives? Under what conditions will there be an identifiable electorate in the University, representing well-organized interests and well-informed "citizens," as well as political and societal acceptance of university autonomy based on internal, representative arrangements? Under what conditions are markets perfect enough (few frictions, perfect knowledge, easy entry, etc.), and oriented towards academic quality rather than low prices, so that competition rewards excellent research and teaching and eliminate low quality?

Arguably, the area in which the critical assumptions underlying each vision are realistic is considerably smaller than the area where they are assumed to be applicable by their proponents. While there has been some convergence in rhetoric, few are likely to be completely committed to a single vision under all conditions. Often various models will supplement each other and the task is to understand how different systems balance different concerns, and how they develop power-sharing arrangements rather than allocate all power to faculty, students, administrators, public authorities, stakeholders or customers.

In a democratic society there are probably long-term adaptive processes that make internal and external conceptions of the University's autonomy and social responsibilities converge to some degree. If so, an existing balance is most likely to be challenged in periods of radical regime change. Not unexpectedly, for example, the South African government wanted a break with the past by restructuring higher education and changing government-institutional relations as part of moving away from apartheid (Muller et al. 2006). One may hypothesize that implementing national priorities may be more legitimate in periods of war and crises than in normal times, that some government objectives are more legitimate than others and that it is more legitimate to intervene in some activities (e.g. capacity-issues) than in others (e.g. the content of research and education). Universities, disciplines and individuals with strong academic credentials and high status are less likely to have their autonomy challenged than others. Disciplines that are highly dependent on outside funds (many natural sciences) are probably more vulnerable to outside influence than those who

---

Contemporaries are said to regret that those who were supposed to stand for education and scholarship had become businessmen, that Harvard was run like a department store, and that the college president had become the tool of business (Veysey 1970: 346). Warnings against the intrusion of business ideals, aims and methods in higher learning and the pervasion of scholarly values by the ethics of the business community is also a well-known theme in Thorstein Veblen's writings (Veblen 1918).

are not (many of the humanities), and they are in particular so where there are attractive alternatives to the University. Systems with strong trade union traditions and general acceptance of workplace democracy, such as the Scandinavian countries, are also likely to be most willing to accept representative schemes in the University.

If support is conditional and a question of degree and the four visions are both competing and supplementing each other, there will in some periods and contexts be a balance among the different visions. In other periods and contexts one vision may generate reform efforts, while others constrain what are legitimate and viable solutions. Ongoing European-level debates and reforms aimed at developing a European Higher Education Area (EHEA) and a European Research Area (ERA) provide a setting for studying such issues. Which, if any, effects is European cooperation and integration – including ambitions of European coordination of research-, higher education- and innovation policies, the development of a European Institute of Technology and support structures such as a European Research Council – likely to have upon the development of European universities, their identity, organization, financing, cooperation and competition?

EUROPEAN-LEVEL DEBATES AND POLICIES

The European case illustrates that debates and reforms concerning the future of the University can evoke several, competing visions of the University and that they can be driven by a confluence of processes taking place in different organized settings, and not by a single dominant process taking place in a single setting.

The Confluence of Reform Processes

On 18 September 1988, the *Magna Charta Universitatum* was signed in Bologna by more than 400 Rectors of European Universities and later endorsed by many others from different parts of the world. The occasion was the 900th Anniversary of the University of Bologna. The initiative had been taken by the University of Bologna in 1986 in a proposal to the oldest European universities. At a meeting in Bologna in June 1987 delegates from 80 universities elected an eight members board to prepare the Charter and the proposal was drafted by a group of academic leaders in Barcelona in January 1988. An Observatory has also been established to monitor future developments.[30]

The charter laid out the principles seen to define "the University." It celebrated the humanitarian values of university traditions and aimed at strengthening the bonds among European universities. The Rectors pledged loyalty to ideals such as the University's moral and intellectual autonomy from all political authority and economic power; teaching and research in universities as inseparable, and cooperation across political and cultural borders. The spirit was one of confidence. The University had

---

[30] Observatory, Magna Charta Universitatum, http://www.magna-charta.org/magna.html. See for example, Observatory 2002; Felt 2004; Lay 2004 (http://www.manga-charta.org/autonomy-public.html).

proven its ability to adapt to changing circumstances and it was assumed that it will be able to do so also in the future. An appeal was made to European governments to follow up the principles formulated in the Charter in their policy making.[31]

Humboldtian ideals were not seen as a hindrance to an active role for universities in the search for a new European order and a European identity. The universal values and the European roots of the University were not seen to conflict. On the one hand, the University transcends geographical and political frontiers and universities from other regions of the world were invited to join the Charter. On the other hand, Europe was asked to unite around the University as a vehicle of unity and a trustee of the continent's intellectual and normative legacy. Reaching back to the early years of European university history, the Charter supported the mutual exchange of information, joint projects, improved mobility among teachers and students, and a policy of equivalent statuses, titles, examinations and awards of scholarship.

These were also core themes in the Bologna Declaration on the creation of a European Area of Higher Education by 2010, but this time the initiative came from a different source. While the Charter was initiated by the academic community, the Bologna Declaration was a pledge taken in 1999 by the ministers of education from 30 countries.[32] The expressed aim was to reform national systems of higher education in order to promote mobility, employability, and European dimensions in higher education. The aspiration was to insure compatibility and equivalence, not to develop a common European higher education policy or streamlining national systems. Focus was on structures rather than content – the development of a system of readable and comparable degrees, a system with two main cycles (undergraduate and graduate), a quality assurance system and a credit transfer system. European cooperation was linked to a cultural as well as an economic dimension and a "Europe of knowledge" was seen as a means to consolidate and enrich European citizenship. Rather than being forced by the imperatives of global competition, ministers did what was politically possible at that time (Allègre 2002: 18).

To some degree the Bologna process has changed the terms of the debate and provided elements of a common understanding. Some have also seen the process as a turning point in the development of higher education in Europe.[33] In 2005, 45 countries were members. Themes have been added (chapter 7), such as lifelong learning, the participation of institutions of higher education and students in the process, making European universities more attractive for non-European students, doctoral studies, creating a synergy between the European Area of Higher Education

---

[31] The Charter is more concerned about the autonomy of the University than the freedom of the individual professor. Peter Maassen has also called my attention to the fact that European Rectors as a collectivity usually supports Humboldtian principles, yet as individuals many of them embrace the entrepreneurial style and are more positive to trade with educational services than are national politicians.

[32] A forerunner was the Sorbonne Declaration, signed by the ministers of higher education in Britain, France, Germany and Italy in 1998, at the occasion of the 800th anniversary of Sorbonne University.

[33] Haug 1999; Hackl 2001; Banchoff 2002, 2003; Neave 2003; Amaral and Magalhães 2004.

and the European Area of Research, and balancing the social dimension and social cohesion against the efforts to improve economic competitiveness.[34]

The Bologna process has so far primarily been an intergovernmental process. Ministers of education have been the key participants and national control over policy making has been emphasized. The removal of barriers to mobility is, however, consistent with aspirations of European integration and making European higher education more competitive in global markets. There has also been a gradual shift in the meaning of "diversity" – from diversity among national systems of higher education to a European-wide diversification in institutions and programs with different profiles (Hackl 2001: 114). The Europan Commission has, furthermore, played an increasingly important role in the follow-up process. The academic community is involved and several institutions and organizations are consultative members.[35] To some degree the process has also become institutionalized. Working structures and a series of meetings with time-tables attached have been set up.

Compared to the ambitious but delimited aspirations of the Bologna process, the Commission wants a general debate on the role of European universities with the aim of developing a vision for university-based research and innovation for the next 15–20 years (Commission 2003a, 2004b, 2005a, 2006b). The backdrop is the emerging knowledge economy and doubts that the universities will be able to play a constructive role in making the European knowledge economy competitive at the global level. The Commission wants to build a single market for research and to mobilize the brainpower of Europe in order to enabling universities to make their full contribution to the Lisbon Strategy (Commission 2005a). A key task is "to deliver" on the "modernization agenda" (Commission 2006b). As often before in EU documents, there is no lack of big words: "A new age is about to dawn." We are in the Century of science and technology and the world is more variable and unpredictable as one society gives birth to the next (Commission 1995a: 73, 2000a, 2003a).

The Commission claims both necessities and consensus. A permanently changing economy and technology *compel* the system of research and higher education to

---

[34] The European Area of Research was decided by the European Council in Feira in 2000, at that time called European Area of Research and Innovation, as part of the attempt to pool scientific and technological resources to improve the economic and technological competitiveness of the member states.

[35] These are the Council of Europe, the European University Association, the European Association of Institutions in Higher Education, the European Centre for Higher Education and the National Union of Students in Europe. *The Council of Europe's* web-site provide much relevant information about the Bologna process: http://www.coe.int/T/E/Cultural_Co-operation/education/Higher_education/Activities/Bologna_Process/default.asp

The European University Association (EUA) has 759 members from 45 countries (January 2005, www.eua.be/). In comparison, the UNESCO-based world-wide association of Universities founded in 1950, The International Association of Universities, in November 2004 had 602 members, 43% from Europe (not all members carry the label "university" but they are degree-conferring higher education institutions; http://www.unesco.org/iau/members_friends/index.htlm).

The European Association of Institutions in Higher Education (EURASHE) organizes National Associations of Colleges and Polytechnics and individual institutions in 18 countries but do not have information about the exact number of institutional members (e-mail from EURASHE and www.eurashe.be/).

change. Increased demands for higher education, the internationalization of education and research, the need to develop effective and close co-operation between universities and industry, competition following from the proliferation of places where knowledge is produced, the interdisciplinary reorganization of knowledge, and the emergence of new expectations make European universities face an imperative need to adapt and adjust (Commission 2003a: 6–9). The Commission also claims that the time of "heated debates" over university organization has come to an end and that there is agreement about the need to "modernize" universities (Commission 1995a: 42, 2006b: 4), thereby framing reforms as technical questions of finding efficient organizational forms consistent with necessities and shared goals.

The situation is assessed as worrying. While Europe aspires to become "the most competitive and dynamic knowledge-based economy in the world," there is a lack of university adaptation and innovation that contributes to a loss of economic growth and competitiveness, as well as brain-drain. European universities are not globally competitive. They have not learnt to compete in world markets and handle structural change and most of them lack the competitive mindset. The picture is not exactly flattering:

"After remaining a comparatively isolated universe for a very long period, both in relation to society and to the rest of the world, with funding guaranteed and a status protected by respect for their autonomy, European universities have gone through the second half of the twentieth century without really calling into question the role or nature of what they should be contributing to society. The changes they are undergoing today and which have intensified over the past ten years prompt the fundamental question: can the European universities, as they are and are organized now, hope in the future to retain their place in society and in the world" (Commission 2003a: 22)?

A sustainable level of competitiveness is seen to require many different and not easily reconcilable things: concerted action, better investment in knowledge, adequate and sustainable incomes, ensured autonomy, professionalism in academic and administrative affairs, priority to excellence, contributions to local and regional needs and strategies, closer co-operation between universities and economic enterprises, and the fostering of a coherent, compatible and competitive EHEA and a ERA (Commission 2000a, 2003a: 2–3).

The Commission observes a trend away from the Humboldt model and towards greater differentiation and specialized institutions concentrating on core specific competences (Commission 2003a: 6). In Europe there are some 3,800 higher education institutions and some 300 of these have a significant research capacity (Commission 2004b).[36] The Commission accepts that the link between research and teaching continues to define the ethos of the university, but the link does not need to be identical in all universities, for all programs or for all levels (Commission 2003a: 18). Managing a modern university is also a complex business and universities should be open to

---

[36] In comparison, Clark observed 3500 accredited institutions of higher education in the United States, 200 of them granting doctoral degrees (Clark 1995: 139–141). Of course, much depends on the criteria and classifications used. Here we are primarily interested in institutions of higher education with a significant research component.

professionals from outside the purely academic tradition, provided that confidence in the university's management remains strong (Commission 2003a: 17).

The Commission, finally, sees itself as surrounded by ignorance and a lack of commitment. The creation of a ERA, attempts to create an "internal market" in research, better coordination between members states and development of a European research policy, have been hampered by insufficient participation by the member states (Commission 2002c). Public opinion perceives scientific ventures and technological progress as a threat – an "irrational climate" and a fear "which has some parallels in the transition from the Middle Ages to the Renaissance" (Commission 1995a: 25).[37]

The Co-existence of Competing Visions

The Commission invites a general debate on the universities but remains within an instrumental economic-technological framework. Consistent with the international neo-liberal reform ethos, the University is an enterprise in competitive markets. This vision is also seen to coincide with the vision of the University as an implementer of market-oriented economic policies, even if some emphasize the value of competition in general, while others view universities as an instrument for supporting *European* industry in the global competition. The Commission's approach can partly be understood on the basis of its limited legal competence in research and higher education. Competition and vocational training are accentuated because these are areas where the Commission's competence is strongest. Still, it is surprising that the Commission seems ignorant about the university-debates during the 1960s and 1970s; that the Magna Charta process is not mentioned when "The role of the universities in the Europe of knowledge" is on the agenda. The support of the Humboldtian model is overlooked and the cultural dimension of the Bologna process is largely ignored.[38]

Among commentators, there were voices in support of the Commission's focus on economics, markets and management and the need to promote competitive European research universities.[39] In order to compete globally, universities had to be granted more autonomy from government within stable financial and legal frameworks, and the "management deficit" required stronger leadership and improved strategic capacity. Unsurprisingly the Commission's assumptions, analyses and conclusions also created criticism and confrontations with the academic community.

---

[37] In contrast, Banchoff (2002) argues that European-level institutional legacies and not solely national interests (or popular ignorance) have undercut efforts to create a European Research Area.

[38] The Draft "Treaty Establishing a Constitution for Europe" says that "The arts and scientific research shall be free of constraint. Academic freedom shall be respected" (Article II-73). The Treaty, however, does not mention the autonomy of the University. Universities are mentioned in Section 9 "Research and technological development and space" (Article III §§248–253) and the formulations are closer to those of the Commission than to the Rectors' Magna Charta. (http://www.eurotreaties.com/constitutiontext.html).

[39] I rely here on documentation from "Stakeholders' consultation" which involved 140 responses in September 2003 and all in all 150 responses (Commission 2004a) and the proceedings from the follow-up Conference, attended by more than 1000 participants (Commission 2004b).

Where the Commission assumed consensus, respondents saw a number of dilemmas, tensions and paradoxes of a nature that cannot easily be solved, suggesting that the future of the University in Europe is a contested issue where power relations as well as good arguments count. The Commission was, for example, attacked for vulgarizing the debate. It presented higher education solely as an instrument of economic productivity and growth. The Commission did not take seriously the possibility that the University could be corrupted by strong economic interests and it gave a too narrow interpretation of the University's basic mission, including its role carrier of European civilization and its role in molding individuals into informed, critical and responsible democratic citizens. The overall negative description of European universities was rejected, and so were the TINA-perspective ("There Is No Alternative") and the consensus assumption. One comment was that "far too many questions in the Commission's Communication asks 'how' instead of 'why' or should we."[40]

As distinct from the Commission's view, the Humboldtian model was seen as still valid. The pledge to the University as a universal, united and autonomous institution, whose identity and integrity should be protected against external groups, was strong. Research and teaching should be linked and individual freedom defended. Support was given to a public service model and it was argued against making higher education solely market-driven, because the market logic does not apply easily to education. The Commission was also attacked for giving too little attention to education as a cultural good with a contribution to social cohesion.

One conclusion was that today there is no ready-made model likely to address all current challenges. The Humboldtian model needs rethinking and adaptation to new circumstances and a possible renaissance for the European University requires that Europe finds its way forward on the basis of its own strengths. Europe should learn from, but not copy the USA. The solution is to be found in a diversity of models, reflecting the diversity of European cultures and perspectives. Diversity is an asset and imposing a single model will threaten the diversity. There are also several roles for universities. The Commission had not considered what should happen to the losers – whether full systems, individual universities or individual academics. Yet, competition creates losers, as well as winners, and it would be a serious mistake to focus on the brilliant few and forget the rest. One should not aspire for a hierarchy of excellence but a system of excellence in diversity, and there is a need for a massive effort to raise the level of universities' missions in training and research across Europe.

Support for Humboldtian ideas was (again) seen as reconcilable with instrumental concerns, as long as utility was not assessed solely in terms of economic competitiveness and growth. The EUA, for example, portrayed the University as an autonomous institution with a distinct European mission and underlined "the fundamental role of the university in building Europe, and in further defining and developing the European social model" (European University Association 2003). Others claimed that there is a need to strike a balance between diverse university missions, including regional development and an equitable geographical distribution.

---

[40] The response of the Learned Societies (Brussels 8 September 2003).

Absent in the comments was strong support for the representative democracy-vision. This was so even if current reform efforts involve a reversal of many of the accomplishments of the 1960s.[41] For example, new hierarchical elements have been introduced, egalitarianism has been played down and the anti-capitalist rhetoric against a University that produces "cogs in industrial wheels and brained-washed middle-class consumers" (Parsons and Platt 1973: 348) has been replaced by market rhetoric. Voices of the 1960s may be absent due to the institutions and individuals invited to respond to the Commission's Communication. The silence may also reflect that faculty and students have become less concerned with participation and representation, as illustrated by the Dutch case. At the end of the 1960s a management-inspired reform bent on coordination, effectiveness and efficiency was swept aside by demands for more democracy. Arguably, the 1970 Act on university governance passed by the legislature took the Netherlands closer to a democratic model than what was the case in any other country. In comparison, the new Act on modernizing the organization and governance of the University, put in effect in 1997, represented a "counterrevolution" with its emphasis on strong and unitary executive leadership. There were some protests, but neither students nor faculty took to the streets (de Boer et al. 1998, 1999). A query then is whether the market and management ideology will also turn out to be a fad, or whether it will establish itself within the University (Amaral et al. 2003: 293).

The European case displays that a new level of university debate and reform has been added. Different contested visions and legacies, partly located in different institutional settings and carried by different types of actors, are evoked simultaneously at the European level. Universities are not solely seen as national institutions (Hackl 2001). For example, the Commission wants Universities to be enterprise-like tools involved in global economic competition and rectors reach back to a past where geographical and political borders were of lesser significance. The EU's funds, Framework Programs and network-building have already had consequences for academic contacts, cooperation and co-authorship, making Europe a more significant entity (Smeby and Gornitzka 2005). A European Research Council, possibly modeled on the National Science Foundation in the USA, may strengthen these developments, depending on their agenda, budgets and autonomy (Caswill 2003) and so may joint degrees, external quality assurance and accreditation. A development from national block-grants to European competitive funding has increased the time and energy spent on applications, reports, monitoring and control, and the trade-off between academic excellence and European "added value" is problematic.

In several respects the European situation is unsettled. There is a multitude of partly inconsistent criteria of "success" and competing understandings of what forms of organization and governance will contribute to good performance. There is also a confluence of processes, and the European case illustrates the difficulties of disentangling the effects of global, European, national and local processes and thus comprehending

---

[41] Interestingly enough, the democratic aspect is emphasized more strongly in documents coming from Africa and the United Nations than in documents from Europe (Kallerud 2006).

university reform and change. The tensions and collisions between competing visions and legacies may have a potential for renewing the European University, but the TINA-interpretation of an inevitable transformation from a scholar-governed mode of research and governance to research governed by political and commercial actors and organizational forms (Gibbons et al. 1994), has to be scrutinized. It is important to distinguish among an observed trend, its inevitability, and its normative validity (Gustavsson 1997). It is also important to make efforts to disentangle the explanatory power of environmental dictates, deliberate reforms and institutional structures, processes and actors (March and Olsen 1989, 2006a, b; Olsen 2007).

THE SEARCH FOR AN INSTITUTIONAL IDENTITY

The claim that universities must reorganize and deal more imaginatively with problems ahead is well known from history. So are warnings against meeting criticism and reforms with romanticizing an alleged ideal model and demonize others. The University needs to avoid the pitfalls of "platitudes and nostalgic glances backward" (Kerr 1966: vi) and being "fogged by noble sentiments and high rhetoric" (Searle 1972: 169). Just like the turn of the nineteenth century, there is a need to rethink carefully the current and future role of universities on the basis of scholarly, institutional and political realities, such as increasing specialization and fragmentation of modern university life, "deep-seated tensions in the very conception and operation of the University" and a gulf between acknowledged models and university practices (Wittrock 1993: 331).

It is beyond this chapter to discuss in detail how the heterogeneous group of organized activities called "universities" and "institutions of higher education" in everyday language will develop in the future, the processes through which change will take place, and the factors that are likely to favor or hamper changes of a particular kind (Enders et al. 2005). The future of the University will be affected by many factors and some are obviously outside the control of the University. Still, universities, and different parts of each university, have responded differently to changing circumstances and attention is here primarily focused upon what discretion universities have and the possible impacts of the University's own actions and institutional characteristics.[42]

Institutions and Environments

A key distinction in the literature on formally organized institutions is the extent to which a perspective views institutions as epiphenomena that mirror environmental circumstances or deliberate willful (re)organization, and the extent to which a perspective pictures institutions as partly autonomous and reproduced with some reliability, independent of environmental stability or change and deliberate reform interventions (March and Olsen 1984, 1989, 2006a, b). The institutional perspective

---

[42] See, for example, Olsen 1998; Kogan et al. 2000; Marginson and Considine 2000; Amaral et al. 2003; Currie et al. 2003; Tomusk 2006.

used here views processes such as competitive selection and rational structural choice and adaptation as less than perfect. They also interact in complicated ways (March 1981). To understand institutional dynamics then means understanding environmental effectiveness in eliminating sub-optimal institutions, the latitude of purposeful institutional reform, and institutional abilities to adapt spontaneously to changing circumstances (Olsen 2001a: 196).

The idea of influential, or deterministic, environments gets support from the fact that universities have never fully controlled the direction, substance or speed of their development. Large-scale processes such as the industrial, democratic and scientific revolutions and the development of the nation state have fundamentally affected universities. Nevertheless, developments have not merely reflected functional responses to macro-forces and national styles, educational ideals and cultures, or differentiation within science itself. The University has been influenced, but not determined, by their environments and we have to consider to what degree reformers promoting specific programs and visions of higher education have had an impact (Kerr 1966; Veysey 1970; Parsons and Platt 1973; Wittrock 1993; de Boer et al. 1999).

The idea that university organization and governance can be designed and reformed through deliberate intervention is a key assumption behind the recent promotion of strong university leadership, the formulation of clear, consistent and stable goals, and the development of long-term-strategies for managing change. In contrast, students of university organization and governance have called attention to the limits of understanding and control and the complications of rational intervention where there is no agreed upon and stable meaning of "improvement." Causal chains between formal structures and university practices and performance are usually indirect, long and complex; formal and informal structures can only to a limited degree be deliberately manipulated; and successful universities tend partly to be loosely coupled "organized anarchies" (Cohen and March 1974; March and Olsen 1976; Kogan et al. 2000). Furthermore, what looks like revolutionary change in the formal organization of University governance, may turn out to be a codification of practice, with uncertain effects upon actual behavior and academic performance (de Boer et al. 1998).

This view is also found in interpretations of the historical development of the successful American research university. Veysey, studying late nineteenth century institutions in the United States, observed that there was a lack of self-consciousness over the emerging new organization, rather than manifest intentions. Much was taken for granted and Veysey (1970: 267–268) warned against interpreting good results as the outcome of intentions and foresight. Kerr (1966: 9, 49, 102) argued that no one created the multiversity, or even visualized it. Developments were unplanned and governed by circumstances more than shaped by plan and conscious design. Jencks and Riesman (1969: xiv–xv) claimed that American educators "have seldom been able to give coherent explanation for what they were doing. Even when they had a consistent theory, the theory often had little or no relationship to the actual result of their actions." The general responsiveness of American universities to society has also been seen to stem not from explicit policy, but from "the habits of flexibility and adaptability that have well served American universities throughout the first century of their history" (Geiger 1991: 215).

Shaping the University's internal organization, performance and role in society through long-term plans and strategies is today further complicated because debates and policy making impacting the future of the University take place in a multi-level and multi-centered setting, involving a myriad of actors, institutions and processes. For decades the single university setting and the nation state setting have been supplemented by premises from international organizations, such as the OECD, UNESCO and the World Bank. More recently, European-level processes have increased in importance. The GATS negotiations (General Agreement on Trade in Services) within the framework of the World Trade Organization may turn out to have huge consequences (Oosterlinck 2002) and it is not unlikely that security policies in the wake of 9/11 will have more important consequences for faculty and student mobility across national borders than policies based on educational concerns.

Processes of change can be well ordered and driven by a single logic. However, they can also be more or less loosely coupled. Sometimes they operate separately and in parallel. At other times they flow together in more chaotic patterns, as participants, problems, solutions, and choices are connected through timing and simultaneity more than through intention and plan, and seemingly accidental outcomes appear. The consequences of such processes depend on whether they take place in more or less institutionalized settings, more or less constraining the confluence of processes, actors and concerns (Cohen, March and Olsen 1972, 2007; Cohen and March 1974; March and Olsen 1976, 1989).

Change, then, is affected by how strong the University is as an institution. Does the University have an integrating self-understanding and shared sense of purpose, an organization and resources that make it motivated and able to impact the multitude of processes potentially affecting its future?[43] Is it likely to be able to counteract institutional imperialism and invasion of alien premises and reexamine its identity and pact with society?

One possibility is that the University gets involved in confrontations and a power struggle over its future. Then the questions are: How united, resourceful and attractive is the University? How relevant is it for other significant actors – what can it offer to others – and how relevant can it be made? Who are likely to come to the rescue of the University and what coalitions and alliances are possible? What opportunities are there for playing different opponents against each other – public and private and local, national, European and international actors?

Another possibility is a public, free and critical debate about the institutional identity and autonomy of the University – its foundational principles, the appropriate forms of organization and governance, and what a legitimate role is for the University in a democratic society. Then, the University involves itself in processes inspired, not by a predetermined vision of a specific organizational form and system of governance or

---

[43] In a similar vain, Nybom is concerned whether the University has the moral, intellectual and organizational strength to defend and deserve *Lern- und Lehrfreiheit* (Nybom 1997: 225).

a shared normative ideal, but by the processes that define the character of the University: communicative rationality, reason-giving, deliberation and learning (Habermas 1987). While the prospects are hampered by the lack of a shared "public sphere" in the University (Kalleberg 2000), such processes may under favorable conditions have a potential to unite highly differentiated and specialized sub-cultures around a shared conception of what a successful university can be and what it means to be a faculty-member, an administrative and technical employee, or a student.

Dilemmas to be Faced

If it is assumed that the future of the University (at least partly) depends on how convincing the University argues for its institutional identity, constitutive principles and rule-governed autonomy, a first step may be to call attention to four dilemmas facing the University. They are, how to balance: (a) the search for unity of purpose and the proliferation of identities and accounts, (b) the desire for unity of action and for protecting individual freedom, (c) the need to secure adequate resources without being seduced or being abandoned, and (d) the desire to embrace self-renewal as well as continuity.

Unity of Purpose and the Proliferation of Identities and Accounts

The University is a specialized institution with limited legitimate purposes. "Institution" implies some degree of internal coherence. Yet there are tensions and conflicts in all institutions. Insuring that a shared sense of purpose does not disintegrate is a constant challenge and it has to be inquired to what degree the University constitutes a rule-governed community with a strong identity and a shared sense of institutional purpose.

There are competing loyalties, logics and accounts. Some are "cosmopolitans," committed to the University as an institution. Others are "locals," committed to a specific university (Gouldner 1957), or a department, discipline or profession. Massive growth and differentiation are claimed to turn the University into an accidental agglomerate of co-habituating fields and individuals at the price of reduced community-feeling (Kaplan 1964) and to create a danger of make-believe-universities (Gardner 1962: 79). "The Humboldt University" has become a myth and a life-lie as its ideals have been incapable of coping with the theoretical and institutional expansion of the natural sciences.[44] Appeals to a unitary, self-governing academic community and the scientific ethos are used for justification rather than for governing the University (Gornitzka 2003).

In this perspective it is important to ask whether faculty, other university employees, and students are able to define what their common, institutional identity is. Do they know, and agree upon, what are the constitutive principles, values, structures and rules by which they want to be organized and governed, what they wish to share as an

---

[44] "The assertion of unbroken faithfulness to Humboldt is the life-lie of our universities. They no longer have a formative idea" (K. Reumann in Frankfurter Allgemeine Zeitung 24 March 1986, referred to in Habermas 1987: 4. Also Gumport 2000; Nybom 2003).

academic community and how they want to be different? To what degree do they, for example, embrace the principles of academic values, excellence and freedom, the unity of knowledge, the linking of research and teaching, the tenure-principle, and the principle of free education? To what degree are such principles related to the University's institutional identity and not solely to individual or group self-interests?

Academic communities, like democratic communities, have problems combining excellence and equality. There are many defenses against competition and against rewarding individual performance and superior individuals. Excessive competition can tear a University or a country in pieces. Excessive egalitarianism can make a university or country ineffective in competition with other universities or countries (Gardner 1962: 24–25, 112).

Historically, universities have not always given priority to high quality nor been willing to differentiate between more and less competent professors and more or less motivated and skilled students. Weber, for example, found a predominance of mediocrities in the German university (Weber 1970: 132). In the United States it was observed that "most university presidents and many professors at the end of the nineteenth century were downright hostile towards eccentric geniuses" (Veysey 1970: 428). It has also been argued that many faculty-members failed to effectively defend high academic standards during the 1960s campus turmoil because they had no overall vision of the University or philosophy of higher education (Searle 1972: 204). During the 1960s, educators were less sure than they were before that their tradition and values were worth defending. Many students were alienated from the University: "they had no sense of identification with the institution, no stake in improving it, and no reason for wanting a voice in its operation" (Jencks and Riesman 1969: x).

An implication is that the University's ability to impact its own future and its ability to defend the position as a fiduciary institution dedicated to academic values, freedom and excellence will depend upon factors such as: How strong is the academic community today? What is its content – what foundational values and principles are it likely to give priority to? How well does the University itself understand the processes and conditions that facilitate an academic rule-governed community that honor academic quality and how are these principles explained to an audience largely ignorant of the nature of academic work and scholarly identity? How widespread is the belief that university employees and students can achieve influence by engaging in genuine discourse and rule-driven, non-strategic and non-coercive behavior?

Unity of Action and Individual Freedom

The current enthusiasm for strengthening academic and administrative leadership and introducing more hierarchical elements as a condition for organizational autonomy is also based on a perceived threat to the coherence of the University. The suspicion that the University is unable to manage its own affairs in a coordinated and unitary way is, however, not new. For example, as unity of purpose disintegrated, a uniformity of standardized practices came into being in the US University around the end of the nineteenth century. There was fragmentation and centralization and bureaucratic administration made possible a new epoch of institutional empire-building without recourse to shared values (Veysey 1970: 311). While the different developments of French and German science during the nineteenth century have been attributed to changes in the German way of organizing and governing the University (Clark 1995), Weber observed that the German loss of academic leadership to American universities at least in part was caused by the latter's organizational and technical advantages (Weber 1970). The same type of argument was evoked during the 1960s. The institute directorship was labeled "the last strong-hold of feudalism" in Europe (Consolazio 1965: 326). The decentralized, live-and-let-live system and the oligarchy of senior professors and academic guilds were seen to contribute to the stifling and decline of basic science in much of Europe and cause a loss of talent to the United States (Kaplan 1964: 111).

Strengthening internal University leadership and external representation and weakening collegial and discipline-oriented organization, is likely to impact individual freedom and creativity. On the one hand, it is a paradox that individuals and small groups in universities account for a considerable amount of innovation, while the University as a corporation has been seen as "unconscious" (Olsen 1966) and even a "stronghold of reaction" (Kerr 1966: 98). There is also little hard evidence showing that New Public Management reforms have successfully contributed to academic success (Amaral et al. 2003: 292–293). On the other hand, academic success is reconcilable with a variety of funding schemes (Liefner 2003) and it is a paradox for many European universities that reforms perceived as threatening, such as externally recruited boards of trustees and appointed presidents, deans and chairs are integrated and legitimate parts of some of the best American research universities that the rest of the world take as a model.

Traditionally, scholars have wanted to be left alone, but today it is difficult to imagine a well-working university that does not have a well-functioning administration. As argued decades ago (by an administrator), it is important to get beyond the old pitting of faculty against administration, simply because it reflects an outmoded idea of the university (Perkins 1966: 88). It is then important to understand how different organizational arrangements and forms of governance are likely to function in different historical and cultural contexts. Under what conditions is it, for example, likely that university administrators come to think of their activity in generic leadership-terms (currently dominated by the ideology of the market-oriented private firm), or come to see university management as special, requiring principles and rules of its own? The ability to reconcile academic and administrative values and skills will also depend on what kinds of leaders, including external representatives, are recruited; what role-conceptions they develop; and how they are they made accountable. These are questions were few well-documented answers are available.

In principle, one way around the management-dilemma is to restrict the scope of the University. An old theme is to rescue basic research and learning by driving out undergraduate teaching and professional schools, by differentiating between professors who are competent to do high-quality research and those who are not, and leaving the writing of a dissertation to the relatively few students who are able to do original work (Veblen 1957; Wolff 1969). In practice, these proposals will produce tension and conflict and it is likely to be difficult for Universities to make such decisions. The proposal that there should be built a limited number of European elite universities (Nybom 2003; Commission 2003a, 2006b), together with the already existing stratification between universities and the development of relatively autonomous research institutes, laboratories and centers within universities, nevertheless indicate that universities have to face a difficult question. Where on the continuum, the Research Academy (generating new knowledge and seeing all knowledge as hypothetical and imperfect) and the School (transmitting established knowledge) do universities aspire to place themselves? The answers given are likely to have consequences for how unity of action and individual freedom are balanced in the future.

Resources; Being Seduced or Being Abandoned

The prospect of a loss of institutional purpose, direction and integrity has a resource aspect. The fear of seduction linked to the University's inability to say "no" to funds was typically voiced in the American context during the 1960s.[45] Facing a plurality of sources of support and a perceived problem of uncontrolled growth, it was asked whether the University should accept the goals and values of whoever could pay. It was also asked to what degree it would be possible to reconcile being an instrument for national purpose or community groups with free inquiry and critique (Perkins 1966; Wolff 1969).

In contrast, the primarily state financed European universities now tend to define their problem as financial more than a question of identity. They are concerned about being abandoned by public authorities – that national governments abdicate their traditional role as the universities' guardian angle and that public funds dwindle so that the University becomes dependent on private sponsors, alumni support and student tuition (Veld et al. 1996; Nybom 2003). Future generous support is certainly not guaranteed (Enders et al. 2005; Gornitzka and Olsen 2006). The University's days of almost unquestioned pre-eminence as an instrument for coping with society's problems have gone (Wittrock 1993: 344). Excellence has been developed in other institutional settings and the University is not necessarily the preferred site even for basic research. The distrust of public sector professionals has to some degree also spread to university employees and generated demands for external quality assurance, accreditation and cost efficiency controls (Kogan et al. 2000) and massive expansion in the number of students has made it impossible for the University to guarantee upward social mobility for all students.

---

[45] During the 1960s a number of writers on university governance illustrated the dilemma with the following Limerick:

There was a young lady from Kent
Who said that she knew what it meant
When men took her to dine
Gave her cocktails and wine
She knew what it meant – but she went.

Slack resources buffer conflicts and make it easier for an institution to live with conflicting goals and principles (Cyert and March 1963). In periods of austerity, budgetary struggles over cut-backs create more visible winners and losers and easily strain feelings of community. Adaptation of specific parts of the University to their task environments, sponsors and customers is also likely to make University-wide coordination difficult and weaken the sense of internal community and shared purpose and identity. Pay-per-unit financial systems can give incentives for growth, independent of internal consistency, academic quality and labour market opportunities for candidates.

A challenge for the University is to balance between the Scylla of being seduced and the Charybdis of being abandoned and at the same time defend its identity and integrity. Potential contributors of funds, and the population at large, have to be convinced that it is worthwhile to support the University in the future. It has to be clarified to what extent and under what circumstances there is a contradiction between academic values and self-governance and various social and economic objectives, and a line has to be drawn between what are legitimate and illegitimate demands and arrangements. This balancing act is not a one-time-affair. It is a continuous challenge linked to the ability to combine self-renewal and continuity.

Self-Renewal and Continuity

The belief in the self-regulatory capabilities of markets stands in contrast to the wide-spread belief that the University is unwilling or unable to change and that its structures are too rigid in an era of rapid scientific and societal change. The University has not changed itself; it has been changed (Kerr 1966: 102; Nybom 2003: 150). The European University in particular has had few if any self-correcting mechanisms (Kaplan 1965: 358) and governments in Europe have leaned over backward in their effort not to interfere with university autonomy (Consolazio 1965: 329).

The perceived rigidity of the University is curious, given that universities are strongly overrepresented among the longest-living formal organization in the world and that they therefore have documented their ability to survive under very shifting circumstances. The rigidity-claim is also surprising given the unprecedented growth and change that has taken place in universities over the last half century.

On the one hand, change in itself is not a valid normative standard. Any change is not necessarily better than status quo and there are few good reasons for generally embracing the current enthusiasm for rapid adaptation, for example by establishing research centers that can be easily established and dissolved (Clark 1998). On the other hand, protecting the identity and integrity of the University cannot simply mean a defense of status quo and in particular not a defense of a specific form of organization or system of governance. It is highly unlikely that a single arrangement can guarantee good performance indefinitely, under all circumstances, and for all parts of the University. Furthermore, concepts such as "University," "institutional autonomy" and "academic freedom" are not completely static. They have changed slowly over time and developed somewhat differently in different political and cultural contexts. Their content, and what are seen as reasonable reciprocal expectations, cannot be determined by universities or any other single group alone. They evolve in the interfaces between the academic community, public authorities and society at large, including the power relations typical for those interfaces.

In democracies the confidence of citizens and elected representatives is in the last instance decisive for how far institutional autonomy will reach and what will be an institution's legitimate role in the social order. The University therefore must balance change and continuity in a way that is acceptable both internally and to the outside world. Overly strong identification with a specific institution or organization can threaten the coherence of the larger system and there are legitimate reasons for guarding democracy against non-accountable experts and functional elites. Universities have to be accountable for the research and education they provide and there are no moral or democratic arguments for accepting mismanagement and eventually the collapse of universities with reference to the principle of institutional autonomy (Pandor 2004). The issue is the balance between autonomy and the degree and nature of democratic intervention and one way to generate support for the University is to convince the public that a well-functioning democracy requires a (partly) autonomous university and that both universities and democracies are constituted by processes of free discussion, opinion building and sharing of information (Gustavsson 1997).

Historically, there is ample evidence that the University's identity and integrity can be threatened from outside. But conflicts are not necessarily between the University and the rest of society. More likely there are disagreements within the University, among political actors and societal groups. Neither is it obvious how different universities will cope with the dilemmas they face and that they will always give priority to academic values, excellence and freedom. Actors within the University can also threaten its identity and integrity, for example through purely self-interested rather than principled rule-governed behavior, or by rejecting academic ideals such as truth and objectivity as unrealistic or outdated. It is an empirical question under what conditions external or internal threats are most likely and most dangerous for the University.

The future of the University then depends on how its autonomy is used in practice. The learning and self-reforming capacity of the University affects both the likelihood of external interventions and the prospect of being abandoned. The challenge is to protect the University's foundational purpose, identity and integrity and simultaneously develop and maintain flexibility and adaptation, including possible long-term change in established conceptions of what a good University is all about. Universities need to distinguish between legitimate and illegitimate demands for reforms. They also need to distinguish between legitimate defense of constitutive values and principles and defense of privileges, self-interests and ordinary laziness. In brief, both reform proposals and resistance to change have to be justified within a valid theory of the University as an institution (Searle 1972: 211), in particular in a democratic setting.

INSTITUTIONAL SUCCESS, CONFUSION AND CRISIS

Institutional change is often seen as driven by perceived failure – the institution fail to meet expected functional performance or there is an erosion of its normative basis and legitimacy. The chapter, however, suggests that institutional success may also carry the seeds of institutional confusion, crisis and change.

The University has in many ways been a success. It has never before attracted more students and resources and has never before been asked to fulfill more roles, take on more tasks and solve more problems. The University, not industry, is made responsible for the practical and marketable use of new knowledge. The University, not the students, is made responsible for student employability. The University has developed into a key institution that impact most aspects of democratic societies and many organizations want to use the name in order to improve their status and attractiveness.

Yet, the success has also created problems. Success has made aspiration levels raise rapidly, creating what may turn out to be unrealistic expectations. A result has been work overload and institutional confusion. The vision of the University as an enterprise embedded in global economic competition has gained strength, but other visions also have their more or less resourceful spokespersons. There are many and inconsistent purposes, expectations and success criteria. It is more unclear who has legitimacy to define academic quality, to talk on behalf of "society" and to define what social needs are. Governments are often unable or unwilling to formulate clear priorities and provide necessary resources; societal groups have different expectations and demands and only few of them are likely to be accommodated through market competition and price systems. Universities are uncertain about their identity – what they are, what they want to become, and in what direction to go. Boundaries between institutions are blurred and it is difficult for universities to find their place in a larger order of research and higher education institutions and in the political system and society at large. Institutional confusion, in turn, generates disappointment, criticism and sometimes an atmosphere of crisis.

Historically, universities have survived by turning institutional confusion and crisis into reexamination, search, innovation and rejuvenation. There is no guarantee it will happen again. Developments will, as before, depend upon many factors the University can not control. What the University can do is critically to re-examine its self-understanding as an academic institution: its purposes, core values and principles, its organization and governance systems, its resources and friends, and its social obligations. A possible starting point is to focus upon the University's work processes (and not solely its processes of governance) and its participation in a European and global intellectual competition among ideas (and not solely its role in economic competition). A key question is: What are the organized settings that attract highly qualified people and encourage academic excellence and free inquiry and also make the University take seriously its social and cultural responsibilities in a democratic society? The answer is most likely found in a mix of visions and principles and improved analytical frameworks, and better comparative data are likely to be of great help in such an endeavor.

A RULE-GOVERNED COMMUNITY OF SCHOLARS: THE HUMBOLDT VISION IN THE HISTORY OF THE EUROPEAN UNIVERSITY

Thorsten Nybom

INTRODUCTION

Whenever rapid, fundamental, and seemingly irreversible changes occur, or at least seem to occur, in politics, art, technology, or in different types of infrastructures and institutional formations, we are almost instantly inclined to start talking about "x-revolutions," "x-quantum leaps," etc. By doing so we are not only indicating that in "our age" we are experiencing an undisputed and measurable quantitative change in our daily private and professional lives, we are also convinced that the impacts of these processes will be extremely rapid, far-reaching, and indeed unique in a qualitative historical sense.

Thus, before discussing the question of continuity and change in European higher education and research and in particular the role of the so-called Humboldtian model, it is only befitting to once again make a humble reminder of the fact that concepts, such as "revolution" and "evolution," "change" and "continuity," are notoriously tricky to use in an actual analysis and explanation of historical events, actors and processes, and, hence, they are also hotly and almost incessantly debated among scholars. Historians have, for instance, not reached even a moderate or provisional form of consensus on the matter *when – or why –* a process of change in politics, economy, culture, or technology should be defined as a "proper" revolution.

Not least because of their powerful psychological appeal and notorious ambiguity these very concepts are – and have always been – used and abused, not only as unproblematic analytical and descriptive tools and categories, they have also been frequently used as potent ideological and political instruments to promote certain contemporary policies and political goals. Those among us, both scholars and other so-called experts, who are the most naive and not seldom notoriously lacking even the most rudimentary form of historical knowledge will usually maintain that they are not only able to predict the *precise outcomes and consequences* of these alleged revolutionary processes in practically every walk and dimension of human life, but are also quite capable of presenting the *"proper" remedies and solutions* that these more or less "revolutionary" and seminal changes crave.

The ongoing European debate on the need for rapid and fundamental changes in higher education and research funding, organization and policy planning during, at least, the last decade has certainly not been an exception from this particular historical

55

P. Maassen and J. P. Olsen (eds.), University Dynamics and European Integration, 55–80.
© 2007 *Springer.*

rule of ideological abuse (Ash 2005). On the contrary, many of the most frequent European arguments in this debate – both on the national and supranational level – have had clear political or ideological connotations. This is perhaps most obvious when different protagonists have resorted to historical arguments to promote their own particular reform agenda and recommendations (chapters 2, 4, 5 and 6). Most notably this has been the case in regard to the perpetual and sometimes heated discussions on the relevance/irrelevance, impact – negative or positive – actual significance and, even existence of the so-called Humboldt University both in the history of European higher learning during the last two centuries and regarding its present-day role and repercussions in European higher education organization and policy making.[46]

Despite the precautions and pitfalls listed above I, nevertheless, believe it is quite possible to identify at least six "revolutionary" periods, including the one we obviously are witnessing at present, in the history of European higher education and research, that is, periods when European university systems went through different types of fundamental changes.[47] However, my ambition is not only, or even primarily, to recreate a condensed and sketchy historical record of European "university revolutions," but rather to point to the fact that these fundamental changes certainly had a variety of internal and external causes or prime movers as well as different outcomes and consequences, which reshaped the institutional, professional, ideological, and political preconditions for the existing and emerging higher education institutions in a variety of ways.

By using a fairly broad historical perspective my ambition is, at least, to complicate the discussion on the multi-facetted long-term effects of structural change on the private and public lives of higher education institutions and knowledge production, as far as their fundamental organizational and curricular structures, pedagogy, main societal obligations, and basic self-understanding are concerned. For all analytical purposes the so-called "Humboldt Revolution(s)" of the nineteenth century will constitute the centrepiece and historical node of my deliberations. The discussion and characterization of the other identified "revolutions" in the history of organized higher education in Europe will indeed be very sketchy.

Thus, the first two "pre-Humboldtian revolutions" should primarily be seen as historically and culturally defined starting-points and preconditions for the institutional reforms and ideological transitions that were first introduced in Berlin at the beginning of the seminal nineteenth century. In many central aspects the starting-point for Humboldt's passionate ambition to restore the German universities into proper places of higher learning, was the deeply felt conviction, not only by Humboldt but by most of his intellectual contemporary *Mitstreiter* that the existing German universities,

---

[46] The Humboldt literature has, not least in the last few years, become almost boundless. For an overview, see Nybom (2003), Bartz (2005) and not least Ash (1999) and Schwinges (2001), as well as the contributions by Nybom, Jonsson, Henningsen, and Wittrock to Neave et al. (2006).

[47] The standard works on the history of the European University are of course the four CRE-volumes, *A History of the University in Europe* (Ridder-Symoens 1991, 2003) and Rüegg (2004). The fourth Volume, edited by Walter Rüegg, is forthcoming.

with a few exceptions, had deteriorated to intellectually stagnant local duck-ponds.[48] One could perhaps even go so far as to argue that his ultimate intention was *not to mend* but indeed to *smash* the existing universities – to create something entirely new (Walther 2001: 35).

Apart for being interesting in their own right the two "post-Humboldtian" examples might also further illustrate the continued relevance and persistence of the Humboldt model. Hence, if one wants to understand the arguments for institutional and ideological change discussed and propagated today, a closer and more complex study of the developments during the "long nineteenth century"[49] is crucial, simply because this particular period in the history of higher education has in a curious way played a central role in the ongoing discussions on the future of the European University – Wilhelm von Humboldt certainly continues to cast a very long shadow.

UNIVERSITY REVOLUTIONS – PRIME MOVERS AND BASIC CONSEQUENCES

Among the many possible internal and external *driving forces* or *prime movers* in the history of higher education and knowledge production a good handful of the more obvious and uncontroversial ones can be singled out:

(a) Political
(b) Ideological
(c) Technological
(d) Economic
(e) Scientific/Cognitive
(f) Demographic.

Even if these general societal forces usually are intertwined and, thus, very difficult to separate from each other when it comes to their actual historical impact, I nevertheless believe it can be quite instructive to discuss their *relative* importance and *possible* impact on different levels and dimensions of higher education and the pursuit of knowledge, such as:

(a) Institutional
(b) Curricular/Pedagogical
(c) Professional
(d) Social/Mental
(e) Policy/Political.

---

[48] His first very short academic experience in Frankfurt an der Oder was deeply disappointing and he subsequently suggested that after the establishment of Berlin this and other "provincial" institutions, which "could never gain any international repute should be closed down." See Steinberg (2001: 13, 72).
[49] The label was coined by Eric J. Hobsbawm (1987) in the 3rd volume of his brilliant exposé of world history since 1780.

As regards the major consequences of the categories I have identified they are equally floating and interrelated. However, it is in this way possible to identify and illustrate, at least tentatively, the multivariate and uneven character of the historical process of institutional change that has gradually transformed European higher education.

THE GUTENBERG REVOLUTION, 1460–1560

My first case takes its starting-point with an equally well-known, and never really disputed, revolution in the field of *Information and Communication Technology* (ICT) quite comparable to the one we have experienced in the last decades: Johann Gutenberg's invention, or rather development, in the 1450s of the printing press in Mainz. This technological innovation did not only revolutionise the production and distribution of knowledge and information (Febvre and Martin 1976; Eisenstein 1980), it also had far-reaching *professional* and to some degree *curricular* implications. In fundamental ways, this technology not only changed the *content* of education but also the *role* and *self-understanding* of both students and university teachers. For the university professor, one could say that this innovation marked an important first step from being mainly a *transmitter* to becoming an *interpreter* of existing knowledge and to some extent even a producer of new, original knowledge. From now on, the professor could no longer exclusively stick to his old trade of reading out loud from canonical texts, because, even if he still was using the traditional form of lecturing, his main obligation had become to *make personal comments*, and preferably even original and intelligent interpretations, on texts that were already available to, and sometimes even read by, his students.

As regards the students, the *ideological* impacts of Gutenberg's innovation can hardly be overestimated. It can be argued, for instance, that it would be quite impossible to understand and explain the "student revolution" of the late fifteenth and early sixteenth century, instigated primarily at the Wittenberg University by that notorious young theologian Martin Luther, and which soon became the prime mover of Protestantism, without Gutenberg's innovation. Likewise, it would be equally impossible to explain the massive expansion and transformation of scientific knowledge starting roughly at the same time. But even if the ICT-revolution of the mid fifteenth century obviously played a decisive role in changing the societal role and standing of higher education and systematic knowledge, surprisingly perhaps, it did not had any visible effect or any substantive impact on the overall organization, institutional, and curricular structure of higher education, and perhaps even more surprising, nor did it lead to any substantial reforms of the pedagogical content of higher education. As many historians have pointed out, this path-breaking innovation in ICT did not have *any* visible or substantial effect on the existing mode of teaching and educational thinking at the university. The actual delay from Gutenberg's invention to the introduction of new pedagogical and educational forms and methods made possible by that very technology was roughly 350 years, that is, when the modern Seminar was introduced as a central form of teaching and instruction.

THE SCIENTIFIC REVOLUTION, 1600–1750

As the second revolution, and in many ways, closely linked to the first – not least when it comes to the distribution of knowledge, one would certainly be inclined to reclaim the so-called "Scientific Revolution" of the seventeenth and eighteenth centuries.[50] Gradually, this scientific revolution had an enormous cognitive and theoretical impact by introducing the methods/*praxis* of modern natural sciences as an independent body of knowledge. But apart from its revolutionary *cognitive/scientific* drive it also, gradually at least, had fundamental *economic/technological* repercussions. Eventually, it also had deep – if in our particular context paradoxical – *institutional consequences* on the organization and political embedding of higher education and knowledge production, both regarding the *standing and institutionalisation* of scientific work and of its distribution,[51] Furthermore, and not least, it had a far-reaching and lasting impact when it comes to the *habitus* and *self-understanding/mentality* of the individual scholar. It is thus only befitting that Francis Bacon published his treatise *New Atlantis* in 1627.

This intellectual revolution witnessed the founding and rapid expansion of the first, at least, semi-independent, institutions for the systematic pursuit of *new* knowledge and research, that is, the European Academies of sciences starting with the establishment of *L'Académie française*, 1635, the Royal Society, 1660 and the *Académie des sciences*, 1666 (McClellan 1985). These were soon to be followed by sister institutions in practically every European country. It also, at least in rudimentary forms, witnessed the birth of the *modern scientific man* and simultaneously a growing insight that the pursuit of knowledge was a *common international enterprise*. Science and research were certainly not performed or did not prosper in *Einsamkeit (isolation)*; these activities were rather the outcome of intense international cooperation and permanent scholarly correspondence. Carl Linnaeus in Uppsala and the Royal Society in London could almost be designated ideal-typical individual and institutional representatives of this "sociological" development.

Furthermore, it has even been argued that this seminal shift in intellectual mentality and *habitus* should actually be regarded as *the* steppingstone to the European "Sonderweg" (unique path) to modernity and eventual hegemonial, political and economic global power. If so, it is almost exemplary that when Carl Linnaeus in the mid eighteenth century defined the *Homo Europaeus* as *"levis, argutus, inventor"* (quick, shrewd, innovative), that is, a supreme being – he was primarily, and indeed proudly, thinking of himself, that is, the *modern scientist* (Lepenies 1998: XVII and Huff 1993).

---

[50] See the contributions in Crosland (1975).

[51] Usually the *Philosophical Transactions*, 1661 of the Royal Society is considered to be the first regular scholarly journal. For an overview of the forms and ways of distribution, see Sörlin (1994), esp. chapters 3 and 4.

Strangely enough perhaps, the existing European universities, with the possible exception of two untypical examples of Leiden and Göttingen,[52] were not only side-stepped but to a high degree the victims of this profound intellectual and institutional revolution, which eventually led to what probably could be described as the most serious crisis that the European University has hitherto gone through in its almost millennial long history. The transformation of the medieval University system had already started with the emergence of the European centralized territorial state in the late sixteenth and early seventeenth century, which turned the University from an almost exclusive prodigal of the church into an institution *instrumentally* directly linked to, and in the service of the early modern absolutist state. In this connection it was primarily seen as a crucial *Kaderschmiede* of civil servants in different branches of the growing state bureaucracy. The Swedish development could serve as an almost ideal-typical example (Frängsmyr 2000: 330; Neave et al. 2006: 52–55).

The gradual emancipation of the University from the church changed the role and the (self-) understanding of what a university, a university professor and a university student were, or should be. The process of instrumentalization/"vocationalization" or what Germans probably, then and now, would give the label *Verschulung* of the university combined with the rise of independent scientific academies led to a gradual decay of the existing European university systems as research institutions from which it, at least in my view, never fully recovered. Thus, the ensuing transformation process in the history of higher education that characterized the next century was not primarily a period of reform of the *existing* institutions but should rather be seen as an era of *reorganization* and restoration of all three major European university "systems": the French – where the university in everything but name was side-stepped by the Napoleonic Reforms, the German with the "Humboldtian" revolutionary reforms, and the English with what Sheldon Rothblatt (1981) has described as the "revolution of the dons." The only place where the existing universities actually flourished during this particular era was probably Scotland.[53]

THE HUMBOLDT REVOLUTION: PART ONE
PROFESSIONALIZATION AND VERWISSENSCHAFTLICHUNG, 1810–1860

The first and perhaps still most famous of these seminal shifts during the "long nine-teenth century" occurred in 1810, in the then not particularly illustrious Prussian *Krähwinkel* of Berlin. The immediate driving forces behind this truly revolutionary break in the history of the University, which has gone down in history as the estab-lishment of the so-called Humboldt University, can be found in a combination of a number of integrated and random historical factors:

---

[52] And possibly Uppsala simply because of the presence of Carl Linnaeus, Anders Celsius, and Torben Bergman; for an overview and further references, see Frängsmyr (2000), and chapter 4.
[53] On the particular Scottish University and the Scottish Enlightenment, see Sloan (1971). For a comparative dimension, see Rothblatt (1997).

- *Ideology*: An almost unique combination of aggressive neo-humanism (classicism), *Spät-Aufklärung* and pre-romantic German idealism. (The most important intellectual point of departure probably being Immanuel Kant's satirical pamphlet *Streit der Fakultäten*, 1798).
- *Politics*: Prussia's national catastrophe after the Napoleonic wars and the ensuing political and institutional reconstruction of central functions of the state (vom Stein – Hardenberg reform era).
- *Mentality*: A historically – possibly unique – concentration of creative intelligence and a general interest in – almost obsession with – education in general.
- *Institutional*: The total external and internal intellectual and institutional decline of the German university system.

I am prepared to state that this seminal and even revolutionary importance did *not* take place primarily at the institutional level but at the *ideological* level. Thus, the main and enduring achievement of Wilhelm, *Freiherr*, von Humboldt was that he, out of the almost innumerable philosophical and pedagogical ideas on knowledge and learning floating around, was able to deduce and articulate and produce a consistent *Idea* of the University. Traditionally the defining properties and basis of the "idea" of the Humboldt's University/vision have rightfully been described as:

- Knowledge as a unified indivisible entity.
- *Einheit von Forschung und Lehre*. (Unity of research and teaching).
- Primacy of *Wissenschaft* and research, which also presupposed a new institutional order and cognitive hierarchy.
- The individual and common pursuit of "truth" in *"Einsamkeit und Freiheit"* (Solitude and freedom).[54]
- *Lehr- und Lernfreiheit* (Freedom of teaching and learning).
- The creation of a unified national culture with *Wissenschaft* and University as the centre-piece: *"Bildung."*
- *Wissenschaft* and (higher) education as the second categorical imperatives of the central state beside national defense: as the basis of a modern *"Kulturstaat."*[55]

The Humboldtian reforms, nevertheless, also had far-reaching institutional consequences. As regards Wilhelm von Humboldt himself his main institutional dilemma and concern could be formulated as follows: How is it possible to establish a *socially integrated yet autonomous institutional order for qualified scientific training?* An institutional order, which, at the same time, could guarantee an optimal and perpetual

---

[54] It should be pointed out by *Einsamkeit* von Humboldt certainly did not mean individual *intellectual isolation*. On the contrary, Wissenschaft = the never-ending search for truth, was indeed seen by both Humboldt brothers as a common enterprise of the republic of scholars/students. The claim for *Einsamkeit* entailed the right to devote oneself to scholarly work without any intervention from external forces.

[55] Apart from the argument of a superior "critical mass" the decision to locate the new University in the capital also reflected the central strategic position of the University in the nation state, Schwinges (2001: 59). This pattern was soon to be followed in other German and European states.

growth in knowledge but also provide a dimension of *Sittlichkeit* (virtue) to the individual?

Wilhelm von Humboldt's pragmatic solution or even functioning historical compromise was: *The regally (state) protected and fully endowed Ivory Tower combined with an elitist and gate-keeping Gymnasium/Abitur.* And even if the label Ivory Tower has gradually, nowadays become one of the most frequently used degrading metaphors for the supposed societal and even cultural irrelevance of the Humboldtian University, it certainly had no derogatory connotations for Wilhelm von Humboldt. On the contrary! The creation of an Ivory Tower was precisely what he ultimately was striving to achieve. Accordingly, the state must be persuaded that it was in its own well-founded, long-term interest to optimally promote the expansion of scientific knowledge, and this could only be accomplished by securing the individual freedom of the scholar. Reciprocally, the king should keep the prerogative of appointing professors – not primarily as a means of control but in order to protect the institutions from succumbing to the vice of internal strife and nepotism. Furthermore, to be worthy of enjoying this extended freedom and autonomy the professors should refrain from the political and other "external" strives, and hence the delimitation of the university from society at large should be clear.

Wilhelm von Humboldt presented two main arguments why the king/state should play the role of a more or less passive guardian angel to an institutional order with unparalleled autonomy in an absolute monarchy. First, there was the "philosophical/moral" argument that new and original knowledge could only be pursued and produced in *"Einsamkeit und Freiheit."* Second, and logically following the first, he also presented the purely "utilitarian" argument, which is usually forgotten in the present deliberations on the Humboldt University: since the intellectual *and* economic prosperity, and even physical existence of a modern *Kulturstaat* was directly and inexorably linked to the optimal pursuit and production of qualified knowledge, the principle of individual autonomy was not only a *desirable* institutional solution but an *utilitarian necessity* and central *moral obligation* of the central state – *sine non qua.* To pull off this political *"Meisterstück"* Wilhelm von Humboldt used both ideological/moral *and* purely economic and utilitarian arguments – sometimes originally invented by his brilliant younger brother, Alexander.[56] This "utilitarian" side of Wilhelm von Humboldt may perhaps surprise his present day academic admirers, who tend to believe that Wilhelm von Humboldt did not care about such "worldly things" as instrumental usefulness – he certainly did.

Contrary to Wilhelm von Humboldt's original proposal and repeated pleas for a fully endowed and thus economically autonomous university, the Prussian *Staatsrat* decided to treat the new University as just an ordinary state agency with annual and hence politically controlled allowances. This decision was a major disappointment to von Humboldt who considered economic autonomy as a necessary precondition also

---

[56] See for instance, Alexander von Humboldt (1845: 3–40), *Zaunick* (1958: 344). For a brilliant condensed introduction to Alexander von Humboldt, see Lepenies (1999).

for academic autonomy. The governmental decision was probably the main reason why he quite suddenly and promptly decided to leave his office as Secretary of state in the *Section des Kultus und Unterricht* after only 16 months in office, and he officially declared that he wished to have nothing to do with the further planning arrangements of the new institution of higher education (Steinberg 2001: 81). This definite demission has been reason enough to ask how much "Humboldt" the "Humboldt" University actually contained – all the more so as it was not until almost a century later that the Berlin University was hailed as the outcome of Wilhelm von Humboldt's genius.[57]

Last, but not least, a strict state control of student admission (*Abitur*) should be established. Modern academic "politicians" tend to forget that Wilhelm von Humboldt's greatest and lasting *institutional* achievement in education was probably not the reorganization of the Berlin University, but laying the foundations of the German *Humanistisches Gymnasium* (Vierhaus 2004: 63–76; and Mittelstrass 1994: 149–174).[58] The European secondary school thus became totally integrated in, and dominated by, higher education, and subsequently also the real gatekeeper and guardian of excellence. From now on the *Abitur* became the only, but still powerful selection mechanism for the comprehensive, "open" Humboldtian but nonetheless highly elitist university system (Müller 1990: 306). The illusion that the present day European secondary school systems are actually still performing this crucial gate-keeping task is very much alive in many parts of continental Europe, which has contributed to aggravate some of the structural dysfunctions in European higher education.[59]

In the initial five decades (1810–1860) of its existence the "new" German University underwent a gradual institutional and professional transformation, which eventually and in different degrees, would permeate and influence almost all Western university systems.[60] At the institutional level the modern organizational and hierarchical triad of *Fakultäten* – *Disziplinen* – *Lehrstühle* (Chairs) was formally established and cemented, where the actual power rested with the full professors (*die Ordinarien*). The European University then became a rule-governed community

---

[57] The actual Humboldt heritage becomes even more ironic and dubious when the Professor of Pedagogy Eduard Spranger in *Über die idee der Universität*. Leipzig 1910 – one of the many "Gedenkschriften/Reden" published at the centennial anniversary – boldly declares: "The great achievement of Wilhelm von Humboldt was that he was able to cog (Verzahnung) *Wissenschaft* and state together into an organic whole." (XLI), and even more so in the light of one of Humboldt's most frequently quoted statements: "The state must always be aware that it … is always a hindrance as soon as it becomes involved in things that would go so much better without it" (257) – and one of those "things" was precisely the University/*Wissenschaft*. For an early classic study on the "Berlin-type" University, see Paulsen (1902).

[58] From 1810 all German Gymnasium teachers had to get their degree from the university, see Lundgreen in Ash (1999: 148).

[59] One interesting case of the lack of serious consequential, long-term analysis would be how Sweden from the 1970s gradually changed its secondary school system from a "German" into a US-type high school system.

[60] The modern statutes of the Uppsala University from 1852 could serve as a typical example; see Blomquist (1992).

of scholars – a loosely coupled institutional framework without an administrative centre of gravity within which individual professors remained more or less autonomous.
The *Rektor* remained a purely representative position, and the *Kanzler*, as administrative head, did not even formally belong to the university but to the ministry. In
due course this institutional fragmentation would turn out to be one of more decisive
institutional differences between the European University and its rapidly expanding
North-American sisters and competitors. When it comes to *pedagogical* change the
introduction of the Seminar could be seen as an ambition to establish an ideal-typical
form of free, discursive and common scientific inquiry of professors and students.

From having been regarded as "*Trivia*" the Philosophical Faculty was elevated
to the indispensable core of the "new" University. A revolutionary transformation,
which although it had deep-set institutional consequences, primarily reflected the
epistemological and ideological corner stones in German Neo-humanist thinking. The
unity of knowledge was not only a cognitive and epistemological pillar of German
idealistic philosophy; it also constitutes, in some respects, its basic philosophical and
moral foundation. This unity should primarily be achieved and secured through the
reign of philosophy.[61]

This did not just mean that the natural and cultural sciences could be merged on
the higher philosophical level. Philosophy – together eventually with history – was
also given the central task or duty to supervise the so-called "*Brotwissenschaften*,"
that is, Medicine, Technology, and Law. These fields of study should not be able to
corrupt, or even influence, the institutional order and the intellectual content of higher
education, since those disciplines – to quote Wilhelm von Humboldt: "don't have their
immediate, spiritual home in *Wissenschaft* but in qualified handicraft." This Kantian
idea actually meant that the existing medieval university was turned on its head when
the traditionally "lower" Philosophical Faculty suddenly became top dog. In reality,
one could say that this Faculty, from now on, constituted the genuine and "real"
new University, since, according to Kant, and von Humboldt *et al.*, the Philosophical
Faculty was the only one immediately connected with "truth" while the other three had
their rationale in instrumental "usefulness" (Mittelstrass 1994: 22, 43; Müller 1990:
294, 306). Eventually, this also quite early led to an institutional differentiation.[62]
"Thus, the dual identity of the modern European University became established: it
was supposed to be at the same time a place for research and an educational institution
for *civil servants*." (my italics, TN) (Neave et al. 2006: 99; Schnabel 1964: 207).

On the *professional* level it has been argued that this period signified the emergence of the modern competitive academic career system and consequently also the
establishment of an informal but nevertheless obvious institutional hierarchy. Until

---

[61] Vierhaus in Treue-Gründer (1987: 69).

[62] But the dream of an indivisible body of knowledge lived on and, accordingly, when the soon much
envied German *Technische Hochschulen* were given the right to grant doctorates, in the second half of
the nineteenth century, they did so only on the condition that they established chairs in philosophy and/or
history "to secure their scientific quality." These chairs are, by the way, still with us today, see Lundgreen
in Ash (1999: 157).

the mid nineteenth century the recruitment of professors had in the German realm been extremely local – and to some extent even a family affair (Baumgarten 1997). In the second half of the century Germany had become a national academic labour market where professors pursued highly competitive academic jobs and careers. It was also now that the Berlin University gradually established itself as the pinnacle of academic excellence and fame (Baumgartner 2001: 105–129). Simultaneously, the individuals devoted to the noble task of perpetual "truth-seekers" that is, university professors – advanced markedly in social and economic status until they, eventually, in the imperial era attained a mandarin-like position – or in the words of the German professor of philosophy, Jürgen Mittelstrass (1994: 83): "What God was among the angels, the learned man should be among his fellow men."[63]

Finally, it must be pointed out that the driving-force behind the broad and massive international impact of the German University in the second half of the nineteenth century was not primarily a matter of any formal organization or institution building but rather an effect of an almost instant and exceptional expansion of scientific knowledge in Germany in practically all scholarly fields, which seemed only to accelerate over time. And since nothing succeeds like success also in academia, in less than half a century the *Friedrich-Wilhelms-Universität zu Berlin* became the undisputed model institution for practically all university systems in the world.[64]

The explanation of scientific productivity has long been a central concern of the history and the sociology of science. Should the undisputable success of German science and scholarship, in the nineteenth century and onwards, be explained by specific or generalisable cultural and/or economic factors?[65] Although there are many different theories accounting for scientific success performances, social scientists seem to agree on at least this one factor: "advance was dependent upon the number of talented individuals who select science as a career" (Cole and Phelan 1999: 37). But even if one certainly can find a fair number of scientific geniuses in German nineteenth century intellectual history, such geniuses, nevertheless, are in need of milieus where their genius can thrive and where their achievements can be duly acknowledged. So, the question remains: what are the factors that seemingly influence and possibly

---

[63] On the German Mandarin, see Ringer (1969) and the ensuing debate, for example, Habermas (1971: 239–251). Also Mommsen (1994).

[64] To illustrate the self-understanding and the almost unbounded self-confidence of the German professoriate already in 1869 one can quote from a speech "Über Universitätseinrichtungen" by the Rector of the Friedrich-Wilhelms-Universität, Emil Du Bois-Reymond: "It is reasonable to maintain that in the field of higher learning the German universities are superior to those of any other country. Indeed, given the fact that none of man's works is perfect, the German universities have such an organizational strength that they could only have been created by an act of the most fundamental legislative wisdom" (My trans.), see Bois-Reymond (1887: 337). As an illustration of the long term international impact one can quote Abraham Flexner's (1930: 305) "self evident" introduction to the German chapter in his famous book *Universities American – English – German*, "Of the countries dealt with in this volume, Germany has in theory and practice come nearest to giving higher education its due position."

[65] The same question is applicable in the case of Ireland showing a staggering R&D growth and publication rates in the last couple of decades – or for that matter also the cases of Finland and the Netherlands, see Bertilsson (2002).

increase the pool of scientific talents? In the history and sociology of science, there are at least three different types of theories: cultural, organizational, and wealth-oriented.

One classic theory in the sociology and history of science is the cultural theory, which Merton (1938, 1970) advanced already in the 1930s. His study of seventeenth century English science showed that after the Reformation in England, the rate of scientists increased considerably. Implicit in Merton's theory was the hypothesis that Protestant societies place a higher value on scientific activity, and hence, these societies will profit from that greater activity. But before applying this handy theory modelled on Max Weber's study of the affinity between Protestant Ethic and Capitalism, we need to consider the fact that many European countries had been Protestant for centuries without showing a similar development, at least not in the nineteenth century.[66] Nevertheless, even if it is no longer Protestantism and related religious and moral values that are significant in explaining scientific success, I maintain that Merton's theory has a certain historical significance for nineteenth century Prussia, and indeed the North-western parts of Europe in the sense that education became a central national state priority in most countries during the first half of the nineteenth century (Neave et al. 2006: 94, 51–60; Wehler 1987: 405–485).

In Prussia, furthermore, after the above mentioned defeat in the Napoleonic war it became a deep conviction among the reformers around Freiherr vom Stein and Fürst Hardenberg that the state must be reformed and rebuilt from within, or in the words attributed to King Friedrich Wilhelm III himself, Prussia had to "... make up in spiritual strength for the physical strength it has lost" (Wehler 1987: 473), which certainly included the notion or concept of national education as an absolute centre-piece (Ibid: 405–485, and Schelsky 1963). Thus and in summa one could quote a fellow German scholar:

The Prussian imperial desire to strengthen the "spiritual strength," the humanist-idealist demand for "national education," and the reformers' aim of having a tertiary educational institution in the service of civilian society all came together and formed the amalgam, which ran like a red tread through the university success story of the 19th century ...(Neave et al. 2006: 95).

However, we need to be highly cautious as to "motivational" factors that may operate in the case of young talents choosing a science career simply because of "higher" idealistic reasons. So it is most probable that apart from inner driving-forces external, material stimuli were also in operation, such as good research facilities, good salaries, good career opportunities; and such a (materialistic) motivation structure is linked to some other kind of theories. In the late 1950s Joseph Ben-David, advanced a theory of scientific success linked to structural-organizational factors prior to motivational-cultural ones (Ben-David 1960). In order to increase the pool of talented scientists, the crucial mechanism is institutional/educational reform. When more universities

---

[66] Concerning a negating case as regards the continued relevance of Merton's thesis of religious connection one could point to the contemporary German situation, where the Roman Catholic south is considered to be far more successful in science (e.g. The outcome of the recently carried through national "*Exzellenz-Initiative*" where the three selected universities are located in Baden-Württemberg and Bavaria!).

are created in a country, competition between these universities increase, and talented youth are offered richer opportunities. Hence, the pool of talents expands and intensifies; a motivational structure of high performance is the result.[67]

Ben-David's theory seems easily applicable to the development of the Prussian and the German higher education system in general in the nineteenth century (Paletschek 2001). Likewise, many have also pointed to a growing tendency to expand and reform the higher education and research systems in response to rising and changing demands and requirements of a rapidly growing and innovative industry, which would also be consistent with the rapid German industrialization process in the second half of the nineteenth century. And even more important, in this second phase of the industrial revolution the new electro- and chemical industries became the "cycle leaders" that is, industrial undertakings that not only craved sophisticated skills but even scientific knowledge to flourish and expand (Wehler 1987).[68]

Taken all these factors or driving forces into account, it actually does not matter if the different international followers often had a less well-grounded or even non-existing knowledge of the actual Humboldtian ideas and their implications and significance.[69] Thus, it would be quite possible to make the argument that the next flash of genius in University history – the establishment of the North American Graduate School – is, at the same time, both absolutely inconceivable without and fundamentally at odds with the *Friedrich-Wilhelms-Universität* (Parsons and Platt 1973: 304–345; Muller 1999: 199). To make the argument a little more provocative I believe one could, quite convincingly, argue that the Graduate School, and subsequently the great American research university, was founded on one of the most successful and productive "misunderstandings" in modern intellectual history! Hence, Daniel Coit Gilman, Abraham Flexner and other US-reformers could serve as instructive illustrations to Friedrich Nietzsche's warning of the dangers of knowing too much history if you wish to be an active and successful political and social actor in our own time.

"Bildung": A Necessary Ideological Excursus

An almost endlessly discussed key concept in Humboldt's thinking and reform plans is *Bildung* which, eventually, would have such a powerful, but at the same time imprecise, impact not only in German culture and public debate for almost two centuries. The Humboldtian concept of *Bildung* was not only a matter of understanding the

---

[67] This was not only how Ben-David explained the lead of United States from the 1920s and forward but also how he explained the success of German universities in the nineteenth century: a federal structure that promoted competition, which in turn promoted adequate funding and innovation, Ben-David (1983: 3–6).
[68] In this connection one should neither underestimate the constant impact of war and armament as an "ultimate" driving force also in the development of national higher education and research systems, for the US case, see Geiger (1993).
[69] For a systematic discussion on the impact of the German university in different parts of Europe and over-seas, see the contributions in Schwinges (2001).

rational features of knowledge and *Wissenschaft*, but also the possibilities of developing a person's natural abilities through an unlimited, spontaneous, spiritual process of self-cultivation guided from within (Ringer 1992: 95–108). *Bildung* involved more than the narrow learning process; it was also related to a particular concept of the human being that emerged in the closing decades of the eighteenth and the first decade of the nineteenth century. As a matter of fact, *Bildung* became the catchword for a whole philosophy of pedagogy, and indeed national culture, spreading from German-speaking cultural circles to the Nordic countries and Russia. The original power of the *Bildung* concept was that it referred to the objective, as well as subjective, aspects of knowledge. Thus, on the one hand, the subjective aspect of knowledge was emphasized, but at the same time *Bildung* would serve as a barrier against arbitrariness.

Inspired by the Swiss educationalist Johann Heinrich Pestalozzi the central aim in Humboldt's "*Bildungs-vision*" was the establishment of a national three-level educational system *(Nationalerziehung)* where the university was the third and final level.[70] In this comprehensive system the first or elementary level should only be concerned with *Menschenbildung*. The secondary schools should, through the intense study of languages (classic), history, and mathematics, primarily teach the students *how* to learn, since mastery of the learning process was absolutely necessary for the kind of university education Humboldt wanted to establish where the student is striving to attain "pure knowledge" in "*Einsamkeit und Freiheit*." At this third and highest level the most a teacher could do was to awaken the student's natural will to learn and act as an experienced counsellor and *Meister*.

The Humboldtian ideas and the ensuing German *Bildungsideal* never created a unitary national culture – if there ever was such a thing anywhere in the world. But it did contribute to the rise of a specific national "super-ideology." Research and higher education became integrated in, and were a central component of, a well-structured societal status- and power brokering hierarchy (Neave et al. 2006: 101).[71] In this extraordinary ideological brew it is possible to find, at least partly, the roots of the peculiar German ideological "*Sonderweg*," which in the second half of the nineteenth century was condensed into the conviction – or illusion – of a unique German road to modernity – *Kultur*. The allegedly unique German development was not only and in many and fundamental ways supposed to be different from, but also superior to the "normal," Anglo-French process of "*Civilization*." This hierarchical, not to say aristocratic, national ideology got its perhaps most ideal typical expression, in 1918, in Thomas Mann's equally brilliant and chilling treatise *Betrachtungen eines Unpolitischen*.[72]

---

[70] The central elements in Humboldt's educational thinking were presented in the "white paper" *Der Königsberger und litauische Schulplan* from 1809, see Liedman (1997: 227) and Björnsson et al. (2005: 217).

[71] For a uncompromising and negative evaluation of the impact of the "Humboldtian Bildung-Ideal," see Litt (1955).

[72] For a penetrating discussion, see Lepenies (2006), also Henningsen, in Neave et al. (2006: 101).

THE HUMBOLDT REVOLUTION, 1860–1920: PART TWO
THE RISE OF THE MODERN RESEARCH UNIVERSITY AND
COMEBACK OF WILHELM VON HUMBOLDT AS MYTH

The second "revolution," the emergence of the modern research university, which in reality brought about a gradual restructuring and reorganization of all university systems, at least in the so-called Western world, took place in the period between 1860 and the outbreak of the First World War in 1914. The driving forces behind these fundamental and simultaneous changes came not least from *within* science and scientific theory itself. With the emergence of the modern – and post-newtonian – natural sciences and their gradually demonstrated industrial potential it became virtually impossible to define the scientific endeavour and the academic profession as "the pursuit of curious individual gentlemen of ingenious minds." After Justus Liebing and subsequently, Herman von Helmholz, Robert Koch, Louis Pasteur et al. (laboratory), Albert Einstein, Max Planck, Niels Bohr, Ernest Rutherford et al. (theory), and also Wilhelm Röntgen, Carl Bosch, Fritz Haber et al. (application) the pursuit of knowledge had become a central concern for almost every sector of modern society. Hence, the combined effects of the fundamental breakthroughs and revolutions on the scientific-cognitive level and the demonstrated and potential impact on the macro-economic and eventually also political level, had deep-going ideological, professional, institutional and policy consequences, which in many ways collided with the basic Humboldtian ideas and ideals.

• First, science had turned into a collective task or "intellectual industry," which demanded scale, organization and, perhaps above all, money and where the notion of *"Einsamkeit und Freiheit"* seemed to be utterly obsolete.
• Second, and for more or less the same reasons, the ambition to amalgamate *"Forschung und Lehre"* gradually became almost impossible.[73] The most striking illustration and manifestation of this fact became the establishment of the *Kaiser-Wilhelm-Gesellschaft* and its string of more or less autonomous research institutes in 1911. It was, perhaps also, the ultimate indication of the deplorable fact that "excellence" had actually started its gradual exodus from the Humboldt University.
• Third, the steadily growing costs and societal impact of research did not only lead to institutional changes but also to innovations in research policy and (targeted) funding, which had consequences for the institutional autonomy (vom Brocke 1988).
• Fourth, and perhaps, even more seminal, modern science finally and irrevocably crushed the illusion of the "unity of knowledge under benevolent aegis of philosophy" and was gradually superseded by the idea of two distinct scientific "cultures." Significantly enough, it was in Germany that this distinction between *"Natur- und Geisteswissenschaften"* was discussed and philosophically codified in the second

---

[73] For instance, when Albert Einstein was called to Berlin in 1913 he had no teaching obligations, and he was not the only one, see Vierhaus in Treue-Gründer (1987: 73).

half of the nineteenth century by scholars, such as Wilhelm Dilthey, Heinrich Rickert and Max Weber, while it was also discussed by intellectual industrialists, such as Werner von Siemens (von Bruch 1999: 46).

This process of cognitive disintegration and specialization was, furthermore, institutionally manifested by the foundation of the modern *Technische Hochschulen* responding to the rapidly growing demand for a new type of qualified professional training and skills.[74]

However, in our context it is equally interesting and remarkable that this process of cognitive and institutional disintegration, which in many respects signified a fundamental brake with the original Humboldtian ideals, was not only explicitly presented as the ultimate fulfilment of Humboldtian dreams, it also, ironically enough, marked the reinvention and even canonization of Wilhelm von Humboldt himself as the spiritual *and* practical founding-father of the German (European) University.[75] Accordingly, it is typical that when the prime intellectual and bureaucratic movers, the theologian Adolf von Harnack and the almighty *Ministerial-Direktor* Friedrich Althoff, instigated the institutional revolution of the *Kaiser-Wilhem-Institute*,[76] they were nevertheless very keen to use and stress all the supportive arguments they could possibly find in Wilhelm von Humboldt's rediscovered and immediately canonized *Denkschrift*. Luckily enough, in his deliberations Humboldt had indicated that a complete science organization should have three major institutional components or levels: beside the free Academy and the University, there should also be "Hilfs-Institute." But with these "leblose (life-less) Institute" Humboldt had hardly meant the powerful centres of excellence that were now established.[77]

It is also at this point in time, especially in connection with the centennial anniversary in 1910 that Wilhelm von Humboldt's ideas and ghost were transformed into some kind of "universal weapon" (*Allzweckwaffe*) (Paletschek 2001: 103) in the German and gradually also the international debate on higher education institution building and higher education policy. It is perhaps interesting that this ideological innovation process or transfer was already from the start driven and promoted not in scholarly works by professional historians but primarily in interventions and pamphlets by academics with a "university political cause" or education politicians on the national

---

[74] Lundgreen in Ash (1999: 157). See also chapter 4 in this Volume.

[75] During the entire nineteenth century *Wilhelm* von Humboldt was hardly a reference point, or even mentioned, in the University policy discussion. The Humboldt that indeed was often referred to was his brother *Alexander*, whose crucial importance regarding the development of sciences in Germany was frequently emphasized, see Paletschek (2001: 98–104). (It is in this connection perhaps significant to note that even if the two brothers have remained almost equally illustrious and constantly referred two, each epoch of German political history has crafted its very own Alexander – and sometimes (1949–1989) even more than one – while Wilhelm, on the other hand, seems to have always remained the unchangeable "neo-humanist genius and university-builder"! On "The many lives of (A) von Humboldt," see Nicolaas Rupke (2006).

[76] On the KWG, see Vierhaus and vom Brocke (eds) (1990).

[77] See Vierhaus in Treue and Gründer (1987: 72). On Althoff's central position in research and university policy-making, see vom Brocke, in Treue and Gründer (1987: 195–214).

level. In the German context this became particularly true in the reoccurring times of national or institutional euphoria, deep crisis and ongoing restructuring.[78]

Even if technological innovation *per se* cannot be said to have played an important role in the process of restructuring university life between 1860 and 1920, the short- and long-term *technological consequences*, of the internal scientific revolution were to become almost "cosmic." From now on, and increasingly so, "Big science" did not only become heavily dependent on modern, sophisticated technology, it also became the absolute necessary prerequisite for, and power-house of, this path-breaking new tool, soon to be called "high tech." Or to put it differently in more socio-political terms: As the English crystallographer and historian/politician of science, John Desmond Bernal *hoped* already in the 1930s, and MIT-President and Scientific Advisor the President, Vannevar Bush *feared* in the 1940s,[79] the demonstrated tremendous impact or obvious and immediate "social function of science" had ultimately made science and scientific training too important a matter to be left to the scientists and so it was eventually turned into a separate sector of national policy making. In this connection, one should also contemplate the undisputed historical fact, that without the boys and the odd girl (Lise Meitner) on the banks of the rivers Spree and Cam, and of Öresund – a little bit later, also, on the banks of the San Francisco Bay and Lake Michigan – the university and research system would certainly not have enjoyed the enormous political and public good-will – and equally enormous investments – that it actually had the good fortune of doing in its golden age from 1945 to the mid 1970s.[80]

THE MASS-REVOLUTION, 1965–1975

The next revolutionary change in the history of the University was what the Berkeley sociologist Martin Trow in his classic article from 1974 defined as the ultimate shift from elite to mass higher education. It started in the USA already after World War II, with the introduction of the GI-bill, (Geiger 1993) and gained momentum in Europe in the 1960s and early 1970s. This shift was primarily caused and driven by external political, economic and demographic forces and had, at least initially, very little to do with internal cognitive or educational factors. It was both a consequence of growing popular demands (equality of life-chances) and of the immediate intellectual and professional needs of the emerging welfare state. This development was by no means confined to Western Europe but it was rather a general process that included,

---

[78] As a starting point one could choose the above mentioned *Gedenkschrift* by Eduard Spranger from 1910. In 1919 the Prussian *Kultusminister* Carl Heinrich Becker published *Gedanken zur Hochschulreform*. In 1946 the philosopher and university ideologue Karl Jaspers published his important *Die Idee der Universität*. In 1963 the sociologist and University reformer Helmut Schelsky published his equally seminal book *Einsamkeit und Freiheit*.

[79] Bernal's influential book *The Social Function of Science*, appeared in London, 1939 and Vannevar Bush' equally important *Science – The Endless Frontier* in Washington, 1945.

[80] For the USA as the leading nation, Geiger (1993), esp. chapters 6 and 7.

more or less, all industrialized parts of the world. In the European case, however, the massive growth of the higher education systems took the form, not of structural renewal but of a rapid expansion of the existing institutional and organizational forms. Or as the German sociologist Thomas Ellwein (1985: 238) has summarized the German development: "*Ausbau statt Umbau*" (Expansion instead of reconstruction)! At least in the German case the most frequent explanation for this obvious lack of structural reforms has been attributed to the lasting and overpowering impact of the "Humboldtian ideals."[81]

But also in countries where the higher education system was quite substantially transformed, as in the Swedish case, its comprehensive and monolithic character was, nevertheless, retained and even strengthened, partly as an effect of the deliberate ambitions to "vocationalise" almost all types of higher education (Neave et al. 2006: 52–55). As long as the European states were prepared to fully finance this rapid and massive expansion, the institutional consequences remained limited. However, when – after 1980 – this was no longer the case, an institutional dissolution process became inevitable (Nybom 1997: 140). All in all, it is not unreasonably unfair to maintain that in the European case the rapid and massive changes have generally been carried out with few if any detectable signs of higher political wisdom or of institutional prudence and professional insights, at least not during the last 25 years and certainly not in comparison to other higher education systems.[82]

The undisputed success of the North American research universities in the last century and particularly in the last 30 years (the same period in which their European sisters declined) could, at least to a certain extent, be explained by their readiness and superior ability to react to social, economic, scientific, and political changes (Kerr 1991, 1994).[83] The European University, on the other hand, *has not changed* in the last 50 years – it has *been changed*. Paradoxically enough, this has been achieved rather by systematic negligence than by bold intervention on part of the politicians, but the end result is, nevertheless, that the European University has become a seemingly helpless political football.

---

[81] Schelsky (1963) had invoked and endorsed the Humboldt Legacy as the basis for future university reforms, was, only four years later in his *Festrede* at the bicentennial anniversary of Wilhelm von Humboldt's birth inclined to warn against the tradition to make Humboldt to the eternal litmus test for higher education policy: "In our considerations on education (*Bildung*) we have elevated Humboldt to the rank of Church Father, and subsequently, every attempt or suggestion to change anything in what is held to be the founding elements in his University structure, is condemned as blasphemy." (Schelsky 1969: 152). For a discussion, see Bartz (2005: 105–110). For the Humboldt "heritage" in the GDR, see Connelly in Ash (1999: 80–104), and Wittrock, in Neave et al. (2006: 119–123).

[82] For a general account of the "massification" process in the USA and esp. of the much envied California system, see Douglass (2000), Kerr (1991, 2001), and Geiger (1993).

[83] Even if Clark Kerr sometimes has argued that the US-universities also have changed mainly due to external pressures, I do, nevertheless, humbly maintain that the North American research universities and central university actors have shown a relatively remarkable ability to act and reform. Not least Clark Kerr himself (the California Master Plan) must be considered to be an almost ideal typical example of this capacity. See also Trow (1991: 156–1972) and Keller (2001).

The most immediate and deep-going impacts of these primarily quantitative changes were visible on the professional, mental and political levels. The academic profession, which hitherto had been extremely homogenous gradually split up into different levels and tasks. This, in turn, gradually led to a declining social and economic status of the academic workforce. I would go so far as to maintain that this eventually also included a slow but irreversible process of "de-professionalization/ de-academization" in what had been regarded as "the highest profession,"[84] and subsequently either led to a gradual shift from collegiate, academic to bureaucratic governance or in some European cases to political neglect.[85] The latter was also manifested by the massive introduction of new and different types of semi-academic vocational programs as well as by the, at least sometimes, reformed admission requirements and examination forms.

This could be illustrated by the transformation of university governance from a meritocratic collegiate to a quasi-democratic representative system (chapter 5) as in the German case where the traditional "Ordinarien-Universität" was abolished in favour of the representative, so-called "Gruppen-Universität." The perhaps most fundamental changes, however, took place on the political or policy level. Due to its steadily rising costs and size, and its growing social and economic relevance higher education no longer was perceived as primarily a national cultural investment but rather regarded as an integrated part of the ordinary education system where manpower planning and not academic excellence became the highest priority in higher education policy and planning. In 15 years time this revolution had changed, or in certain cases even severely damaged some of the European higher education systems – with the possible exception perhaps of the English where the changes occurred later.

Curiously enough, if there were interrelations between innovation/business and the ordinary European universities in this entire process, it was perhaps primarily a negative one – with the obvious exception of medicine and some of the technical universities. From now on, and increasingly so, the sophisticated branches and producers of the emerging information communication technology, and other high tech branches, did not intensify their collaboration and interactions with the ordinary European University.[86] This process of estrangement, together, of course, with other interrelated political, economic, etc., factors, is certainly not unimportant when trying to explain the constantly widening scientific/technological gap between the USA and Europe after the Second World War, and particularly since the 1980s.[87]

Even today, politicians and academics, who should know better, seem to forget that if there was a gap in technological and scientific know-how in 1945 then it was

---

[84] In the sense that the Academic profession actually trains and examines all other professions.

[85] For primarily the Swedish case (Nybom 1997: 121–127) and Nybom (2001: 63–66), and for Norway see Olsen (2000: 231–249).

[86] The establishment of Fraunhof-Institute organisation in Germany, and similar initiative in the 1960s and 1970s in other European countries are instructive cases.

[87] One possible explanation to this development could perhaps be the historically close connection between the European universities and the state/civil service.

probably to *Europe's* advantage. To deny, like many European academics *still* do, the fact that the quality and performance of the respective higher education systems has played a crucial role in bringing about this rapid and massive shift in the distribution of intellectual power, is not only a sign of historical ignorance but also an example of institutionalized continental, mainly academic, arrogance or even sheer ignorance.

Considering the natural delay of causes and effects in research practice and research policy planning, there are good reasons to believe that something happened in European or American research policy planning in the 1970s. And it most certainly did! Starting in the late 1970s many European countries gradually and consciously replaced the existing Vannevar Bush model of science policy and research funding with a variation of more or less explicit versions of instrumentally oriented research-funding policies, which were supposed to secure and boost the immediate "social function of science." This shift did not least have, and continues to have, profound and lasting detrimental consequences for the norms and values, such as disciplinarity, peer-review, for institutional autonomy, and eventually also for the level of intellectual creativity and hence the life and well-being of the European University.[88]

The first, which could be labelled "the technocratic phase" started in the mid-1960s and lasted until the late 1970s. This development constituted no immediate threat to the primacy of basic research, traditional academic values and the university. Instead, it was seen as a complementary but supposedly more "socially relevant" form of knowledge production that was funded and administrated outside the traditional research sector, but often under the qualitative supervision of academic research. It could, perhaps a little simplistically, be regarded as an attempt to fulfil the old social democratic dream of the "good society" governed by a scientifically based and enlightened form of social engineering.

THE UNIVERSAL REVOLUTION–AND THE RISE OF NEW PUBLIC MANAGEMENT, 1980–2006

Finally, I will wage the risk of getting into even deeper waters by talking about the present state of affairs and indeed also about the future, fields where the historian can claim no exclusive or superior competence.[89]

First, during the last 25 years there has been a sharp rise in student enrollment, which means that several of the European higher education systems have turned from being mass to become almost universal higher education systems. In most European cases this has happened without any fundamental structural and institutional changes in

---

[88] For the Swedish case until the 1990s, see Nybom (1997). For a discussion on more recent European developments, see Krull in Neave et al. (2006: 146–151) and Scott in Neave et al. (2006: 130–142). For the Swedish case in the 1990s and onwards, see Benner (2001), Bennich-Björkman (2004), Leijonhufvud, in Neave et al. (2006: 153–158). Also the discussion on recent Nordic research policy planning and universities in Nybom and Stenlund (eds.) (2004: 175–213).

[89] For detailed and certainly more sophisticated analysis of the present situation, see the other contributions in this volume.

the existing, often unitary and inflexible, European state-controlled higher education systems. Accordingly, this growth has caused substantial structural, institutional, and intellectual dysfunctions and deficits.[90]

Second, and to make things even worse, this rapid growth of the student body has been accompanied by unchanged or, in many cases, even reduced levels of state funding. This could be seen as an undisputable indication of the European states' and central governments' massive retreat from their traditional "Humboldtian" obligation of being the ultimate guardian angel of their national higher education institutions. And additionally, the resources which eventually were allocated to the universities and research gradually turned from a system that had included a substantial share of block grant funding into a system where so-called "competitive funding" became the standard operating funding procedure. This meant that the possibilities of long-range research planning at the university level became more or less illusory, and, eventually, also to a reduced capacity to function as independent and autonomous institutions.[91]

In the last 15 years, European central governments have become just another "stake-holder" who is primarily treating the universities not as a public good *as such,* but rather as just another political means for achieving all sorts of political ends. It is, for instance, quite clear that at least some European governments have expanded their higher education systems in the 1990s *primarily* because they wanted to reduce the unemployment level among young people.[92] Paradoxically, this development has almost everywhere been accompanied by a trend of sometimes massive politicisation of higher education and research,[93] which in some cases has led to a redefinition of the ultimate role and mission of higher education institutions. These are no longer considered to be responsible and invaluable academic and national *cultural* centres. They are rather primarily seen as instrumental means; to function as "development or innovation centres" in national or even regional economic policy (Kogan et al. 2000). In addition, this process has been accompanied by an almost explosive growth of numerous evaluations and accountability schemes, which have turned the traditional

---

[90] The chronology of this development has differed between the European countries, but, generally, one could maintain that there has been a substantial rise in the number of students in the last 25 years.

[91] The sharp increase in competitive funding and the relative decline in public funding in the last decade has certainly not been without complications and detrimental effects also in US-University system. Yet there are fundamental cultural and historical differences between the US- and the European systems both when it comes to experiences of multivariate, competitive funding and the societal embedding of the universities. These fundamental differences also mean that the institutional impact and consequences in the two systems tend to be different. On recent trends in the USA, see Geiger (2004), as well as Slaughter and Leslie (1997) and Slaughter and Rhoades (2004). For the Swedish case, see Engwall and Nybom (2006).

[92] Obviously explicit statements by politicians to confirm this are nowhere to be found, hence it would be interesting to make a serious empirical study on the correlation between f.i. Swedish unemployment rates and the governments repeated decisions to increase the number of "student-places" during the last decade.

[93] For an interesting and penetrating discussion and for references, see chapter 7 in this Volume.

European system of exclusive and strict "input control" into different types of "output control" where practically "everything that moves is measured."[94]

Furthermore, and in a European "etatist" university context and tradition certainly not least important, it remains an undisputable fact that, as of today, very few if *any* of the present European central governments can be said to articulate, and much less pursue, any form of conscious national research and (higher) education policy, even in the most rudimentary form, with the possible exception of Finland and Switzerland. Instead European politicians are standing on the ruins of their crumbling university systems delivering one joint statement after the other on the strategic importance of knowledge, research, innovation, education, etc.

Third, during the same period of time research funding has undergone a second period of massive bureaucratisation and instrumentalization. This is primarily but certainly not only manifested by the constantly growing importance and direct and indirect impact of the so-called "frame-work" EU-Research Programs. It has also to a very high degree become a dominant trend in research policy and research funding at the national level. The "Policy for Science" that characterized the first three decades after World War II has in practice been abandoned for something that rightfully could be labelled "Politicised Science." This has gradually led to a growing tendency in research funding to replace the traditional criterion of academic excellence by more nebulous criteria sometimes labelled "strategic," sometimes "social and economic relevant," sometimes "mode 2" research or "the production of socially robust knowledge."[95] Subsequently, this has affected public research funding in the sense that politically controlled "earmarking" and "strategic allocation of resources" has become the rule rather than the exception (Forman 2002).

Ultimately, this has had fundamental consequences for discipline formation and for other dimensions of the internal life of science including the self-understanding and professional ethos among scientists and scholars.[96] Thus, it is not only relevant to talk about a gradual demise of the University but also, at least in relative terms, of a decline of the disciplines, particularly in research policy planning. Even if the traditional disciplinary structure is still well anchored in academic life and prestige structures it has, nevertheless, gradually lost its favourable position in the research (policy) hierarchy. In a system where politically defined "socio-economic relevance" has gained the upper hand as the ultimate criterion of quality, disciplinary based peer-reviewing and expertise is not only considered to be inadequate and even obsolete, it can also quite easily be dismissed as nothing but a means of illegitimate power abuse on part of the scientific community (Forman 2002).

---

[94] Peter Scott's apt characterization at a Bank of Sweden Tercentenary Foundation Seminar, at Krusenberg 05/25/2003 also Scott (2000). For international comparison, see also the contribution in *Sociology of Science Year-book* (2006, fall).

[95] For an intresting discussion and references, see the contributions by Scott, pp. 130–141 and Gustavsson in Neave et al. (2006: 159–162), also Elzinga (2004: 277–304).

[96] For a notable shift among Swedish academics during the 1990s and the early 2000s, see Blomquist et al. (1996) and Bennich-Björkman (2004).

Against this total background, one could very well start wondering if the euphoria among national and European politicians and higher education bureaucrats over the alleged unlimited possibilities opened up primarily by the jointly agreed upon implementation of the Bologna process in European higher education has *anything* to do with a serious will on part of its academic and political protagonists to promote the pursuit of qualified knowledge (Witte 2006). A more suspiciously minded (cynical) observer would perhaps rather detect a hidden political agenda behind the sudden and massive Bologna-enthusiasm among national and European politicians, bureaucrats, and lobbyists, which indicates that the main objective of the Bologna scheme is simply and foremost that it gives the politicians an opportunity to avoid the risk of having to take the immediate responsibility of a number of necessary but probably very controversial reforms on the national level concerning (a) funding (fees), (b) differentiation, (c) access (master), (d) marketization. Instead, unpopular undertakings can and have been presented as "unavoidable and logical consequences" of Bologna.[97]

This implies that the Bologna process is not only presented as the magic tool for creating an open European Higher Education Area, it is also considered to be the ultimate means for implementing long overdue, fundamental structural reforms in European higher education. In the worst of all possible cases the politicians – together with their allies in academia – will succumb to the illusion that Bologna will, in itself, *both* raise the quality of higher education and research *and* at the same time take care of the constantly growing needs for qualified vocational training and lifelong learning structures.

CONCLUDING REMARKS

Coming back to the Humboldt revolutions I would, in this connection, first like to point to the fact that successful transformations in higher education are not always – and have even seldom been – to expand the number of tasks, duties, and obligations performed by the University. I have the slightly worrying impression, that we, being caught in a curious type of a-historic and simplistic analogy-thinking, have a tendency to believe that the developments of the 1960–70s are forever true and relevant. In short, when, and if, the University has to respond to "new challenges" or is asked to "reformulate its agenda" or "mission," the universities tend to conclude that they must take on any new task or responsibility "society," on an almost daily basis, suggests or demands. *This is not true,* simply because, when it comes to knowledge "*society*" very seldom actually knows what it really needs in 15 years time!

The two Berlin-based "revolutions" discussed above, which thoroughly reorganized and rejuvenated the Euro-American universities and turned them into the real intellectual *and* industrial power houses of their societies, for almost two centuries, had nothing to do with expansion. On the contrary! Wilhelm von Humboldt's

---

[97] This type of argumentation is sometimes called the TINA-syndrome (There Is No Alternative), see chapter 1 in this Volume.

exceptionally successful institutional reforms of 1810 in Berlin meant retraction and "purification." The establishment of the modern European and American research university at the turn of the previous century also meant that the universities defined their core mission in a much more restricted way than they had previously done. So, when we, today, are discussing how to respond to the "new challenges and demands" and to "redefine our new role/mission" in society, we should also perhaps remember that all great universities always have, *at the same time*, been institutionally adaptive, intellectually creative, *and* ideologically conservative institutions.

Sometimes the impact of intellectual or mental transformation is so powerful that actual reality is more or less superseded by this projection and thus becomes a myth. Certain concepts and ideas may acquire an "afterlife" that makes them significant far beyond the times in which they were created and sometimes for reasons far different from those the original creator probably envisioned. This is most certainly the case with Wilhelm von Humboldt's *Denkschrift* and his final proposal, *Antrag auf Einrichtung der Universität Berlin Juli 1808*. These few and scattered pages, written in clear and beautifully unbureaucratic German, have triggered off an almost innumerable number of more or less qualified scholarly, political and other reflections during the last 200 years. In these two centuries there has probably not been delivered one academic *Festrede* – at least on the European continent – that did not mention either Wilhelm von Humboldt or the "Humboldtian Idea of the University."

But despite the never-ending deluge of speeches, essays, and books from both Humboldt's friends and foes I do, nevertheless, believe that it is necessary for the European academic community to discuss and confront this overpowering and nebulous image repeatedly, simply because of its continued presence in almost every European discussion on the mission and future of higher education and research. In some curious way the central question then is perhaps not Wilhelm von Humboldt's *actual thoughts* but rather why these ideas have come to play such an exceptional role during two centuries almost regardless of how far from his original thoughts the European university systems have moved.

One tentative answer to this fundamental question would be that Humboldt was not only able to formulate a comprehensive idea of what institutionalized higher education and the systematic pursuit of knowledge should be, but he was also able to convincingly argue why it must be considered as one of the central interests and indeed obligations of the nation state to support such an undisputed public good. This is very different from our era in which almost everybody in politics, business, civil service, and academia is almost incapable of delivering a single speech without referring to the alleged strategic importance of "research, education, knowledge, competence, and excellence" in the present and future "knowledge society." At the same time, most European universities neither seem to have a formative idea nor are they adequately supported or trusted by their formal political owners and masters. As a consequence, ideological references to the "noble Humboldtian ideas" can either be used as an eternal source of moral and intellectual legitimation or be dismissed as an obsolete and detrimental institutional European heritage, which is hampering the necessary restructuring of European higher education and research.

As we have seen, this is nothing new in the history of German and European University politics, it has been going on for more than a century (chapter 4), or at least since the turn of the previous century when the then existing Berlin University almost officially was declared to be the institutional and physical embodiment of Wilhelm von Humboldt's *corpus* of ideas and ideals. One of the reasons why this ideological traffic has persisted is, in my view, precisely because von Humboldt was primarily interested in *pursuing and realising a coherent but nevertheless imprecise body of neo-humanist ideas*. His actual interest in institution building was secondary or at least not concretely and precisely articulated. And, however brilliant, a slightly nebulous set of ideas can readily and steadily by used and abused in ideologically infested conflicts.

So, if the other important University ideologue of the nineteenth century, John Henry, Cardinal, Newman, who incidentally formulated his vision of the University in direct opposition to the German/Humboldtian "*Wissenschafts-Universität*," could be said to have taken an existing formal *institutional order*, the Oxford College, and transformed it into an *Idea of a University*,[98] then Wilhelm, *Freiherr*, von Humboldt's major achievement was to *synthetise a number of ideas on science, Bildung, and learning*, which 100 years later were transformed, or elevated, or perhaps even perverted into *an institution* soon to be decreed as *the* University, and which another 100 years later is freely and indiscriminately used in the European debate on higher education; either hailed as an eternally valid ideal-type or disdained as a suitable scapegoat, which is responsible for nearly all our alleged present miseries. From this saga we may thus learn that not only "institutions matter." This is equally true of ideas.

---

[98] For a penetrating analysis of Cardinal Newman and his important *The Idea of a University* from 1852, see Rothblatt (1997).

CHAPTER 4

AN INSTRUMENT FOR NATIONAL POLITICAL
AGENDAS: THE HIERARCHICAL VISION

Åse Gornitzka and Peter Maassen

INTRODUCTION

The vision of a University as an instrument for shifting national political agendas represents a specific kind of instrumentality, that is, the University as used by democratically elected governments. As such it differs from the instrumentality identified by the "University as a representative democracy" and the "University as a service enterprise" visions. It sheds light on the complexity of the government-University relationship by linking the university's mission, aims, and direction of growth through a government hierarchy to shifting political priorities and funds.

While there is great inter-country diversity in the recent adaptations of the national governance approaches with respect to higher education, the common feature in continental European countries[99] is the move away from the government hierarchy model with respect to the University. In the vision underlying this model the government is responsible for the funding and regulation of the University's operations, which limits the level of institutional autonomy in procedural as well as substantive matters, and allows the supervisory authorities, especially governments, to steer the universities in a hierarchical way in technical-administrative as well as professional-academic matters.

As such the government hierarchy vision with respect to the University forms a complement to the Humboldtian vision on University organization (chapter 3). It was an important element in the transformation of the European nation states from the end of the feudal period (around 1800) to the First World War. The period brought, certainly after 1850, the development of national social and economic strategies. The result of this transformation was that the state funded the universities, guarded them against direct intrusion from powerful economic and social groups, and granted the academic staff a relatively high level of individual academic freedom, as long as the universities were willing to follow the procedures prescribed by the government for running their organization, and accept the interference of the government in teaching and research matters. The latter was an important aspect of the development of national policy traditions with respect to higher education.

---

[99] The governance situation with respect to higher education in the UK is different, in the sense that the Jarratt report from 1985 marked the beginning of the period of greater instead of less hierarchical government interference with higher education (Fulton 2002: 193).

P. Maassen and J. P. Olsen (eds.), University Dynamics and European Integration, 81–98.

Different countries developed different traditions in this period, and these traditions have continued to form the basis for specific approaches in using the University for national purposes until today. The three main national traditions that also influenced other countries' efforts to use the University in the implementation of national agendas were the German, French and British traditions.

Resistance of the University to this state interference was not unusual, implying that the nineteenth century saw many conflicts between governments and University (Gerbod 2004a: 98–99). It often was difficult for the state to "use" the classic University in a direct, instrumental way. In a number of cases university resistance made the state set up new types of organizations, such as specialized technical, agricultural, medical or economic institutions that initially in Europe did not carry the name University, or new extra-university research structures. After 1945 the relationship between the state and higher education further intensified on the European continent, until governments decided from the mid-1980s on to introduce the notion of "steering at a distance" (Maassen and van Vught 1989) and increase the autonomy of universities in various core areas. Since then universities have operated "between government and market" (Gornitzka and Maassen 2003); but the move away from the hierarchical governance model does not mean that it has been completely replaced in practice by a service enterprise governance approach (chapter 6). Instead of European governments fully abdicating their central steering role with respect to higher education, they have taken measures that have led to a serious repositioning of all actors involved as well as the institutional arrangements developed for the governmental steering purpose.

The hierarchical chain of command in the instrumental model raises a number of questions on the aims and expectations of the state with respect to the universities. What are the main national policy traditions with respect to the University? What was seen as the main purpose of the University? What were the national agendas that the University was expected to implement? What were the conditions under which the hierarchical vision could operate in a stable way?

The chapter will address these questions, first by reflecting upon the historical position of the instrumental vision on university organization at the national level. Second, by discussing the relationship between state and higher education in areas of direct instrumental interest to the state. Third, by discussing the extent to which the instrumental vision on university organization is part of the current state governance models with respect to the University. Fourth by presenting some developments in the internal organization of universities related to the change in governance approach.

FRAMEWORK FOR ANALYSIS

In chapter 2, Olsen introduced four visions on the University as an organized system. These visions provide different answers to the questions: What is the University for? And: Under what conditions will it work well? Three of these visions interpret the University as an instrument for different groups. In this chapter the vision that regards the

University as a tool for shifting governments and national political agendas is taken as a starting-point. The organizing principles of this vision are hierarchy and command. In the two-by-two matrix presented in chapter 2 of this Volume the "University as an instrument for national political agendas" cell represents the combination of shared norms between various actors, and dominant external factors (chapter 2, Table 1).

In this hierarchical instrumental vision two core functions of the University are the training of employees for the growing professional bureaucracy and the production of knowledge in areas that provide the basis for the state's wealth and welfare, especially agriculture, defense, education and health. A key element in this vision is the idea that the University is functioning best from a societal point of view when it is steered up to a point by the state. The underlying assumption is that the state is best positioned to represent the public interest and on the basis of that set up national agendas and identify national priorities.

This vision is related to an instrumentalist view on politics (March and Olsen 1989: 3, 6–7) which sees choice making and resources allocation as central issues in political life. There is limited interest in this view for the symbolic side of politics. The basic underlying question is: Who gets what, when and how? The assumption is that the state is best positioned to make the choices concerning resources and the regulatory framework within which universities have to operate. Choices are claimed to be made rationally on the basis of knowledge and information provided by experts, and through careful consultation, analysis and planning. The state gets its legitimacy on the basis of its position as main if not sole funder of the University. This position allows the state to take a hierarchical position towards the University and steer it through a set of regulations that can conditionally be linked to the funding regime. The primacy of outcomes implies that "Action is choice, choice is made in terms of expectations about its consequences, meanings are organized to affect choices, and symbols are curtains that obscure the real politics, or artifacts of an effort to make decisions" (March and Olsen 1989: 48). Consequently the outcomes of the governmental interference in the University's technical and professional matters are not an aim in themselves, even though they are presented as such, but the real intention is to strengthen the legitimacy of the government of the day as the authority that is responsible for the political life of the nation state. The more effective the contributions of the University to the implementation of national agendas, the more important the University as an instrument for the government in maintaining and, if necessary, strengthening its legitimacy in the political decision-making arenas.

THE RISE OF THE HIERARCHICAL INSTRUMENTAL VISION

The often difficult relationship between state and University under the government hierarchy model that allowed the University to be both a Republic of Science and a national instrument with specific social, political and economic aims, has a history that goes back to the beginning of the nineteenth century (Olsen 2000; Gornitzka 2003; Gerbod 2004a: 83). Until that time European universities were self-financing, independent institutions (Neave 2001; Gerbod 2004a: 84–85). The period from the early nineteenth century until the beginning of the Second World War showed a gradual growth of state interference in universities and a subsequent loss of organizational autonomy. This was also the period, especially in the second half of the nineteenth century, when the modern University was firmly established and recognized as a knowledge-producing institution (Wittrock 1993: 305). This development was closely linked to the emergence of the democratic nation state as we know it today in Europe as well as the USA. The technical arm of these nation states became to a large extent dependent on the knowledge produced and transferred by universities, especially in areas such as agriculture, defense, health care and education.

However, these were not the first examples of European universities being directly linked to national priorities. In the seventeenth and eighteenth century various monarchs or other supervisory authorities had taken measures that indicated the growing importance of the University in the building of European nation states. Sweden was, for example, the first state to introduce the direct link between its public functions and University training: from 1655 on access to its civil service functions was restricted to national citizens that had obtained a qualification from one of the national Swedish universities. This example was followed before the end of the eighteenth century by Prussia, Piedmont, Austria and Russia (Frijhoff 1992).

Another important development from this period was the establishment (in 1773) of the *Ecole des Ponts et Chaussées* in France (Neave 2001: 23). This event provided the model for the elite training schools *Ecole Polytechnique* and *Ecole Normale Supérieure* that were set up 20 years later. As such it lay the foundation for French higher education as it still exists today, with the "technical arms of the state" having their own elite training institutions outside the University. In addition, the establishment of this school showed very clearly that if the University remained insensitive to the demands of government for the push of relevance, it ran the risk of being bypassed. Finally, the establishment of the *Ecole des Ponts et Chaussées* forms one of the first examples of the explicit development of a national "state sector" of higher education. Efforts to nationalize the existing universities had not been successful until that time: as indicated above, the European University of the late eighteenth, early nineteenth century was still a "private, self-governing, property-owning and self-financing corporation" (Neave 2001: 23).

Among the main reasons why governments in the end were successful in their attempts to integrate the universities in their national state structures was the expansion of the European universities. While it took, for example, the French universities 400 years to double their level of enrolment, that is, from around 6000 in 1400 to around 12,500 in 1789, in the following 150 years student numbers multiplied rapidly: in 1937 the University of Paris alone had more than 32,000 students (Gerbod 2004b: 101).

A large part of this expansion was the result of the growing demand of public institutions, including national Ministries, for highly trained, competent staff. As such the rapid expansion in student numbers marked in the first place the end of the possibilities of the University to operate as a self-financing institution and allowed the state to take over at least partly the control. But in the second place it gave the state a number of arguments, including the need to guarantee the quality of university graduates, to legitimately reduce the autonomy of the University.

The growing importance of the "usefulness" of the University was accompanied by efforts to adapt the internal organization, including the setting up of new, hitherto absent faculties, for example, in natural sciences. In addition, it led to the introduction in the higher education arena of specific "utilitarian" fields and disciplines, such as engineering, agricultural sciences, education and medicine. However, in most cases the existing universities refused to open up their organization for these new fields that they looked upon with a certain disdain. In many cases this led to the establishment by the state of new, specialized institutions that, as indicated before, were fully state controlled and administered.[100]

The resistance of the University to governmental interference in its internal affairs was possible on the basis of the traditional principle of academic self-governance through councils and other bodies. Even in countries with a very tight state control, such as France and Russia, the traditional universities were allowed to continue some form of self-governance. This was not the case with the non-university higher education institutions that were established in the nineteenth and early twentieth century. They were totally controlled and administered by the state (Gerbod 2004b: 91). This difference, that is, the University being managed by full professors with a certain level of autonomy (depending on the country and institution in question), and the other type of institutions being fully administered by the state, had its effects on the extent to which the state in practice used the University as an instrument for specific national purposes.

THE UNIVERSITY AND NATIONAL POLICY TRADITIONS

When looking in more detail at the relationship between the state and the development of the university sector in a number of countries the following main policy traditions can be observed. In France and Germany a strong, large professional bureaucracy was developed that formed the main driving force of socio-economic developments. The main difference was that in Germany policies were developed through an "organic-corporatist approach" based on a strong coalition between state, church and industry, while France knew a more "centralistic, state-driven policy tradition" with a more coherent elite forming the core of society (Vijlder 1996: 110). In England the aversion against the involvement of the state in education remained strong, implying that a liberal-capitalistic policy tradition was developed with a limited involvement of the

---

[100] Ruegg (2004: 691–702) provides a list of 167 important other institutions of higher learning (non-university institutions) set up by national European governments between 1745 and 1944. About 70 of these were technical/engineering institutions (incl. mining), many of which are leading European Technical Universities today. In the same period 110 new European Universities were established (Ruegg 2004: 682–691). Even though most of these were set up by their national government, contrary to the non-university institutions they were organized as the traditional universities with a certain level of organizational autonomy.

central government in policy processes. The Anglican Church that throughout much of the nineteenth century held a firm grip on the education sector, was replaced in much of the twentieth century by local education authorities (Ringer 1978; De Swaan 1988). The English tradition had obviously a strong influence on the development of the US policy tradition with respect to higher education.

The influence of the national policy traditions on the modernization of national higher education systems in the nineteenth century can be illustrated by the following brief descriptions of some of the main aspects of this modernization. In Germany the new technical schools (*Technische Hochschulen*) increased in economic importance after 1850. They contributed in many ways to the technological and other innovations that formed the basis for the economic growth of Germany in the period until the First World War (McClelland 1980). However, during the entire nineteenth century their status and organizational structure remained different from the traditional universities. For example, only after a century of opposition from the traditional universities did the *Technische Hochschulen* in 1899 get the right to elect deans and rectors instead of having them imposed by their Ministries (Gerbod 2004b: 120).

The modernization of higher education in the Netherlands resembles the German developments. Also in the Netherlands a strong development of technical higher education can be observed in the second half of the nineteenth century. Like in Germany this development does not take place in the traditional universities, but in newly established *hogescholen*.[101] However, in the Netherlands the relationship between the traditional universities and *hogescholen* was less conflictuous than in Germany. In 1905 the term *hogeschool* was incorporated in the law referring to programs with a scientific character, but aimed at application. This meant the factual recognition of the higher education status of *hogescholen*.[102]

In France the structure of the higher education system established during the Napoleonic time was very different from the German situation. The core characteristics of the French system consisted of centralized state control, isolated faculties that took the place of universities, and the central position of specialized schools (*Grandes Écoles*). Only in 1896 did the French Universities become institutions with inter-faculty connections (Weisz 1983). Because of the stagnation in the university sector gradually the *Grandes Écoles* underwent a development comparable to the German *Technische Hochschulen*, that is, their status was growing and they became central institutions in the development of the French economy. Contrary to the *Technische Hochschulen* the *Grandes Écoles* were never formally integrated into the university sector.

In England the dominance of Oxford and Cambridge continued also in the nineteenth and twentieth century. The only national competition came from private

---

[101] In addition to technical institutions in this period (1880–1930) also economic and agricultural *hogescholen* were established (Idenburg 1960).

[102] Most original Dutch *hogescholen* have in the second half of the twentieth century been transformed into Universities. The current Dutch *hogeschool* sector consists of institutions for higher professional education. Outside the Netherlands these institutions use the term University of Applied Sciences.

colleges and the private London University (set up in 1826). However, the Humboldtian model did not bypass the dominant English universities. They became fully devoted to the importance of scientific research from the end of the nineteenth century on (Ruegg 2004: 12).[103] However, this does not imply a growing importance of technical university education and research in England. The rise of technical higher education took place later than on the continent. The general view in this was that industrial techniques should not be taught at universities – because of the fear for company espionage – and that training-on-the-job was preferable (Vijlder 1996: 100–101). Another difference between England and the continent was that the government only started to fund the newly established universities from 1889 on. The liberal British governance tradition with respect to the universities was continued after the First World War with the establishment of the University Grants Committee (UGC). This body was dominated by academics and played an important role in the allocation of public funds to the universities until the time of the Thatcher government. Consequently, until the late 1970s the English universities enjoyed a much larger level of autonomy than their continental counterparts.

An important difference between the developments of the modern University on either side of the Atlantic was that in Europe the University became an essential part of the state structure, while in the USA the initial efforts to include the University in the emerging new federal structure as well as the rising US state structures were less successful (Trow 2003: 17), resulting throughout the nineteenth century in a decentralized US University system that was more autonomous and more market driven than its European counterparts. However, this was a conditional autonomy since the US states clearly expected their universities to serve the general public. As a reaction to the refusal of the classical private and public universities of that time to provide the education and research in areas of immediate relevance to the US states, the Morrill Act was accepted in 1862. It radically altered US higher education by establishing land-grant institutions or programs in every US state. These were expected to be "allies of their state governments in furthering the economy, health and cultural life" (Moose 1981: 8; Nevins 1962).

The Morrill Act changed US state universities fundamentally in at least three ways, that is, their disciplinary basis, their teaching styles, and their accessibility. As a consequence of the act programs in new areas were established, such as agriculture, engineering, business, forestry, education, architecture, education and mining. The act also brought an element of professional training to the US campuses through the

---

[103] Of relevance here is the interpretation of Brockliss who states that "the idea of the modern research university advocated by Humboldt was implemented more authentically in the universities of Oxford and Cambridge than in the institutions in Germany, since Oxbridge retained corporate and collegiate autonomy, as well as their primary mission of non-professional education. On the other hand, the continental universities subjected to state authority served first and foremost to train doctors, teachers of law and other academic professions, and only the most gifted students benefited from a scientific education through research undertaken in co-operation with their professor" (L. Brockliss, *The European University 1789–1850*, in: Rüegg 2004: 12).

introduction of discussion classes, experiments, field trips, and laboratories, as well as through the emphasis on English as the language of instruction instead of Latin and Greek. Finally it opened up higher education to non-traditional students. An important consequence of the "land-grant" Act was that from 1862 on the states could use a large number of their universities for the implementation of specific political agendas and the realization of priorities that had to do with their economic, medical and cultural development. The act brought science and engineering into the University leading to major improvements and modernizations in agricultural and industrial production, sanitation, water supply, and transportation (Moose 1981: 5–8). The effect of the act on the institutional landscape of US higher education after 1862 was rather diverse since around half of the states established their land-grant universities separate from their state universities. In these states the state universities were preserved as centers for the study of classics and humanities, while the land-grant universities became a second layer of more professionally and practically oriented universities. In other US states the land-grant idea was integrated into the existing public universities leading to the first comprehensive universities that combined "classical" with more applied disciplines and fields.

Diversity in the State Driven Modernization of the University

These developments show that the current diversity of European universities and higher education systems can in many ways be traced back to the diverse ways in which various countries handled the need for a more instrumental function of their autonomous University system. On the one hand we can see the liberal British-US policy tradition with at least initially a minimum involvement of the national (UK) or state (US) government in the development of the universities and the higher education system. The assumption in both traditions was that the University would contribute most effectively to socio-economic development of the society if it was granted a high level of autonomy from the state. In the USA the major interference of the states in the development of the University in the nineteenth century was through the so-called land-grant act that "corrected" the rather autonomous development of the traditional university sector through the establishment of a specific set of "instrumental" universities and university programs that were explicitly expected to contribute to the implementation of political agendas. The British government did not interfere directly in its university sector, implying that the establishment of technical, agricultural and economic programs in higher education took place much later than on the continent or in the USA.

On the other hand there is the state-driven continental European higher education policy tradition in which the state governed its higher education system through a centralistic state approach, aimed at creating a homogeneous national elite that would take the lead in the development of the economy and the bureaucracy. France was the first country in Europe that deliberately tried to set up a state sector in higher education, and it tightly steered, regulated and funded its higher education system from the early nineteenth century on. An important consequence of the focus on national elite creation was the central position of the professional colleges (*Grandes*

Écoles) in the higher education system, implying that the core of the French higher education system was formed by technical, educational, economic and other types of applied oriented institutions, instead of by the universities. The German situation was different in the sense that the core of the German higher education system was formed by the traditional universities that resisted the integration of the new applied oriented, mainly technical institutions, into the university system. The state granted the traditional universities a high level of substantive autonomy, and focused its efforts to use higher education for socio-economic priorities mainly on the non-university institutions and centers.

THE LIMITS OF HIERARCHY AND THE POST-WAR EUROPEAN UNIVERSITY

The way in which the hierarchical utilitarian vision on higher education and research has been expressed by governments in Europe displays what can be interpreted as the limits of this vision as applied to the University. The result is a significant organizational differentiation in the field of research and higher education. Two core dynamics of organizational differentiation in this are on the one hand the development of a conception of higher education as serving national agendas but organized outside of the realm of the University, and on the other hand the differentiated research organization that is the result of the government's desire to use scientific research for the purpose of national priorities.

The Hierarchical Vision and the Alternatives to University Education

Beginning in the 1960s European societies were faced with an increasing demand for higher education among a growing number of young people with qualifications to enter higher education. As a response governments started the build-up of public alternatives to the universities, especially in the shape of vocational colleges and the upgrading of specific secondary education institutions to tertiary education status (Kyvik 2004). These alternative institutions were expected to cater for government perceived labour market needs through shorter degree programs and practice-oriented courses. This happened to the degree that by the end of the 1990s Italy had remained the only EU member state that had not introduced some type of professionally oriented higher education institution besides the university sector.

The establishment from the late 1960s and onwards of a "non-university" higher education sector should not only be seen as an autonomic response of European governments to demands for system expansion. The underlying government rationale for polytechnics, colleges and other non-university higher education organizations contained a strong element of instrumentality, especially as part of national priorities in regional policy and social equity in access to higher education. These organizations were also subjected to political-hierarchical control to a larger degree than the established universities at the time. In UK, Sweden and Norway the governance of regional colleges and polytechnics was tightly linked to regional political control. The hierarchical vision embedded in the regionalisation of higher education started in the 1970s, continued in the 1980s and lasted well into the 1990s – by establishing new colleges or polytechnics and with increasing emphasis on building stronger regional units through mergers. In the national innovation policies and strategies that were introduced in the 1990s and 2000s the instrumental view on higher education resurfaced in the shape of the much acclaimed role of regional colleges in regional development (Kyvik 2004).

THE HIERARCHICAL VISION AND THE INSTRUMENTALITY OF ACADEMIC RESEARCH

A basic goal attached to higher education and academic research is that it can provide a knowledge basis for public decision-making. As providers of knowledge and scientific information, research organizations and universities as a prime site of knowledge generation and dissemination serve as a core element of the nation state as an effective and legitimate political system. In the field of higher education studies this perception of the role of academic research has been associated with the interventionist state or model of state control (van Vught 1989). Granted the centrality of research and higher education for governments, such activities have to be subjected to government control. Science and academic research have been funded and organized according to national political agendas and as an instrument for reaching economic or social goals harboured by the nation state.

In modern democracies there is a mutual dependency between science and the state. The scientific community is largely dependent on government funding. In addition, the state is responsible for establishing and securing institutions within which a large part of the scientific activities are performed. In return the nation state relies on science and technology to secure its core cultural, political, economic and strategic viability (see, e.g. Solingen 1994). Science is thus a considerable political resource. It offers a knowledge base for policy making. In specific areas of politics and policy, the role of science is looked upon as essential, most notably in the military and defense sector, in public health care and agriculture (Hanney et al. 2003). The history of the university – government relationship is also a history of how governments have had designs for the use of academic research as a knowledge basis for public decision-making. Through the university the government would have access to "intelligence and research" (Skoie 2001: 10).

The 1960s and 1970s have been identified as a period during which governments and scientific communities alike had strong beliefs in the ability of research to solve societal problems that reached national political agendas (Albæk 1988). Hence, a strong belief in the instrumentality of science identified with the linear model of science. It also paralleled a trust in government ability to affect society through its policies and this legitimated *a policy for science in policy*. This vision has been most apparently visible with respect to other organizations within higher education and research systems than the research-intensive universities. This speaks to the limit of the instrumental concept of the University in which research organizations should be tightly controlled, with a strong emphasis on them being accountable to political authorities. In practice the relationship between government and science within this understanding of the role of science for government has entailed varying organizational solutions and affected *university* research in diverse ways in different national systems.

This is evident in the way in which sectoral research has been organized in the post-war period. An overall model for organizing science as an instrument subordinated to the needs and priorities of societal sectors consisted of functionally organized Ministries and government departments with strong vertical steering of research and less horizontal coordination. The telling example of medical research and government in Britain (Kogan et al. 2006) shows how the social engineering of the 1960s and 1970s *in part* was played out as a hierarchical relationship between government and science. First of all, the dominating doctrine of science policy at the time was to make a principled distinction between basic and applied science.[104] The former having its home within the universities and national research councils and the latter requiring a hierarchical relationship where government identified its priorities and informational needs and science undertaking the work. In the case of Britain in the 1970s the dominant organizational model for applied science was the customer-contractor doctrine ("the Rothschild formula") where government departments should define their needs, fund their own sources of knowledge and set the goals for science (Kogan et al. 2006).

In the Nordic welfare states in the 1970s and 1980s the research organized according to a sectoral logic played a significant role in the national research system. In Denmark and Norway sectoral research was organized mainly outside the universities, as the guiding organizational principle for science as instrument for public policy was to channel state determined research needs to government research institutes. Sectoral research had little foothold within university research. Examples of this specific form of organization can be found in the way in which sectoral research was organized, especially in the agricultural sector (Gornitzka 2003), but also predominantly in other core public policy areas, such as health and transportation (cf. Brofoss and Wiig 2000: 91–94). In Sweden sectoral research was steered and funded directly by sector ministries and agencies, but conducted within the universities (Kyvik and Ødegård 1990). The organizational arrangements left no doubt that research is organized to be a link in a hierarchical chain going from the politically elected leadership via the state bureaucracy in the sectors in question down to research performance level. In other words, this represents a research structure with its raison d'être in its capacity to be an instrument in an overall sectoral policy in a sovereign state.

The extent to which universities have been enlisted into a sectoral logic of the hierarchical vision of research varies over time and national systems. Overall the experiences with such systems are an illustration of the resilience of the traditional universities to fulfil the instrumental expectations of governments. In line with the

---

[104] The core document for international R&D statistics, the Frascati manual, sees the *objectives* attached to research as the defining characteristic that marks applied from basic science. In other words it is the expected utility and actors having "designs" on research that classifies it as applied and the absence of such instrumentality that is the hallmark of basic research by the definition employed in statistical surveys.

developments in other continental European countries, the University of Oslo, for instance, actively opposed in the nineteenth century the establishment of a chair for agricultural studies because it was unwilling to incorporate this kind of mission-oriented set of activities into its academic profile (Valen-Sendstad 1959). This paved the way for the establishment of what in the end became the Norwegian University of Life Sciences.

The last 20 years, however, with the dismantling or at least loosening of the sectoral cohesion and "iron triangles" between science/professions, public administration and sectors of society, the sectoral logic of instrumentally organized science and higher education is under attack all over Europe (Levidov et al. 2002). Similar de-sectoralisation has happened in "non-university" higher education as the functional principle of organization has to a large extent been abandoned in Western Europe: colleges for professional education, in areas such as engineering, veterinary medicine, nursing and so on, have been merged into multi-disciplinary colleges. This development has also been fed by the idea of neo-correspondence (Saunders and Machell 2000), which severed the traditional link between a specific education and a specific career (Kyvik 2004). That does not imply that the hierarchical vision of higher education and research is dead, but rather that the idea of having a parallel functional organization of higher education and research, and government organization is no longer prevalent.

The history of the organization of government funding of academic research tells similar stories of the changes in the perception of the instrumentality and state regulation of research. A significant change in organizational fields of knowledge production took place in the early post-war period with the establishment of intermediary institutions that linked the state and knowledge production by way of research councils (Rip 1988: 69). National research councils were in most systems devised as bureaucracies to serve as an instrument of state patronage of science, and as such they were part of a hierarchical chain of command that regulated the funding of academic research. However, the general pattern of development implied that the hierarchical state patronage model of research councils was "captured" by the scientific community, so as to become "the parliament of the Republic of Science" and looked upon as a logical component of the institutions of scientific communities (Rip 1993). Furthermore, research councils have varied in the extent to which they expressed the subordination of research to national political agendas. The overt instrumental-hierarchical vision of university research has a strong foothold in the sectorally/functionally organized or mission oriented research councils (Skoie 2001).

The development of research councils exemplifies how intermediary organizations between government and universities have developed both according to an intra-academic model and a top-down interventionist model. Intervention was on the part of government and industry, with the former mediating the interest of the latter (Benner and Sandström 2000). The 1980s brought about another restructuring of the organizational field of academic knowledge production with the introduction of research and development programs, that is, organizational structures explicitly oriented towards giving missions to or coordinating national research efforts. Research programs, although often initiated at governmental level, were hooked up to and based on the already existing intermediary institution of the research councils (Ståhle 1993). It became one of the important ways in which national research councils did their business. The latter development did in fact represent a strengthening of the regulative basis of academic research in the sense that research activities became the object of formal coordination and governance by being connected to national research programs. Grand scale national priority setting for research – that included university research – established itself as a research policy doctrine during the 1980s (Mathisen 1994, 1996). These included not only the political demand but also the industrial demands with respect to research. In practice in many Western European countries reforms of national research council systems and overall national research policy instruments blended with the established structures of research funding and organization, and as such they represent organizational models that mix the hierarchical-instrumental vision of research with the self-regulated state patronage of the scientific community. Nonetheless, the establishment of mission oriented research councils and of large scale research programs and national priority areas were testimonies of continuous presence of the hierarchical instrumental vision of one of the University's basic activities. The organizational differentiation that governments have developed outside the University and as instrument to affect university research could also be interpreted as indications of universities that evaded to a large extent political hierarchical control.

UNIVERSITY GOVERNANCE REFORM AND THE HIERARCHICAL VISION OF THE 1970s AND 1980s

While continental European universities have been regarded as important institutions in national state structures, until at least the 1980s they have not been hard-pressed to justify their existence in immediate cost-benefit terms. Also in the heyday of the welfare state, service provision was not the dominant expectation lying behind academia's appeal to policy makers. There was also not a direct link visible in political and public arenas between the public's willingness to pay higher taxes and, for example, the expectation of greater chances for either their children or themselves to qualify for a course of study that would improve their job prospects, or the improvement of the chance that researchers' discoveries might improve the quality of life. Instead, from an instrumental perspective the University's main tasks were to contribute directly to the satisfaction of specific needs of the state structure, for example, deliver competent and skilled civil servants, facilitate social mobility, and produce at least in some areas, for example, defense, agriculture, and public health care, knowledge of direct relevance to the state (Gornitzka 2003; Hanney et al. 2003). This implied a governance relationship with a relatively low level of organizational autonomy for the University, and a relatively high level of individual academic freedom for academic employees of the universities, despite their status as civil servants.

   The government was focused on making sure that the University as a public institution that was part of the state structure would operate on the basis of the same strict rules as other state organizations, implying, amongst other things, earmarked funding and a budgeting system on an annual basis, civil service status for all university staff and nationally determined labour agreements for university staff, strict reporting requirements, a centrally determined structure of degree systems, etc. As such the state was determining and controlling the organizational input conditions under which universities could operate, that is, the *how* of the University. What happened inside the University, that is, the *what* of the University, was to a large extent left to the academics themselves to determine. According to Olsen (2000) academic self-governance was part of a large democratic-constitutional social order, with partly autonomous institutions. Constitutive regulations defined these institutions and their roles, competence, social and political relationships, and responsibilities. From that perspective the academic autonomy of the University was a condition for legitimate governmental steering of the sector and peaceful co-existence of the University with other institutions.

From the mid-1980s on, various European governments have addressed in Green and White papers, as well as law proposals, the apparent ineffectiveness of the traditional instrumental steering model with respect to higher education.[105] Developments referred to as causes for this ineffectiveness were, amongst other things, the massification of higher education with the accompanying increasing costs, and the growing demands towards the University leading to a complexity that could not be steered effectively anymore by a rigid structure of central planning arrangements and rules. Governments felt that they were no longer able to provide fairly stable and generally acceptable objectives for the University, nor did they have the capacity and expertise to analyze what it would take to reach specific objectives (Maassen and van Vught 1989).

One of the areas around which the steering relationship between the state and higher education was changed was academic program development. The responsibility for approving the programming and adapting of study programs moved in many countries from the state to the universities. In exchange for this the universities were expected to accept the development of a formal quality assessment or accreditation system that would allow for regular evaluations of the way universities handled their increased organizational autonomy in the area of academic program development. The area of quality assessment and accreditation has remained a central policy area throughout the last 20 years in the changing steering relationships with respect to higher education. Also an important part of the European Commission's efforts to acquire governance responsibility with respect to higher education has been organized around the issue of quality assessment and accreditation.

Overall the 1980s and 1990s can be regarded as the era during which the almost 200 year old intimate institutional relationship between state and higher education was seriously reorganized. However, this period does not show any abdication of governments with respect to the steering of the University. Instead it shows a repositioning

---

[105] See, for example, the discussion of the Dutch adaptation of the higher education steering model in Maassen and van Vught (1989); and the analysis of the changes in the relationship between the state and higher education in France, Germany, and the Netherlands in van Vught (1989).

of the governance actors involved and the institutionalized governance arrangements. At the national level governments introduced governance models based on the principles of "government steering at a distance" and "self-regulatory" university systems (van Vught 1989; Maassen and Stensaker 2003). The theoretical basis for these new governance approaches were found especially in systems theory and cybernetics (Maassen 1988), with Habermas, for example, providing inspiration for the new communicative planning system in Dutch higher education (Maassen and van Vught 1989). The autonomy of the University was enlarged in many areas in addition to academic program development, including financial and personnel management. Also the legal basis of the University was in nearly all countries adapted accordingly.[106] This was also the period during which the European Commission built up an administrative executive support structure with respect to higher education; initially for coordinating intra-European mobility programs, later also for developing and implementing activities in other areas.

This marked the end of the traditional input-focused governance approach towards the University. However, it did not mean the end of the instrumental vision on the University as such, instead it meant that the steering and legal relationship between the state and the University have been adapted. Instead of a control over the input of the University, that is, students, staff, resources, governments focused on the output of the University, graduates, publications, services. This implied that the organizational autonomy increased, while the academic autonomy, at least on paper, decreased. The state's governance starting-point with respect to the University has become: "we do not care anymore how you do it, as long as you achieve the outcomes we expect you to achieve." What is it that Universities are expected to achieve? Here we can point to the remarkable substantive shift that has taken place from a focus on the role of the University for the state and the public sector, with an important emphasis on social aspects, to a growing emphasis on the role of the University for the economy in general and the private sector in particular (Gumport 2000).

As a consequence the state has to reconsider the policy instruments used for governing higher education. Instead of relying on legal instruments, states seem to prefer nowadays alternatives such as "the power of the purse" (financial instruments), and bilateral or multilateral contracts or performance agreements.

EUROPEAN UNIVERSITIES IN THE 1990s – LIVING THE HIERARCHICAL VISION?

In the government hierarchy vision of university organization and governance it is assumed that universities' operation and dynamics are governed by national political agendas and priorities; the University is an implementer of predetermined political

---

[106] Implying in the first place that universities became independent public corporations instead of state-controlled organizations. In the second place it meant that many detailed university laws were replaced by one comprehensive law.

objectives. What do the experiences of European universities tell us about the track record of universities in achieving national purposes? In the post-war period universities have been extraordinary successful in implementing the overall political objective of system expansion as well as specific structural objectives. This has been a major source of change within universities, changes that in most likelihood would not have occurred if left to the traditional structures of academic self-governance (cf. Gornitzka et al. 2005: 9–11). At the same time, the development of alternatives to university organization and the stronger instrumentation of research funding and organization on the part of national governments we have already taken as indications of university resilience to and ineptitude for being malleable policy instruments. There is very little doubt that governments continue to harbour expectations towards the University and express confidence in the political ability to affect change through higher education reform and through more targeted governmental programs (Maassen 2006). However, a remaining question is how this affects the basic activities of the University and how such hierarchical attempts have to be seen from the side of the universities? Have great expectations in corridors of national ministries been crushed in lecture halls and research laboratories of the university, to paraphrase the subtitle of Pressman and Wildavsky (1973)? Studies of policy implementation in higher education have in the past (Cerych and Sabatier 1986) and more recently (Gornitzka et al. 2005) given mixed answers to the general question.

Main observations from a study into the effects of the growing policy emphasis on the economic role of higher education on university organization (Gornitzka and Maassen 2000a, 2003) can illuminate the complexities of "being a living instrument of political agendas." This study shows that universities respond in different ways to changes in their environment, depending on the signals that governments and other actors have given, and the unequal internal conditions for change. Nonetheless, there are two main characteristics in the developments with respect to university organization in the involved 25 case institutions that seem to have general validity, and can be assumed also to apply to universities in Western Europe in general. In the first place, despite all changes universities in the 1980s and 1990s have been remarkably stable with respect to their traditional educational core areas, that is, academically based degree programs. In general the universities have protected this kind of education, and the relationship between universities and the student market has hardly changed at all during the last two decades when it comes to these programs. Governments continue to set core parameters for traditional degree programs, for example, regulations of student intake and numbers, and regulations for the provision of new degree programs, but the call from governments to make university degree programs more adjusted to the needs of the economy did not meet with reliable implementation of such an agenda. Partly, this reflected the rather vague expectations from governments in Western Europe as to what kind of economic role of higher education provision this would entail. Even in the most overt case where the national government did substantiate the declarations of intent with a program for university change – the "Enterprise in Higher Education Initiative" in the UK – universities responded with adjusting the government program to existing university practices.

According to Kogan (2005: 59) the £100 million provided by the British government to "embed enterprise into the curriculum had no effect at all."

The other main conclusion we can draw on the basis of the above-mentioned study concerns the area of lifelong learning. Many universities have introduced the last 15–20 years innovations as a response to calls for developing new structures connecting learning and working to the need for educational activities for non-traditional students, and to the demand for flexible educational course offerings resulting from the rapidly developing "knowledge economy." Governments were not alone in expressing such designs on universities, but they featured prominently in national public policy rhetoric on higher education. Universities have developed new structures and introduced new practices without the availability of dominant national or international examples that could indicate how these changes could be implemented most effectively. In addition, these changes were introduced with minimal financial or other support from the state. A special characteristic of universities that have contributed to innovations in this area is that their lifelong learning and other non-traditional education activities have not been integrated in the traditional university organization structure. These new activities were carried out next to traditional university units, in a generally marginal position at universities. The accommodation of lifelong learning objectives has created internal organizational tension as such activities were seen as "everything the University is not" (Gornitzka and Maassen 2003).

CONCLUSION

The developments in the governance relationships between the European University and the state of the last two decades have led to a situation where universities operate between state and market (Gornitzka and Maassen 2000b; Maassen 2006). However, this does not imply that European universities are moving along a continuum from central government control and steering to a market dominated form of governance, as is for example, suggested by Clark's triangle of coordination (Clark 1983). Universities do not relate to their environment in a homogeneous way. Despite the traditional dominance of the state as an external actor in the continental European context, the interaction between a University and its environments takes place through many internal actors, and with various actors and interests in the environment. Part of the interactions can be characterized as market-driven, while other parts are steered carefully by the state or the institutional leadership. Of importance here is to emphasize that state and University do not form a kind of dichotomy. The developments of the last two decades imply that European governments have started to use more and more market-type of policy instruments, with the aim to make universities operate more efficiently and effectively. But a market-oriented approach is also used for the stimulation of more direct interactions between University and environment, amongst other things, for bringing the University and the economy closer together especially in areas outside the traditional core activities of the University.

The national priorities with respect to which the University is supposed to play a role have become less social and more economic. However, the educational (and to some extent research) core activities of the University have not been adapted accordingly. In order for the University to become an effective instrument for the state in addressing national economic priorities new initiatives have to be taken, new structures have to be established, and new partnerships have to be developed. European universities have been reluctant in doing so, amongst other things, because these new initiatives, structures and partnerships fall to a large extent outside the traditional identity and core of the University. Despite the adaptation of the University governance model European national governments have until now emphasized the continued centrality and importance of this traditional core.

CHAPTER 5

AN INTERNAL REPRESENTATIVE SYSTEM: THE DEMOCRATIC VISION

Harry de Boer and Bjørn Stensaker

INTRODUCTION

In this chapter the focus is on the University as a representative democracy. Universities are also highly politicized institutions – they can be seen as arenas for vested interests and various stakeholders. Such a university characterization – as well as others such as the Republic of Science (Polanyi 1962), the organized anarchy (Cohen et al. 1972; Cohen and March 1974), or the enterprise university (e.g. Marginson and Considine 2000) – refers to the dominance or illumination of particular organizational features. It means that under certain events and conditions specific institutions – formal and informal rule configurations – temporarily repress other value systems. This is also our analytical point of departure. Sometimes institutions collide and a new equilibrium with other prevailing institutions may arise where "a possible outcome of collisions is the fall and rise of institutions" (Gornitzka and Olsen 2006). With respect to such collisions not just external factors but also organizational processes are relevant. In this chapter we focus on the internal aspects of the University.

Institutional change happens because of the emergence of mismatches among existing institutions. As a consequence their legitimacy and performance may be questioned. Usually institutional change is incremental, but because the rate and pace of external change every now and then exceeds the rate of adjustment to it, there are occasional periods of rapid change (see, e.g. March and Olsen 1989: 171). The rise of new institutions does not mean that the new (set of) institutions establish an efficient equilibrium. Usually there are several competing options, none of them perfect. The outcome of this "collision of institutions" requires careful investigation.

This chapter analyses these "collisions," and the possible rise and fall of the University as a representative democracy, with the aim of trying to identify where a possible new equilibrium might appear due to the supposed moral and instrumental benefits of the democratic university (see next section). We would argue that there are good reasons to examine the relevance of such an institution in a policy context in which the future university is seen as a key organization in and towards the knowledge society. In order to see to what extent the University as a representative democracy could still be a relevant and viable mode of organization in an era where universities have to meet a battery of expectations, we will address the rise of this mode of organization and, through reviewing its "performances," its current perceived decline. After that we will discuss the current conditions for and legitimacy of the University as a

99

P. Maassen and J. P. Olsen (eds.), University Dynamics and European Integration, 99–118.
© 2007 *Springer.*

representative democracy, particularly in the context of the European Higher Education Area, before concluding by pointing to possible future aspects of the democratic university.

THE UNIVERSITY AS A REPRESENTATIVE DEMOCRACY

The concept of democracy is obviously highly contested. Based on earlier work (de Boer and Denters 1999), we suggest that a University should have the following characteristics for being called a representative democracy:

- Affected interests should have the right to elect their representatives and should be eligible for such positions.
- These representatives should have substantial powers (otherwise the university demos cannot effectuate its voting right).[107]
- Decision-making powers should not be concentrated but fused or separated among the several; ideally, in a system of horizontal checks and balances the representative council has the upper hand.

In theory "affected interest" means that students, academics, non-academics, parents, the (national) government, industry, and other stakeholders should elect their own representatives for university governing bodies. These representative governing bodies should have legislative powers (including budget power), fused with or separated from an executive (e.g. the rectorate). These executives should be directly elected from and by the university electorate or should be elected members from the representative councils (monistic fusion of powers), or being elected by the representatives.

Olsen has portrayed this kind of university as an interest group allowing representation of university members on governing boards and councils (chapter 2). In his eyes such institutions have a strong focus upon formal arrangements of organization, more than on the special characteristics of work processes. Procedural and authority rules are important. Decision-making is organized through elections, bargaining, compromises, voting, and coalition-building among the organized groups with the aim to pursue their interests. The basic mechanisms for change are shifts in coalitions and successful internal bargaining. The model rests upon the assumption that actors have conflicting norms and objectives and that university operations and dynamics are governed by internal factors and causal beliefs. Hence, it should be underlined that the model is first and foremost a vision of how a university may function, and that it should be understood as an ideal which in practice may have been incomplete or poorly implemented – a point we will come back to in our conclusion. The ideal of the University as a representative democracy is also highly paradoxical in that it

---

[107] Of course one can take this argument further by discussing the different roles representatives (should) play. Burke's well known distinction between trustees and delegates comes to mind here. Trustees, entrusted by their voters, have autonomy to deliberate and act in favor of university interest. The delegate speaks more directly for its constituency, has far less autonomy and is supposed to consult his constituents more frequently before taking a decision. This representation issue will be left aside.

downplays the importance of the authoritative academic hierarchy while at the same time emphasizing that academic voice is important (Kallerud 2006).

However, the model of university democracy has also similarities with the University modeled as a political organization, full of dispute and contention (Baldridge 1971; Cohen and March 1974; Altbach 1992: 1438). The political model of universities stresses the diversity of interests, the lack of consistent and shared goals, and the continuous internal power struggle (competition). Plurality and heterogeneity are emphasized in comparison with collegial university models that stress consensus and collaboration. Resource mobilization and utilization (power, prestige, information, authorities) relative to competing groups determine the actor's potential to be successful. The existence and underlining of interests, values, power and status almost automatically lead to conflicts between the groups: between governors and academics; between students and non-students; between faculties, institutes, schools; and between cost and profit centers. Kinship, solidarity, and intimacy are unlikely to exist. In Middlehurst's concluding words, "The organization itself is seen as no more than a coalition of different individuals and groups, kept together in dynamic tension, but with the potential break as soon as resources and power become unbalanced, or as dominant groups choose to strike out independently" (Middlehurst 1993).

What is the appeal of the University as a representative democracy? In principle, there are two answers to this question. First, the normative view which sees democracy as an end in itself. It is a kind of moral right to give employees a say in decisions that affect them. A representative democracy has an intrinsic value that may contribute to individual growth, feeling of self-worth, or, at macro level, good citizenship. Second, there is the instrumental view that sees an organizational democracy as a means to an end. Democracy may create greater support for institutional policies, for example, by reducing resistance. It this respect it facilitates decision-making, also because of a better use of information available within the university community. Thus, the instrumental view assumes that a democratic system ultimately leads to superior organizational performance through a better utilization of its human potential (chapter 4). Taken together, advocates of organizational democracy argue that influence sharing has potentially positive consequences at three levels: it is good for the individual members of the organization, it is good for the organization, and it is good for society (Heller 1998). However, at the same time both in academia and elsewhere the results of organizational democracy have been largely disappointing, among other things, due to unrealistic expectations and the neglect of necessary antecedents such as adequate laws, experience, skill and trust. In the next two sections we will explicitly address these issues.

THE HISTORY OF THE REPRESENTATIVE UNIVERSITY

The Rise of the University as a Representative Democracy

The origins of the University as a representative democracy stem from the midst of the 1960s and were primarily the consequence of student activism (Altbach

1992: 1438), although younger professors and faculty at a number of universities also can be identified as being active partners in reforming university governance in this period (see, e.g., Olsen 1976b: 334). The reasons for the political activism and waves of rebellious student revolts varied between countries as did their intensity. In some countries it had serious political repercussions (in France and Germany), whereas other countries were to some extent "followers of reform fashion." Apart from the differences, the developments during the late 1960s and their consequences have also common features.

As regards the "revolution" in internal university governing systems a key element often noticed is the resistance and reaction against plans to reform higher education systems in various countries. In many countries the government and the university sector were looking for possibilities to deal with the problems of the *massification* of higher education.[108] In this context advisory committees were installed to study the problems of university governance. Students and junior academics usually played no role in many plans and reform proposals before 1967 (except for some countries). For example, in the Netherlands the Maris Committee, composed of members from the national body of academics (Academic Council), went into this issue and proposed a business-like approach that would certainly fit the "NPM-ideas" of the 1990s. These "managerial ideas *avant la letter*" were critiqued by both the professoriate ("the Maris committee denies the University as a professional organization") and students (missing all the element of democratization). It was so to speak the worst possible proposal at the worst possible time. As a consequence students became even more focused to (loudly) voice their demands for emancipation and democratization, the government started to get more involved, and the old regimes within the universities got increasingly confused.

Key question in these discussions, in the Netherlands as elsewhere, was how to increase the efficiency and effectiveness of the system in order to cope with the large number of students. It meant not only more students but also a more diversified student body pressurizing traditional habits and organizing themselves in different ways, for instance, through new unions (Daalder and Shils 1982). As de Boer et al. (1999: 331) indicate:

"(S)ince 1963 a new student unionism had begun to develop with the aim of ending the more isolated position of traditional student associations. The Dutch student union launched its program in 1964 in the form of a 'Democratic manifesto' promoting the material and social interests of students (...) In 1967 the student union published the 'Syndicate manifesto,' as a spur for protest activities oriented towards democratizing the university."

The massification of higher education also meant a growing academic staff, looking for career opportunities and influence, not at least an increased interest of junior staff to participate in decision-making bodies and to be appointed to management

---

[108] De Boer et al. (1999: 332) also indicate that the student action provided an important breeding ground for thoughts on a new university governance structure, but "it would give the student movement too much credit to claim that the reorganisation of the university was due only to their action. Historically, this is too much a one-sided perspective."

positions. This process was not always opposed by the established professors. For example, Halvorsen (1967), a university director at the time, pointed out that the opening up of non-professors to take on the role as department head also could be viewed as a move that could increase time professors spent on research and decrease time they spent on administration.

But the massification also painfully demonstrated the dysfunction and out-datedness of the prevailing structures. This dysfunction of the old university elite also became embarrassingly clear in the disordered response of the universities to the new challenges imposed by the students in 1967–1969. Daalder (1982: 497) argues that this was one of the reasons for governments to interfere themselves: "universities were unable to settle their affairs without external intervention." And of course an expanding system requires more financial means. The financial claims of the universities started to bear down heavily on the education budget. As a consequence the government became increasingly concerned about the allocation of resources and started to look for possibilities to rationally restructure higher education. Thus, before the real democratic waves in the late 1960s, in many countries discussions were already going on to see what kind of substantial changes in the university organization were needed. In terms of real outcomes these discussions were not very productive. However, this changed radically by the democratization movement that really speeded up the discussion and geared it into a new direction by adding demands such as "one man, one vote."

This student activism focused on both internal and external democratization. It is important to note that the (organized) students were having quite different opinions on these issues. It is, just as the other groups such as the professoriate and the government, a rather heterogeneous instead of a homogeneous group. However, due to limited space we cannot avoid this oversimplification in our description below. One aspect underlying the student protests in this period was, for example, the argument that universities should not loose their critical role in the larger society. There was protest against the Vietnam War, protest on the exploits of the Third World, campaigns against "repressive" authorities as well as use of (neo) Marxist writings, all to create a "better world." As such, student activism was also a revolt against the University being used as an instrument for national political agendas (chapter 4). Paradoxically, the protests were often targeted against national ambitions that, among other things, were enabling more students to attend the University.

In the 1960s student movements, encouraged by media, philosophical intellectuals and Marxist ideologists, developed ideas about the academic organization that were alien to the then-existing university. Students as a political force came completely unexpectedly (Daalder and Shils 1982). This new ideology was taken up by others, such as politicians and junior academics, which sensed an opportunity of gaining power. A collision of institutions was the result. These movements revolted against the feudal authority structure of universities, which were run by the senior academics (teaching and research) and the state (matters of finance and personnel). Universities were greatly decentralized, powers were diffused and there was virtually unlimited power of the professorial "lords" in limited realms.

After the years of agitation the years of codification followed (Pedersen 1982). New laws, in the beginning often as experiments, on internal university governance were put into effect. They introduced various forms of representative democracy (instead of the radical demands for direct democracy). An important event occurred in August 1967 when the *Sozialistischen Deutscher Studentenbund* put forward a new slogan: democratization, worked out in *tripartite representation* in all academic governing bodies (Hennis 1982: 11). This slogan on "parity" left its imprints on the student actions in 1968 as well as ultimately in the internal university governance structures in many countries. For example, in Germany the *Ordinarienuniversität*, governed by full professors and the state, was transformed into the *Gruppenuniversität*, governed by representatives of the various university constituencies. In the period 1968–1976 new laws on university governance passed national parliaments, for example, in Belgium (1971), Denmark (1970), France (1968), Germany (1969–1973 and 1976),[109] the Netherlands (1970), and Norway (1976). In the first half of the 1970s the University as a representative democracy was born and spread all over Western Europe. The costs of implementation were enormous and caused serious problems at both the macro and the micro level (see next section). One of the side-effects of massification and the rise of the representative university was a growth in the number of university administrators during the 1970s and 1980s. These administrative experts took increasingly part in the governance of the university, sometimes adding *"separate sets of roles and interests"* to those of the academic staff and students (Clark 1983: 89), while at other times attending the conflicting interests caused by increased representation (Dill 1992: 1326).

These kinds of changes occurred especially in countries with "state-controlled" university sectors. According to Daalder (1982: 496), Denmark, Germany, and the Netherlands went furthest in meeting the demands for a democratic reform of university governance. In countries that traditionally had less (direct) state interference, for example, the UK and the USA, universities were largely left to themselves to cope with the challenges of that time. According to opponents of democratization, such as Kielmansegg (1983: 47), by and large university management "did better than the politicians and the bureaucrats, simply because they were less willing to embrace the follies of the day." In fact, many "despised" politicians for their lack of knowledge and vision. The University as a representative democracy was far more the result of ideology, prejudices, and political fashion than of decisive, vision-based political action (Hennis 1982: 26).

The Fall of the University as a Representative Democracy

The fall of the University as a representative democracy has basically two reasons. The first general reason relates to the changes in society, that is, the social, technological, socio-economic and political changes, to some extent exogenous to the University,

---

[109] In the years 1969–1973 new legislation was introduced in the German states and after that in 1976 a new comprehensive federal law was put into effect.

that have affected university governance. Such exogenous factors can create new opportunities and expectations or may reveal problems in existing institutions. In other words, they can cause mismatches among institutions. The emergence of mass education was the example mentioned earlier. Other examples that more recently stimulated new modes of governance, in the University and elsewhere, are the fiscal crisis (since the late 1970s), internationalization and globalization, and the dominance of neo-liberal ideologies, including strong preferences for market-oriented values and behaviors. These external factors have contributed to the fall of the University as a representative democracy, since, arguably, they require universities to respond swiftly and flexibly. The widely expressed view is that the democratic university is unable to respond timely to external changes and to satisfy societal demands and for that reason should be abolished.[110] The incapability of representative bodies, such as university councils, to take strategic decisions, particularly in times of headwind, has seriously harmed the "case of the representative university."

The second general reason relates to perceived shortcomings of the democratic university itself. As described in the previous section, the introduction of the University as a representative democracy was a clean break with the past and was in many cases explicitly regarded as an experiment. How successfully did these new authority structures operate? What have been the side effects? In the remainder of this section we address point by point some side effects, expressed worries and perceived shortcomings of the university as a representative democracy. Again we stress that this is the general picture; local situations will differ. We address three general issues: the tensed relationship of a representative democracy (as a political organization) and features of the academic profession (e.g., academic freedom), the difficulty of designing transparent rules and procedures, the qualifications needed to take good decisions, and the commitment of staff and students for university "politics."

One of the consequences of the University as a representative democracy was the emergence of a politicized organization. Especially during the peaks of the democratic university in the 1970s, the politicized nature emphasized competition and conflict instead of consensual decision-making. Obviously, conflicts of interest did also exist in the old regimes, but due to a completely different power distribution and a culture of "decision-making among equals" this was dealt with in a different way. Points of view differ with respect to the desirability of having turned into a real political organization. It is argued that particularly when differences in opinions, interests and positions do exist – and they do! – it is better to be explicit about them and to try to channel and resolve disputes through "politics." On the other hand, it is frequently said that politicized structures in universities have accentuated differences and have lead to more conflicts than necessary. Of course, one should not underestimate that conflicting interest or seemingly consensus also could be the result of different interpretations or misinterpretations of vital issues, lack of participation in decision-making due to the

---

[110] See, for example, Meek and Wood 1997; Askling et al. 1999; Currie et al. 2003; de Boer 2003; and Mignot Gerard 2003.

"cost" side of involvement, or shared academic values leading to "socialization" with respect to how problems should be solved (Olsen 1976a: 310). Still, distraction from teaching and research and extensive fights over rules and procedures have at least for part of the academic staff contributed to de-motivation and non-optimal performance.

One of the consequences at German universities was, for example, increased mutual distrust and hard feelings among the various parts of the institution (Hennis 1982: 19). In France the politicization of university decision-making has been the source of unethical and openly illegal behavior in many areas (Salmon 1982). Councils have gone beyond their sphere of competence and discussed issues that they were not empowered to consider. On these lines Salmon (1982: 83) speaks of "collective misbehavior." Such behavior seems somewhat "odd," but could be observed in other countries too.

In such troublesome contexts academic excellence suffers, or put more mildly, does not flourish. Particularly professors complained that instead of upholding academic standards, or being places for excellence in teaching and research, universities tried to become small democracies or instruments for the democratization of society (Lobkowicz 1983: 27). Academics were increasingly preoccupied with organizational and political questions instead of with scholarly ones, leaving aside the "brain drain" in the 1970s of professors who left their university, even though, seen in retrospect, this was very much a minority phenomenon (Altbach 1992: 1444).

Related to this issue is the supposed threat, or at least tensed relationship, of the democratic university and academic freedom. Particularly professors saw the internal constellation of competing interests as problematic. In the German context Kielmansegg (1983: 48) states that academic freedom was much more severely threatened from within than it had ever been from without. It "was a façade behind which countless serious and sometimes even brutal infringements of academic freedom took place." In the Dutch context Lijphart (1983) analyses the, in his eyes, lamentable deterioration of the universities as a result of the internal democratization: weakening of academic control of teaching and research, politicization of the University, and the gradual decline of academic standards. One of the main reasons for this abominable situation was in Lijphart's eyes the firm institutionalization of "student power" at all levels, in the beginning partly related to the at the time outspoken Marxist ideological driven behavior.

Another consequence of the functional representation has been that professors lost their dominant position, at least in terms of numbers. Of course, this was exactly the meaning of much of the new legislation. However, it was not the intention that professors would "completely" withdraw from formal decision-making. In countries such as Denmark and the Netherlands many professors lost interest in taking a seat in the representative councils. Consequently, many constituencies were formally represented in the university's decision-making, except for the "most important group" (Pedersen 1982; de Boer 2002). This does not imply that professors no longer had any influence. Non-participation in formal decision-making can be explained as an outcome of alternative ways to influence decisions (Olsen 1976a: 283–286). Hence, professors were still influential, but in a more subtle and informal way (de Boer 2003).

After all, equality of participation is not the same as equality of professional tasks and of (external) status (Pedersen 1982). However, it does contribute to the transparency of university decision-making. While democracies intend to be open (e.g. having public meetings) important decisions in the universities were taken elsewhere.

The University as a representative democracy has also had serious problems with establishing clear distributions of authority. Moreover, practice was even tougher than paper. In the Netherlands the division of powers between the legislature and the executive caused many problems and needed adjustments (achieved after more than ten years) (Commissie Polak 1979). This unclearness caused many (procedural) conflicts and bitter fights that have seriously damaged institutional policies, teaching and research as well as people's individual careers. Moreover, unclear divisions of authority paralyzed decisive decision-making, created opportunities for not taking responsibility and blaming the other side; not only inside the institution but for the outside world too. For external parties, such as the state, it was sometimes difficult to find the right "addressee," since, if deemed necessary, the legislating body and the executive were hiding behind each other's back. In other words, it was hard for external parties to "do business with" the University. Similar unclearness in the power structure existed in Denmark between the rector and the senate. The position of the German rector was also troublesome but for different reasons. The intention was to strengthen the position of the rector who should be elected from a university-wide audience. However, the result was that the average rector was in a weaker position as he wanted to please all constituencies at the same time which did not particularly contribute to strong decision-making (Hennis 1982: 18–19).

Another major concern is related to the participation and engagement of the members of the university community themselves. It was argued from the beginning that equal distribution of power throughout the university would increase staff and student involvement. However, after some years it became clear that the "average" member's involvement and commitment are somewhat limited (Schuster 1989). The majority of staff and students are indifferent or keep contemptuous distance, not or hardly being interested in university politics at all. Most of them are not willing to take a council seat. Many of them do not vote. Turnout rates for council elections are low. With the advent of the enterprise university, by and large after the midst of the 1990s, this problem may have grown, but it already existed during the heydays of university democracy (for France, Denmark and the Netherlands, see Salmon 1982; Pedersen 1982; de Boer 2002).

The model of the University as a representative democracy was meant to increase transparency and equality; it became at many places a model of disintegration, irrationality and inefficiency. Concerning the French situation, Salmon (1982: 81) argues that feelings of frustration probably increased among all categories. "All of them have felt that they were not really or sufficiently represented or influential, compared with their expectations."[111] Nasty qualifications as "mud-slinging," "manipulation" and

---

[111] Obviously this says also something about the high expectations of some groups in the beginning.

"inconsequential squabbles over spurious problems" accrued to the "democratic university" (Hennis 1982). Though several of such qualifications may be exaggerations, they can be found in nearly all West European countries at the times of the "democratic university" and this university has never gotten rid off this image.

Also the (lack of) skills and competences of the representatives of the democratic university have traditionally been criticized. This in fact brings the old issue to the surface of what kind of expertise one has to possess for good rulership. Students were, for instance, blamed for a lack of knowledge both with respect to non-academic matters (can we let them decide on multi-million budgets?) and academic matters (do they have to decide what kind of books and how many pages they read?). This amateurism might well be related to another "fact." The University as a representative democracy is not particularly known for its efficiency, that is, it is a very time-consuming system to take decisions, if they are taken at all. There are several studies that indicate the excessive use of time (e.g. frequent and long meetings) (Daalder and Shils 1982; de Boer et al. 1998).

Another aspect of the democratized university was the intention of the abolishment of the Ivory Tower. Universities should be part of the real world. They should be adaptive and respond to societal needs. One way of doing this was to give external members a seat in representative councils. In 1982, Daalder (1982: 508) concluded there is no evidence that university "democracy" has made European universities more adaptive than they were under exclusive professional rule. In the 1980s and 1990s universities as representative democracies were frequently accused of being inward looking ("navel gazing") instead of being external oriented. In 1990s, one of the reasons to strip the representative councils from some of their substantial powers (through legally imposed reforms) was to strengthen the external orientation of the University, that is, to encourage them to behave as "public entrepreneurs" and to strengthen their ties with society. The strengthening of executive leadership aimed to further strategic decision-making and to make the institution more adaptive as the democratic university had failed in that respect.

International studies of faculty participation in university decision-making also disclosed disappointing results concerning the perceived effects of participation. An analysis of academic involvement in institutional governance in England, Germany, the Netherlands, and Sweden (based on Carnegie survey data) showed that those academics that were most involved in administrative matters (faculty from England) also were most dissatisfied with the influence they had over policy processes at their institutions (Geurts and Maassen 1996, 2005). Even though one should be open for the possibility that dissatisfaction also may trigger participation due to an increased mobilization, in all four countries, the general conclusion reached was that although much faculty time was spent on administrative issues, faculty's perceived influence on policy making in their institutions as well as their departments was marginal (Geurts and Maassen 1996: 81).

Hence, the momentum of the "democratization" movement as Daalder (1982: 509) named it was gone in the 1980s. However, in many countries the concept of functional representation in governing bodies with substantial powers would by and large last till the last decade of the previous millennium. After incremental changes in the 1980s and early 1990s, we have witnessed real changes in internal university governance. In a number of countries we saw, at least in a formal sense, a clear weakening of "workplace" democracy within the University, and the introduction of elements such as appointed managers, external representation in boards and governing bodies, and the assignment of increased weight to individual responsibility rather than collective decision-making (Currie et al. 2003; Larsen et al. 2005). As a result, new forms of representation – the rise of, and the inclusion of unions in various governance arrangements – were emerging due to an increased conflict level within universities (see e.g. Kirp 2003). Was such a shift in internal governance inevitable? Could it easily be justified because of bad performance of university decision-making through representation? And has the University as a representative democracy completely vanished?

Whatever the shortcomings of the University as a representative democracy are and apart from the more recent changes towards more managerial-run universities, there is still a substantial amount of influence sharing among the various constituencies in universities. The decline of the democratic university should not be confused with a university in which staff and students hardly have any voice in or impact on institutional policy making. They still have "democratic rights," are still influential and are still represented. In most universities, for instance, staff and students still elect their representatives, and have university councils not been abolished. Moreover, as a practice many university decision-makers tend to consult staff and students before they initiate real action. Some powers are exerted through informal channels instead of through formal procedures.

At the same time, we can observe that the power of representative bodies has declined. They have become advisory bodies instead of decision-making bodies. And power has become more concentrated into the hands of a few executives. Generally, persons on such key positions are appointed instead of elected. Horizontal structures of checks and balances have been replaced by vertical ones. But not, as some would argue by vertical chains of command. In other words, some of the conditions mentioned above are no longer met while others are. These kinds of changes in internal university governance do not imply a return to the *Ordinarienuniversitat*, while at the same time the *Gruppenuniversitat* in its full growth seems history as well.

THE DEMOCRATIC UNIVERSITY AND THE EUROPEAN
HIGHER EDUCATION AREA

Does this mean that the vision of the democratic university is fading away, or will we witness new institutional "collisions" arise as a result of the next phase of governmental reforms in Europe – the realization of the European Higher Education Area? By looking into the changes during the last decades with respect to how universities are managed, there seems to be less belief in the democratic vision of the University (de Boer 2003; Maassen 2003). Looking at the Bologna process or the Lisbon strategy, one is struck by the tendency to overlook the institutional fabric of decision-making structures in universities, while there, at the same time, is a strong tendency to refer to universities as "partners" in the realization of the European Higher Education Area (Nyborg 2002).

"Good Governance" in a European Perspective

Governance is an important topic in the realization of the European Higher Education Area, but the term is nowadays often used to indicate a new mode of governing that is distinct from the hierarchical control model. Rather, it is interpreted as a more cooperative mode where state and non-state actors participate in mixed networks (Enders 2004: 372). In other words, governance in a European perspective is often linked to the relationship between different institutions and European macro-politics, where the development of autonomous institutions responsible for their own future is seen as a key for the future (van der Wende 2003; Commission 2006b).

For those belonging to the university sector, governance often has another connotation, relating more to issues concerning academic freedom, even if organizational autonomy does play a significant part in their understanding of the concept. The "predecessor" of the Bologna Declaration (chapter 7), the Magna Charta Universitatum, signed by the university rectors present at the 900th anniversary of the University of Bologna in 1988, emphasized that the University was an autonomous institution, where academic freedom is a key factor, and that "*To preserve freedom in research and teaching, the instruments appropriate to realize that freedom must be made available to all members of the university community*" (Magna Charta Universitatum 1988).

A reasonable interpretation of this statement is that one of the potential instruments that should be made available to members of the University is access to decision-making structures. In principle, participation in governance structures seems to be supported by the European Commission. In a 2001 White Paper, the Commission (2001) presented five principles that should in general underpin "good governance" in all sectors: *openness, accountability, effectiveness, coherence* and the fifth principle being *participation*.

However, if one consults the European Charter for Researchers (Commission 2005), ambiguity rather than clarity characterizes the EU position concerning participation in higher education governance. While again emphasizing academic freedom as an important condition for academic work, it is argued that participation in governance structures is not, and should not, be a fundamental right for researchers: "*Researchers should, however, recognize the limitations to this [academic] freedom that could arise as a result of particular research circumstances (including supervision/guidance/management)*" (Commission 2005b: 11). Moreover: "*Researchers should be familiar with the strategic goals governing their research environment and funding mechanisms*" (Commission 2005b: 12)

In other words, according to this statement there is not an opening for participation in the development of strategic goals; researchers should "only" have knowledge of the existing goals. Still, the ambiguity is disclosed when the European Charter describes the principles and requirements employers or funders have with respect to researchers: "*Employers and/or funders of researchers should recognize it as wholly legitimate, and indeed desirable, that researchers be represented in the relevant information, consultation and decision-making bodies of the institutions for which they work, so as to protect and promote their individual and collective interests as professionals and to actively contribute to the workings of their institution"* (Commission 2005b: 22)

While the latter statement appears quite positive towards the idea of the democratic university, ambiguity is yet again displayed in a recent Communication from the European Commission on the modernization agenda of European universities. The importance of academic representation in university decision-making is considerably toned down, and a link is created between innovation and organizational autonomy, with the Commission arguing that universities will not be innovative and responsive to change unless they are given real autonomy and accountability (Commission 2006b: 11). The instrument also *"(...) requires new internal governance systems based on strategic priorities and of professional management of human resources"* (Commission 2006b: 11).

As an illustration of what this might mean in practice, the new Danish University Law is mentioned as an example where universities are governed by a self-renewing governing board, where the board appoints the rector, who in turn appoints the deans. Staff and student representation is in the Danish University Law only related to the existence of an Academic Council at each university. However, the latter body is only consultative without any real decision-making powers. Hence, the argument seems to be that change is about establishing more hierarchical lines of command, and creating a more visible management and leadership structure. As Burquel (2005: 4), in one of the conferences leading up to the new Communication from Brussels concluded, there is a request for "strong leaders" and "professional managers" to develop a university vision, a mission, and to implement these.

Organizational Autonomy, Academic Freedom and the Democratic University

Although one could argue that formal documents display ambiguity concerning how universities should be managed in the European Higher Education Area, there is a tendency to emphasize leadership and professional management as a necessity to foster change within the sector. Does this mean the rise of a new equilibrium with respect to democratic governance within universities, or the end of the vision of the democratic university?

Even though one might be tempted to give a confirmative answer to the latter part of this question, the conditions for the democratic university should be discussed more broadly before coming to such a conclusion. However, in a broader discussion, the conditions for the democratic university need to be related to the two concepts it seems to be strongly connected to, organizational autonomy and academic freedom.

Traditionally the relationship between organizational autonomy and academic freedom is seen as two sides of the same coin and mutually dependent (Nyborg 2002: 1; see also Berdahl 1990). Tight (1992: 1384) has noted that it is quite possible to have organizational autonomy without academic freedom, or vice versa as historic examples of Oxford University in early nineteenth century and Prussian universities in the Humboldtian era have demonstrated. Tight concludes that in practice the two concepts tend to be mutually supportive (Tight 1992: 1384). However, when adding a democratic dimension to this relationship, the situation becomes more complex. In their definition of organizational autonomy, Ashby and Anderson (1966: 296) provide a list of areas: freedom from non-academic interference in the government of the institution, freedom to set standards and determine methods of assessments, etc. But in the democratic university, freedom from non-academic interference is rather difficult as representation often includes both administrative staff and students in decision-making bodies. Furthermore, the freedom to set standards and determine methods of assessments becomes limited with the increased institutional responsibility for developing quality assurance systems, often subordinated to external standards and criteria set by external quality assurance agencies emerging partly as a result of the Bologna process. Clearly, even in practice organizational autonomy does not necessarily link up with either academic freedom or the vision of the democratic university. One could rather note that stronger autonomy might mean less freedom for those working at the University. The classic paradox appearing is that *"entrepreneurs justify the privilege of voluntary action and association for themselves, while imposing upon all subordinated that the duty of obedience and the obligation to serve their employers to the best of their ability"* (Perrow 1984: 53–54).

The link between academic freedom and the vision of the democratic university is further complicated if acknowledging that academic freedom also implies duties towards the institution, duties that also should include participating in administration, in elections to decision-making bodies and positions, and volunteering to participate as a representative to such bodies and positions (Tight 1988: 117; Shils 1997: 156). Empirical studies show consistent low levels of engagement and unwillingness of rank and file staff as well as students to participate in university decision-making. For example, in the Netherlands this becomes particularly clear in poor turnouts at university council elections. Turnout rates of between 10 and 20% are common in student elections. The staff electoral turnout rates are usually higher, but still low. Figures also show that the situation in the 1970s, the peak of university democracy, was not rosy and promising. In the Netherlands, a 1978 questionnaire revealed that only 20% of the academics were willing to take a seat in the university council (in those days the most essential powers resided in the council) (Commissie Polak 1979: 84). This percentage was even lower for non-academic staff and students (14 and 10% respectively). The main reasons for this were that it would take too much time or that others would do a better job. A national survey in 2005 showed no improvement. University community members are not enthusiastic to invest in a university as a representative democracy. As Tight (1988: 122) has argued with respect to students *"it would seem that many present-day students do not want academic freedom, or [...] would not know what to do with it if they were suddenly given it."* Hence, it might be argued that in practice the emphasis on stronger leadership and management in university governance will not lead to a university governance structure that is significantly different from the current situation.

Here, one should also notice the fact that even though the "representative revolution" in the late 1960s and early 1970s often has been interpreted as the rise of the democratic university, one should still acknowledge that there are, and have always been limitations to the democracy in that, for example, students often hold a substantial yet minority number of seats on governing bodies. In other words, seats in decision-making bodies have never been distributed according to numerical strength. Hence, the democratic principle of one person one vote has never been the norm in higher education (Bergan 2003). For administrative staff, the number of seats available in governing bodies is also traditionally in minority while the academic staff in general has elected a majority of the members of a given decision-making body. Seen in this perspective, the representative university has never been truly democratic.

This can further be illustrated by a US study on "the University as a site for citizenship," which suggests that there is a general belief among both faculty and students that decision-making within universities has always been concentrated in the hands of an elite few. Consultative processes, anchored in an elaborate and multi-layered committee system, often function and are accepted as legitimate surrogates for direct democratic participation or representation in decision-making (Plantan 2002: 57). In this context, the vision of the democratic university is a concept that conceals more than it clarifies, with the idea of the democratic university being more symbolic (Bergan 2003) than a reality. As reported by the above mentioned US study, often university administrators and academic staff consider aspects of citizenship and democracy to be entirely a personal matter, and not an integrated part of their duties as teachers or scholars (Plantan 2002: 9). Based on this, one could argue that the interesting questions should not be centred around democracy or formal changes in governance structures, but more focused on whether and how various groups of actors are influenced by prevailing models of governance, and on the limits of formal structures (Rhoades 1992: 1381–1382). While the idea of the democratic university holds strong promises concerning participation and representation, the irony is that leadership seems quite critical to foster engagement and involvement by staff and students in decision-making processes (Plantan 2002: 56).

Related to this, one might argue that the emphasis given to new leadership and management structures in European universities actually could be seen as a change where formal structures are more reflecting the empirical realities of university governance where power and control often goes beyond the existence of formal structures, and where influence is determined by informal structures, agenda setting skills, the ability to define the issues of importance, or the solutions that are legitimate (Rhoades 1992: 1379). One could even argue that this is a process that has been going on for a number of years. As Dill (1992) has pointed out, mechanisms for stronger coordination in university governance were established already in the 1970s in a number of countries. Hence, the general tendency is the blurring of distinct governing models into a collection of integrating mechanisms to be applied as appropriate (Dill 1992: 1327). Clark (1998: 137) is only one example of this when he advocates the need for a strengthened steering core of universities combining *"new managerial values with traditional academic ones.*" This suggests that "representation" in the knowledge era is less about physical presence, and more about the presence of ideas in the decision-making process. Maybe the new equilibrium concerning representation is found in "*new forms of academic-administrative relations*" (Clark 2004: 173)?

Interestingly, those defending the more traditional view on the need for a democratic university seem to have changed their lines of argument recently for promoting representation in university governance. For example, while the Council of Europe (2004: 6) is "*supporting innovative practices in the democratic governance of educational institutions [...] including participation in decision-making,*" the new rationale for such decision-making structures is "*(T)hat education for democratic citizenship is a factor for innovation in terms of organizing and managing overall education systems, as well as curricula and teaching methods*" (Council of Europe 2004: 4).

Suggesting a relationship between innovation and democratic governance is an interesting twist when trying to defend the vision of the democratic university in the European Higher Education Area. However, the argument could be empirically defended. As Blau (1955) showed in a classic bureaucracy study, employment security and autonomy are conducive to a positive attitude towards organizational change as well as social change in general (see also Tabatoni et al. 2002: 8).

CONCLUSION

The opening up of the governance structures in the University to others than professors exposed university conflicts to a greater extent than before, triggering studies on participation, power and the people in the new governance system, not least concerning election processes with respect to managerial positions, and how group conflicts were negotiated and solved in the new system (Baldridge 1971; Cohen et al. 1972; March and Olsen 1976). In sum, a picture of universities as loosely coupled systems was introduced (Weick 1976), where the new actors involved in governance sought to deal with the translation of problematic goals, unclear technologies and fluid participation (Cohen et al. 1972). The empirical studies of choice and decision-making in these kind of situations paved the way for an understanding of university governance as a garbage can process where "*various problems and solutions are dumped by participants*" (Cohen et al. 1976: 26).

Partly related to some interpretations of these processes as being poor in effectiveness and low in efficiency (also non-rational), Europe saw the emergence of reforms "inspired" by New Public Management in the latter part of the 1980s and throughout the 1990s. The new governance models that appeared in universities in this period were a result of a changing relationship between the higher education sector in general and the state (van Vught 1989). Stronger self-regulation, increased organizational autonomy and a more "managerial" university were parts of the new recipe prescribed with voices emphasizing the need for a strengthened steering core of the University

(Clark 1998), with increased weight given to individual responsibility rather than to collective decision-making (Larsen et al. 2005). As mentioned before, an often noticed (side) effect of this trend is the emergence of new forms of representation, this time by unions and student organizations having formal rights in the governance structure of universities (Kirp 2003).

Even though the effects of these changes are complex and allow for different interpretations, not least with respect to the practical implementation of more "managerialism" in the university, one could argue that the Bologna process with the ambitions of realising a European Higher Education Area in 2010 (chapter 7) as well as the broader Lisbon strategy (chapter 8), make it important to study and analyse the conditions for university governance as a form of representative democracy. There are several reasons for this.

To start with, one could argue that the Bologna and Lisbon processes are first and foremost structural in nature, and that both are processes in need to be filled with content. Agreeing with Enders (2004) in that much attention so far has been focused on macro-politics and meso-structures, it could be argued that (studies of) new forms of representative university governance are a necessity for establishing and also understanding the micro-processes needed in the implementation process. If universities are supposed to be "partners" in the implementation process one could, especially given our knowledge about implementation in higher education (Gornitzka et al. 2005), question the wisdom of not allowing for more diversity in university governance where the "citizens of academe" could play key roles (Bergan et al. 2004), even in a period where strengthened leadership is seen as a central success factor (Reichert and Tauch 2005: 43).

Second, emphasising and arguing for the need for greater professionalism in university governance does not mean the end of some of the drivers behind the rise of the representative university. Power struggles, battles for influence and control over resource allocation are processes that do not disappear even in the era of "managerialism", and are also issues that could be further fuelled by the Bologna process and its implications. One can easily agree with Altbach in that

"Activism by both students and professors is inherent in the nature of the academic community. The combination of academic freedom and autonomy in universities, the role of ideas (and sometimes idealism) in higher education, the power instilled by the universities' expertise, the relative ease of organizing campus-based activism, and the increasing central role of the academic community mean that academic activism will continue to be a powerful force"
(Altbach 1992: 1444).

Hence, to conclude, one could offer three different interpretations of the future of the representative democratic university. First, one can make the point that "university democracy" was a wrong term describing the changes in the 1960s and 1970s. The University has never been truly democratic, representation was not according to numerical strength, and the system was still open to manipulation by those with power and influence (based on academic expertise). As indicated in our introduction and our analysis, it can be argued that the implementation of the underlying ideas of the

University as a representative democracy has been rather poor. But if this is a viable explanation, then the democratic university cannot be blamed for the perceived lack of efficiency and effectiveness with respect to university governance. Daalder's (1982) argument that increased "bureaucratization" accompanied the "democratization" of universities is in this respect interesting. If university inertia can be related more to university bureaucracy than to university democracy, this opens up for a rethinking of the efficiency aspects of representation in university governance. From this perspective faculty dissatisfaction with their involvement in administrative processes, that is, the more involved they are in administrative decision-making processes the more they seem to be dissatisfied with their involvement (cf. Geurts and Maassen 1996, 2005), can be explained by the bureaucratic "side-effects" of participation, and not by democratic failures.

Related to the first point, could university democracy actually be seen as a necessary condition for innovation as the Council of Europe has suggested? Observing the "Management Revolution" in US higher education during the last three decades, Keller has strongly argued for the virtues of ambiguity as one of the main reasons for the success and the adaptiveness of US higher education pointing to that "an ironclad and historically developed scheme of strictly correct governance procedures would probably have stymied campus changes" (Keller 2001: 318). What he observes is that despite the conservatism of representative governance bodies, reluctance in accepting change and allegiance to established privileges, universities do still change, and continue to adjust to new conditions and external demands. According to Keller, representative democracy in governance creates the necessary equilibrium between the two indispensables of academic life: tradition and innovation (Keller 2001: 320). In this perspective, representation in governance may be efficient in that it secures more "voices" in decision-making processes, providing more information, better decisions, and a smoother implementation when the decision is taken.

There is also a third interpretation concerning the future of the representative democracy. This perspective sees representation as a channel for and the voice of the "powerless" (students and administration) in university governance. If the University continues to have informal power structures which will find their way despite the emergence of a more visible and stronger leadership, then one could expect that the difference between the formal and informal decision-making structures in universities will be even greater than those that might exist today. Somewhat paradoxically, the key to representative influence will in this perspective be in the hands of the new breed of university leaders (see also Plantan 2002).

It is perhaps in the "grey zones" between the three interpretations that the future of the University as a representative democracy is to be found. In the current innovation era where new ideas have to be turned into actions more rapidly, participation in decision-making will still be needed by those controlling important knowledge (Clark 2004). This might likely result in new forms of representative governance, perhaps in more informal settings avoiding some of the bureaucracy associated with the former procedures, and administered by a more professional (but still quasi-elected) leadership. Hence, despite all the discontent and the decreasing interest in representative governance structures in universities, there are strong reasons to keep up our attention to this aspect of university life. Even if the vision of the democratic university currently might seem rather blurred, this might well be because representation in university governance is in a process of establishing a new equilibrium.

CHAPTER 6

A SERVICE ENTERPRISE: THE MARKET VISION

Carlo Salerno

INTRODUCTION

The movement from elite to mass higher education and the accompanying rising costs have both put enormous fiscal and political pressure on governments accustomed to fully funding post-secondary education. Though many European countries would very much like to retain the University's public good character, mounting evidence[112] is gradually forcing policymakers across much of Europe to accept the sobering reality that the continent's capability to compete in the global higher education and research markets is being threatened as a result (Economist 2005). What is more, there are strong arguments to suggest that such a strategy is simply not sustainable in light of rising public expenditures in other publicly-funded and politically contentious areas, such as healthcare.

For universities many believe this shift has created more problems than opportunities. As processes, education and research are poorly understood (even within academe) and the gains from both are difficult to define with any real degree of precision. Cost escalation coupled with institutions' inability to clearly demonstrate the value of their services has done much to erode the public's trust (Ehrenberg 2000; Cole et al. 1994; Massy and Zemsky 1994) and prompted unprecedented efforts to regulate or monitor universities' performance. With buzzwords such as efficiency, adaptation and value increasingly permeating the political rhetoric, universities have found themselves forced to alter the institutional and governance structures underpinning their "community of scholars" image and supplanting (or in some instances replacing) it with a more corporate, business-like structure.

The growing attention given to diversifying universities' revenue streams, promoting competition, encouraging mobility and creating organizations that are far more responsive to their consumers' needs reflect a societal shift in what universities are for and how they are expected to function. It also suggests that at least some of the dynamics being observed today could be better understood by eschewing traditional sociological and political-based frameworks in favor of a more economic one. This of course raises the question, "what type of framework?" Though much research has considered higher education's more service-oriented role, a comprehensive vision is still lacking. What would such a framework encompass? What would it address? To

---

[112] In recent years a number of European Commission communications (e.g. Commission 2002b) or EU-funded research projects (e.g. Conraths and Smidt 2005) have made repeated reference to this notion.

P. Maassen and J. P. Olsen (eds.), University Dynamics and European Integration, 119–132.

what extent can it help explain the ongoing changes and complex dynamics behind European higher education institutions and systems?

A FRAMEWORK FOR ANALYSIS

The starting point of this chapter is Olsen's thinking about the University as a market-driven, service organization (chapter 2). As was shown in earlier chapters, the "University as a service enterprise" vision reflects the combination of high conflict between various actors and strong external pressures. In Olsen's market-oriented vision, institutions are positioned by the regional and global markets they operate in. The institutions' products, education and research in their various forms, are regarded largely as bundles of goods to be exchanged in the market. Competition and profit gain are regarded as core while knowledge is seen less as a public good and more as a private benefit. Change, be it evolutionary or revolutionary, is driven by the need to survive in the market and Darwinian-like natural selection.

This mode of thinking is based on the idea that universities often must undertake rapid adaptation that is buttressed by a unified, albeit professional, leadership. As a rule, the University has considerable freedom to operate without direct public oversight. In place of micro-management, governments limit intervention to providing rules and incentives that parameterize the institutions' operating environment. In return, accountability is shifted largely to the institutions. However, greater organizational autonomy also drives non-government stakeholders to become more scrutinizing; the response is much greater emphasis on externally monitoring output quality and performance. The push for efficiency prompts institutions to increasingly embrace more private-sector and profit-oriented business operating practices. In the end, traditional modes of collegial governance and democratic rule are eschewed in favor of stronger management structures and more interdisciplinary organization. Lay boards play an increasingly important role in the University's upper-level governance. Faculty members are more apt to retain their intellectual property rights.

THE MARKET REVOLUTION

In many respects, the vision of the University as a service enterprise operating in competitive markets strongly captures the essence of how economists have come to view higher education. This helps to shed some light on the subject, but the predominant view still persists that universities' behavior remains a poor fit to textbook economic theories and models (Winston 1997; Rothschild and White 1993). Indeed, explanations behind market phenomena are still inconsistent with, for example, models of individual universities' behavior.

From this standpoint Olsen's framework (chapter 2) is quite useful as it draws on a much broader mix of the many pieces or components that typify analytical frameworks of this sort. Here I want to focus on just what several of the more important pieces actually encompass and, importantly, how they are inter-linked. Doing so will not only provide a more comprehensive elaboration of the University as a service enterprise vision, but also lay the groundwork for thinking about the sometimes unique aspects of European higher education institutions and systems.

In essence the basic framework is developed around the idea that society values what the University produces *relative* to how those resources could be used elsewhere; it helps to explain *why* resources ought to be allocated to such organizations in the first place. The pursuit of free inquiry or the inculcation of democracy are noble objectives in their own rights but they nonetheless constitute activities that demand resources that can be used just as well for meeting other social objectives. The "marketization" of these objectives (including education) produces a set of relative prices for each that reveals, in monetary terms, just how important these activities are when compared to issues such as healthcare, crime, social security or any other good/service that is funded by the public purse. It does nothing to reduce universities' roles as bastions of free inquiry or their promotion of democratic ideals; it only recasts the problem in terms of the resources available to achieve them. As this imbibes the purposes of the University that are outlined in Olsen's other three visions (chapters 2–5), it makes the service enterprise framework appealing even if it is only from the perspective of scope.

From here the processes underlying the dynamics we tend to observe today are fairly straightforward when two key economic principles are adhered to. One, resources for such activities are allocated when, at the margin, the combined social and private benefits exceed the costs. As long as this condition exists then additional investment of resources will continue to impart societal gains. Two, which is inexorably tied to the first, is that keeping the costs of providing those services (or producing those goods) to a minimum not only reduces waste but maximizes the amount of the investment that is made. The tricky part, that which seems to raise most of the analytical problems in university research, is finding an appropriate way to determine (and value): 1) what precisely the benefits and costs actually are; and 2) who precisely reaps the benefits as well as who incurs the costs.

As a rule, economic theory tells us that competition will usually work to ensure that the second principle is addressed, which explains why it has become such a prominent feature of institutions' operations, system-level policy initiatives and consequently, Olsen's vision. Competition provides a mechanism for allocating resources to the units most efficient at producing certain outputs or providing certain services but it is also believed to encourage technological progress. That said, competition is but a means to an end. Its *purpose* is extracting efficiency and more than that, different types of efficiency. Cost minimization (allocative efficiency) is the most common form, but competition works to ensure the efficient allocation of physical inputs (technical efficiency), the combination of both physical inputs and their prices (economic efficiency), operation at the most efficient size (scale efficiency), and the production of the right combination of goods (mix efficiency).[113]

---

[113] The discussion here purposefully eschews notions of input and output quality for two reasons. One, as a factor in higher education production functions, economists generally agree that the notion is not well

Unfortunately, for all of the emphasis policy makers, administrators and even researchers give to promoting competition, in practice it bafflingly fails on two very important levels. One, there has been remarkably little technological progress. Even in the USA which has long had the most competitive university markets, education delivery is still predominantly lecture-based, just as it was a century ago.[114] Two, it has done little to stem rising prices. To draw again on the highly competitive American market, for the better part of two decades annual price increases have exceeded inflation rates with alarming consistency even in the face of both Federal scrutiny and threats by individual US states to impose sanctions where tuition increases exceed inflation.

The failure that more competition on these fronts has had highlights two important aspects of consumers and costs that bear on any analysis of the service enterprise university. First, most education consumers have a strong preference for studying close to home.[115] As such, even though globalization and internationalization efforts have increased the aggregate number of students that study abroad, the size of the overall pie is still remarkably small, which means that education offerings are still largely geared to stable, local consumer bases. Second, higher education is not like the auto industry where advances in technology coupled with mass production leads to decreasing long-run costs. The gradual adoption of information and communication technology (ICT) and the fact that such technology changes rapidly, for example, means that costs rarely decline. Moreover, as science becomes more complex and education delivery becomes richer, both processes demand increasingly more resources, particularly when it comes to education and research in the physical and biological sciences. This in turn helps explain why strategies underlying adaptation and change in the interest of cost reduction usually are less often enacted within the University's core processes, but instead in the reorganization of institutions' sub-units.

An important question, especially when it comes to the provision of education is "competition for what?" Not all institutions compete with one another or in the same markets. For example, prestigious universities are believed to compete heavily for high quality inputs. Faculty searches at these institutions tend to draw scholars from around the world while the filling of coveted enrollment places is equally intense. In contrast, less-prestigious institutions are more apt to compete in output markets; that is, they compete heavily with other (usually regional) providers for the right to sell degrees (Winston 1999).

---

understood; however, a growing body of American-led research does argue that competition and education quality are linked through students' roles in educating their peers and is one of the main reasons behind the concentration of top students in a small number of universities (see, e.g. Winston 1999; and Hoxby 1997). Two, economic analyses of production and efficiency tend to account for quality by assuming some given level of quality and *then* asking how resources can be most efficiently allocated/re-allocated.

[114] See Zemsky et al. (2005) chapter on "Thwarted Innovation" for a good discussion of the economics behind why universities have been reluctant to develop education delivery structures (e-learning) that rely on the growth in electronic media.

[115] See for example studies in both the USA (Hoxby 1997) and Australia (James et al. 1999).

At first glance prestige does not seem to fit neatly into the business-like organizational framework but as it turns out, it is terribly important for understanding universities' internal allocation decisions and consequently both the quality and volume of the different services offered (Massy 1996). The nonprofit status of the overwhelming majority of universities precludes profit maximization as a tenable objective. From an organizational standpoint, even though many argue that universities are increasingly adopting corporate-like organizational structures (Birnbaum 2000), from an economics perspective they are still more like physicians' cooperatives (Pauly and Redisch 1973). One consequence of this is that if universities have a single overarching objective then most economists agree that it is probably to jointly maximize their faculty's satisfaction and institution's prestige (James 1990). The rub is that the two objectives are inexorably linked; the activities faculty members enjoy doing most, research and doctoral training, happen to be the ones that researchers believe do the most for enhancing prestige. The problem is that these activities tend to cost more than the revenues they bring in.[116]

Here a more precise conceptualization of "profit" comes into play. Being nonprofit does not imply that universities cannot earn profits. What it does mean though is that any excess revenues must be churned back into the organization. Since universities seek to jointly maximize faculty satisfaction and institutional prestige, which are gained primarily through costly research and doctoral education, they are believed to produce other outputs (i.e. undergraduate education) using an inexpensive technology like larger classes that allows them to earn a profit. This profit is then used to help pay for the costly but objective-achieving activities. In other words, tuition from undergraduate education cross-subsidizes research and doctoral education (James 1990). What allows universities to do this is the use of lump-sum annual appropriations coupled with the inability of third-party payers like state governments and students to effectively monitor how funding is used once it is distributed.

So, the *reason* that profit is so important to universities is that it allows them to meet their objectives and to jointly produce the various outputs expected of them. It also suggests that organizational autonomy to flexibly allocate resources internally may possibly have deleterious side effects. Coupled with rising prices, this prevailing view has long provided the impetus for claims that universities are effectively shirking what many believe is their core responsibility (undergraduate education) to satisfy more self-centered pursuits.

---

[116] For example, external grants for academic research rarely cover universities' indirect costs (e.g. researchers' office space or electricity). Institutions have to pay for such outlays regardless, so the reasoning goes, hence where indirect cost recovery is possible, as a rule it is usually only a partial reimbursement. As for doctoral education, in many European countries these students usually do not pay tuition fees but are instead hired as university staff. While the trend has been towards more fee-paying doctoral programs, the one-on-one training that students receive and the higher maintenance costs from treating them as staff means that they consume a disproportionately greater amount of university labour and capital than bachelors or masters students.

This idea first emerged in the early-1980s but it was not until the end of the decade before it began receiving serious attention, first in widespread publications like *Profscam* (1989) and later even by higher education researchers (see, e.g. Massy and Zemsky 1994). While the negative image has gradually faded in light of further research, the episode did highlight the importance that information plays in the service enterprise university. Specifically, it probably did much (in combination with the implementation or growth of tuition) to clarify and rationalize greater public scrutiny of universities' activities. Information asymmetry between higher education providers and consumers invariably favors the former over the latter, which is one of the main reasons that nonprofit theories suggest that universities form as nonprofits rather than for-profits.[117] Since education consumers cannot value the quality of the product they are purchasing until long after it has been consumed, they must rely on market signals of quality and trust education providers' claims about the value of their degrees. This essentially gives institutions a competitive advantage since they are well aware of the quality they produce. It creates an imbalanced exchange situation that is really not so different from that between used car salesmen and individuals looking to purchase a second-hand automobile.

As costs rose through the 1980s and 1990s, students and their families (most notably in the USA, South Korea and Japan) increasingly found themselves shouldering a larger portion of the debt. It is no surprise then, given the concurrent revelations brought about by the cross-subsidization hypothesis, that quality assurance mechanisms and performance-based funding criteria rapidly became prominent features of most higher education systems.[118] While greater organizational autonomy provides an intuitively appealing explanation for greater stakeholder scrutiny, the limited available evidence suggests that it was more likely a mechanism brought about by a cultural shift towards greater government efficiency and mistrust with the University's non-transparent operating practices. The most interesting facet of these developments, one that is in dire need of greater scrutiny by higher education researchers, is the remarkably scant empirical evidence to support the argument's logic (James and Rose-Ackerman 1986). The truth is, we do not know that universities are providing

---

[117] Lacking the profit incentive, they ought to be more responsive to their stakeholders' rather than their shareholders' needs.

[118] The correlation between accountability mechanisms and cost sharing is an interesting one. Higher education survived for the better part of 700 years without quality assurance mechanisms and performance measurement and if one looks at the quality of the curriculum, staff and resources even at the turn of the twentieth century they could make a case that such tools have been sorely needed for some time. Yet this has not been the case. The rapid expansion in quality assurance frameworks first began in the mid-1980s (in Northwestern Europe). By some accounts it was driven by the rapid success the practice enjoyed particularly in Japan's manufacturing industries (Schwarz and Westerheijden 2004). Others have suggested that quality assurance frameworks arose as part of the shift in government steering: more organizational autonomy was 'traded' for more formal quality assurance frameworks. By the late-1990s, the phenomenon had subsumed much of Central and Eastern Europe as well, though here it was believed to also be used for helping purge the institutions' strong Marxist-Leninist ideology.

substandard education or that universities' operating practices are productively or cost inefficient.

Given the push towards recognizing universities as service providers, research to-date has failed to account for how consumers' preferences and resource use shape institutional behavior. The airline industry, for example, draws on consumer demand to adjust its in-air food and beverage offerings, entertainment options, flight destinations and seating policies. Restaurants shuffle their menus and food portions in response to consumers' tastes and how much they eat while hotels price rooms based on occupation rates and alter the time schedules of their various amenities (e.g. health clubs, in-house gift shops or hotel bars) based on the extent to which patrons utilize such services. However, when it comes to the University casual observation suggests that neither researchers nor policy makers nor the public seem to consider how university behavior may be affected by the way institutions' consumers draw on their resources.

Yet it *is* important because the limited available statistics, at least for education, suggest that students grossly under-utilize a considerable amount of the resources placed at their disposal.[119] Waste is particularly problematic for organizations such as universities, where a common pool of resources is used for several activities. Once a resource (like faculty time) is allocated to an activity it cannot be used for another. Consumer demands for more student-faculty interaction and greater attention to education activities in general must be weighed against the tradeoff of that individual's potential contribution as a researcher. Why put a Nobel-prize winning chemistry or economics professor in an introductory seminar where students nod off in class, spend little time on out-of-class assignments or only visit the professor's office hours after an exam to barter for additional points? It is no surprise that when given the option, universities more often than not choose to put that individual in the laboratory and increasingly rely on part-time or adjunct faculty to teach undergraduate courses. I am not discounting the uncertainty and resource waste that goes with producing research. Indeed, much of the business is shaped by timing and more than a bit of luck (Stephan and Levin 1992). However, one can argue that incentive mechanisms like tenure and peer review provide institutions with greater control over both the volume and quality of that which is done. From this it is apparent why contemporary explanations for the University's internal resource allocation decision-making are fundamentally deficient – they simply do not account for how certain consumers' habits potentially shape internal decision-making. This raises the tantalizing possibility that the increasingly aggressive climate of university oversight may be somewhat misdirected as are the policies designed to redress the problems. Further research in this area is clearly warranted but it is not beyond the realm of possibility that a behavioral model that explains universities' internal allocation behavior in light of consumers' resource use

---

[119] The most recent findings reported from the National Survey of Student Engagement (NSSE) in the USA show that students spend less than half the amount of time outside the classroom that their professors expect. In nominal terms, both first-year students and those graduating reported spending only approximately 10 to 14 hours outside of face-to-face instruction.

could show universities to be already operating efficiently. At the extreme, it may be that the near global expansion of quality assurance is in itself inefficient.

An additional factor that must be considered when casting universities as service enterprises is the competitive dynamic between public and private providers. Though the two are similar in many respects, the differences that do emerge play an important role in shaping the consumer-seller mentality. Privates' (especially the for-profits') strong reliance on tuition fees is believed to make them more responsive to consumers' demands while the absence of substantial up-front capital (typically provided by states) means they are apt to produce different programmatic offerings that change the industry's competitive dynamic. Especially in transitional or developing economies, privates tend to provide education in a small number of professional programs, for example, business or computer science, and be geographically concentrated in saturated education markets. African countries offer the most illustrative example but this geographic and content clustering is also clearly evident in Central and Eastern Europe.

The bifurcation is particularly important since numerous questions arise about the circumstances under which privates emerge in the first place. In countries with strong public sectors the emerging privates embody the service enterprise, as their rise seems to be related to either niche-carving or exploiting public universities' failure to provide academic programs at a level of quality consistent with consumers' expectations. Again though, many of these new privates are also organized as for-profits. In theory, since quality costs and these institutions primary objective is to maximize shareholder wealth rather than student learning, consumers should not be attracted to their offerings, yet the growth of this sub-sector has been remarkable over the past two decades.

The last point I want to address is the valuation of benefits (information) and how it relates to the service enterprise university. The shift towards greater recognition of the private benefits to higher education over public ones has less to do with any political rationalization for cost sharing practices or a less socially-conscious society. Rather, it has to do with states' abilities to support massive enrollment increases and the ensuing recognition, on behalf of policy makers, about the balance between what individuals and society gain through the process. From an equity standpoint, if we accept the economic axiom that "he who benefits, pays" then the greater emphasis being put on individuals' benefits essentially reflects public dissatisfaction with the rate of return on its current investment. Yes, I will publicly support another individual's university training to the extent that it reduces the chance that that person robs me 10 years from now. Yes, I will fund these persons if their contribution to society will make my life richer down the road (perhaps through a cure for cancer). But no, I am not eager to finance someone's university education through the tax system so that they may live in a bigger home someday or have the wealth to purchase and drink more expensive wines.

This "balancing the benefits with the costs" principle is also evident on the research side. The commercialization of academic research has long drawn on the principle that universities claim eminent domain over research findings because the scientist made the discovery as an employee. As perceptions have gradually shifted to view faculty members more as individual professionals under a larger university umbrella, it has become apparent that allowing individuals to retain partial control over their own findings works as an incentive for faculty to continue making such discoveries and to keep them at that particular university. Scarce resources coupled with intense competition for securing the most able human capital has given the faculty members greater leverage to retain the benefits of their work.

EUROPEAN HIGHER EDUCATION AND RESEARCH

Much of what researchers know about markets, efficiency, the economics of higher education in general and consequently, the service enterprise framework has come primarily from US economists' studies of American universities. Thus, even though the service enterprise organizational model may have its merits, it remains an unresolved question just how broadly applicable such a framework is vis-à-vis the particular cultural, political and social institutions within which different university systems are based. How appropriate then is the service enterprise vision for understanding the University in Europe?

The prestige-maximization hypothesis that governs much of the thinking about competition between US universities does not work as well in the European case for at least three reasons. First, open admission policies prevent top students from clustering in particular institutions, though this is gradually changing in some countries with the introduction of university "colleges." Second, the distribution of wealth is far less pronounced between European universities. The absence of both substantive development efforts and the ability to charge flexible tuition fees have curtailed exorbitant endowments and large percentages of institutional revenues coming from tuition fees. The third reason is that the public character of most European universities has historically created little need for institutions to compete with one another, either at the national or international level. A predominance of public funding and the fact that few students studied abroad meant universities did not need to compete for resources; they had, in effect, geographic domains that allowed them to behave more like local monopolists (which could also explain the lack of technological progress).

Its apparent misspecification in the European context can also be seen when regional differences are highlighted. Among other things, high per-capita wealth in the Nordic countries coupled with relatively low rates of return to higher education have allowed these systems, and their students, to continue enjoying strong levels of financial support from the state. Intuitively, such practices contradict the notion of an imbalance in public versus private benefits, or that excessive public funding promotes resource waste, and would imply that socio-political factors not evident in economic analyses are equally important. Yet one can look to countries like Norway and Sweden and see similar performance-based funding strategies or quality assurance frameworks that demonstrate greater stakeholder focus and a striving for economic efficiency found in European countries with less-endowed systems.

Moreover, Central and Eastern European countries that whole-heartedly embraced market-driven, consumer oriented practices in the early 1990s have spent the better part of the last five years trying to swing the pendulum back towards a more balanced mix of market incentives and state oversight. The point from these observations is that competition and a consumer-oriented mindset have practical limits that inevitably must be balanced by some degree of government intervention (Salerno 2005).

Though these observations cast doubt on the appropriateness of the service enterprise framework, Europe is nevertheless in the process of embracing these very principles. Token tuition fees have begun to emerge and calls for greater freedom to set prices are growing. The establishment of honors colleges within universities, for example, in the Netherlands, shows how institutions are trying to differentiate themselves in systems where the mechanisms for establishing hierarchies are not yet in place. Development offices (i.e. endowment procurement) which have been slow to catch on, are gaining both importance and formal structure within universities. One has to look no further than the UK government's recently established matching gifts initiative to see public support for a more hierarchical university structure based on institutional wealth.

The mold breaker is the United Kingdom where top-up fees have allowed institutions greater freedom to charge differential tuition rates and a new government initiative that provides matching funding for development activities has recently been established. The German initiative to create a class of elite institutions is also noteworthy in that it is being driven by the infusion of a serious amount of research funding and being supported by the federal government. The strategy runs counter to most European higher education policies and, somewhat ironically, represents a 180 degree shift from the late-nineteenth century when the Americans ambitiously adopted the German model. For the purpose here it provides direct evidence that the prestige/wealth hypothesis has at least some applicability in the European context.

The spirit of the service enterprise model is further evident in the forces driving the development of a European Higher Education Area and a European Research Area. The homogenization of educational structures clearly reflects policy makers' preferences for a more standardized education product over universities' preferences for providing what they see as necessary and/or appropriate. Efforts to spur private investment in research reinforce the two-pronged view that society and universities mutually benefit from greater interaction and that encouraging more market interaction will drive universities to be more responsive to their stakeholders. In the end, the real question is one of causality. Is the economic need to more efficiently allocate scarce resources driving changing public perceptions of the University as service provider or has the perception driven the implementation of policies designed to reap the efficiency benefits of a more market-oriented environment?

The challenge that Europe faces in embracing a university world based on the service enterprise model is fundamentally adapting the basic notions of equity and social responsibility underlying the European University (see, e.g. Gumport 2000). Competition, markets and responsiveness to stakeholders' demands will invariably produce hierarchies that give rise to a class system based on perceived quality. The ability to create a group of Ivy League-style institutions will demand student selectivity mechanisms that will impinge on access, the accumulation of wealth will create a system of rich and poor institutions and a set of universities capable of doing world-class research will inevitably force some universities that are the pinnacle in their own country's system today to lose some of their prominence in the broader European Research Area of tomorrow.

The tendency to partially embrace market principles or to treat universities as service enterprises and then hamstring them with counter-productive regulations has been more common than not. The abuse of tuition policies has been the most flagrant example but it is also evident in the mechanisms for distributing research funding. The Dutch government's continued policy of charging a flat tuition fee across academic programs and even institution types limits these higher education providers' abilities to compete on quality that is reflected in prices, which subsequently hinders consumer choice (Salerno 2004). The public backlash from introducing top-up fees in the United Kingdom, the one system in Europe well-accustomed to substantive tuition fees, also demonstrates how well-intentioned policies can fall short when economic and political concerns must strike a balance. Top-up fees prevailed but instead of giving universities unfettered flexibility to establish their own schedules, fears about harming access led the British government to cap the increases. In the end, worries that all institutions would simply raise the fees to the capped level came true. Had the market solution prevailed, the price increases put in place at the prestigious institutions would have made it impossible for lower quality institutions (based on resources) to match the increases without it adversely affecting enrollments.

Where research funding is concerned, the problem is two-fold: one is the misguided belief that investment on its own is the solution to Europe's knowledge economy problem while the other has been balancing individual country's needs against those of Europe as a whole. Germany's effort to create elite universities by pouring money into them ignores a long history of strong state oversight. In the end the available evidence would suggest that the successful recipe involves generous yet equal proportions of funding and autonomy of institutional actors to use those resources as they see fit. It remains to be seen whether the "German experiment" will yield the results that policy makers are hoping for. The same can be said for the Lisbon strategy's private investment objective. This latter issue presents far more difficult challenges. The process of establishing a European Research Council (ERC) and the support for such a body from trans-European organizations, such as the European University Association (EUA) and European Science Foundation (ESF), are logical steps towards building common goals. However, the proposed form of the ERC is arguably a step backward for fostering a pan-European identity, mainly because it seeks to make the ERC *complementary* to the problematic existing structure of national research councils (European Science Foundation 2003). For all of the efforts, the exclusion of foreign scientists from applying for research monies is still the norm, which hurts the quality of the science done. And while there is greater coordination today between national councils' funding priorities, so long as the money is considered Italian, French or Estonian then national priorities will always win out and mediocre academic units will persist. In essence, keeping national research councils and thus national funding streams intact hinders macro-efficiency (on a European level). The problem is that no country wants to subsidize pan-European competition that relegates their most prestigious universities and programs to second-class status, even if the long run gains exceed the short run losses.

In some ways, the conflicts above create the wrongful impression that the service enterprise framework is less useful than it actually is when the real problem lies in Europe's desire to only embrace those market principles that do not hinder its broader social agenda. An economic framework has distinct advantages and the more Europe moves towards a market-oriented model the more relevant the existing literature will be towards explaining the phenomenon currently being observed. It is evident that the service enterprise vision has its place for explaining the European University but its application must somehow still capture the political and cultural idiosyncrasies that cannot be explained with traditional economic models. Clearly this is an area for fertile research.

CONCLUSION

While the idea seems to be borne mainly out of the fiscal problems that first cropped up in the early 1990s, European universities have long embraced at least one principle behind the service enterprise framework. As public entities, universities have always maintained some responsibility for being attentive to their parent state's needs. Today that responsiveness has just shifted, albeit progressively and as some might argue quite rapidly, towards private parties, that is, students, their families and private industry. At the same time, competition and its consequences for university behavior do seem to be the direct result of contemporary social, fiscal and technological changes. Thirty years ago, few could have foreseen Europe's contemporary political landscape or how electronic communication would change the way the University could, for example, offer education to a global audience or provide scientists with avenues for international collaboration. Competition, or as some suggest the fear of what could happen by falling behind (Frank and Cook 1995), has fundamentally altered nearly every aspect of how universities, university managers and academics choose what to teach and whom it is taught to as well as what research is done and whom it is done for.

As an industry the University is just too complex for any single framework. That said, one that treats universities more as economic actors making decisions based on the complex interactions in the markets that they operate in is appealing on several fronts. The service enterprise notion is cruel in that it essentially strips universities of their democratic, social and cultural contributions or their positions as the guardians of free inquiry and intellectual exchange but, as was discussed earlier, it is rather effective for describing many of the dynamics being observed today.

Olsen's visions are based, in his words, on the "different assumptions about what the University is for and the circumstances under which it will work well" (chapter 2, Table 1). Clearly, the University here is treated much like any other firm that is willing to sell its services where demand exists. In this regard process is only important in so much as it is efficient; what is of more concern, at least to the public, are the specific services that universities provide and how they can be exploited to maximize both private and public gains.

The circumstances under which education and research work reasonably well are more complicated but understandable when one takes a much broader view of the existing literature. Competition and efficiency are important but even more so is what universities are competing for and what types of efficiency gains are being sought. Markets are also important, but so is the recognition that market failures are inevitable and not necessarily bad. The "products" on which the service enterprise framework is based complicate analyses because of the temporal gap between consuming and valuing what is being purchased. This justifies stakeholders' growing desire to monitor universities' performance but in the end it probably does more to limit the effective functioning of universities than it does to strengthen or enhance them.

European policy makers recognize the precariousness of the current situation and are putting in place ambitious initiatives not just to ensure that the European University survives but thrives as an engine for economic growth and social cohesion. At the same time, the European University has found itself in the midst of an identity crisis. The institution it thought it once was is gradually being challenged and some believe eroded by those it has long and successfully served. If universities are going to succeed in adapting to this new reality then re-conceptualizing and reframing how we think of universities, like that which has been done here, is both necessary and warranted.

PART 3

EUROPEAN REFORM PROCESSES

CHAPTER 7

THE BOLOGNA PROCESS: AN INTERGOVERNMENTAL POLICY PERSPECTIVE

Guy Neave and Peter Maassen

INTRODUCTION

In this and the following chapter the empirical complexity of the attempts to integrate Europe as applied to the university sector, and very particularly the Bologna and Lisbon processes, will be discussed. Both chapters show that to study any single process of European integration in isolation is problematic. Under some conditions, as both Bologna and Lisbon demonstrate, reform processes interact and intertwine, if not integrate, as several partially interconnected developments intersect, cross and meld.

An important foundation stone in the Bologna process can be traced back to 1988, when university leaders of Europe came together in Bologna to sign the Magna Charta Universitatum. This declaration extolled certain fundamental values of the University: academic freedom, the freedom to teach and learn, and with it, university autonomy. Ten years later (May 1998) the 800th anniversary of the Sorbonne was celebrated in Paris, during which occasion the British, French, German, and Italian Ministers responsible for higher education signed a joint declaration (the Sorbonne Declaration) aimed at harmonizing the structure of higher education in the four countries. One year later (June 1999) Ministers of Higher Education of no fewer than 29 European countries signed the so-called Bologna Declaration. Given that at that time only 15 member states made up the European Union, this was an amazing feat of intergovernmental action and commitment to a joint interest, namely the creation of an open European Higher Education Area (EHEA).

The Bologna Declaration laid out policies and joint measures for establishing the EHEA. It included a schedule for achieving the joint objectives thus agreed upon, and a commtment by the Ministers of the countries involved to meet every other year for discussing and assessing progress. The pursuit of the joint policies and measures is commonly referred to as the Bologna process.

The Bologna process has been one of the most studied, if not *the* most studied European integration attempt with respect to the University.[120] However, such studies usually treat the University as an isolated phenomenon – isolated from the dynamics

---

[120] For an overview of various aspects of the Bologna process, see, for example, Hackl (2001), Neave (2003) and Witte (2006: 123–148). See Corbett (2005), Neave (2003), and Wit and Verhoeven (2001) for analyses of the development of a European-level higher education policy.

135

P. Maassen and J. P. Olsen (eds.), University Dynamics and European Integration, 135–154.
© 2007 Springer.

of science and research policies at the national and European level, cut off from the overall processes of European integration, and in many cases divorced from its specific institutional history.

Given the abundance of studies available we will not present an overview of the nature of the Bologna process in this chapter. Instead we will discuss its changing agenda. First we will reflect upon the way in which the Bologna process has shifted gradually from a project with an agenda dominated by a vision of European integration set down by the university world itself to a process where the agenda reflects a vision of European integration that comes from external sources. The latter suggests in the first place that the main aims of the Lisbon agenda – namely, strengthening Europe's economic competitiveness and bolstering its social cohesion – are filtering into the Bologna process. Since social cohesion has been largely neglected in the "Bologna literature" special attention will be paid to it in this chapter and in particular to the way it has become related to the Bologna process.

CHANGING POLICY AGENDAS

The concept of policy as a moving target is not new (Wittrock and deLeon 1986). Many of the changes in University and State relationships that have been introduced over the past two decades have to deal with this particular phenomenon. The redistribution of responsibility and initiative between central government and the institutional level, between setting the strategic framework on the one hand and increasing the scope for institutional initiative on the other, are justified to a very large degree by the pace of change, whether that pace of change is held to be technological innovation, shifts in the labour market, the redundancy of acquired skills or shifts in various forms of student demand for different modes of acquiring knowledge or updating it. Strategic vision and institutional flexibility are prior conditions for anticipating change and that, in turn, adds a further dimension to the definition of policy as a moving target, a metaphor that Wittrock and deLeon introduced more than two decades back to the process of implementation.

The notion of policy as a moving target can also be applied to the Bologna process. It has shifted from a declaration of intent put out by Ministers responsible for higher education in 29 countries on June 1999, to becoming a regular occasion in Europe's Ministerial round. As a statement of intent, Bologna has currently acquired the endorsement 45 European governments. Every two years the Ministers involved come together to set new goals, insert new ambitions of standardization into the Bologna agenda, and strengthen further, if not agency control, then at the very least the extension of agency remit to coordinate their efforts across frontiers. The biennial Bologna meeting of Ministers allows the success of intentions and policies jointly and previously endorsed to be revealed, registered and feted, and to ascertain where it is we are along the path towards constructing a European Higher Education Area. The Bologna Declaration has become institutionalized, an institutionalization evident in the regularity of its Ministerial and other formal meetings, as well as the studies carried out in the framework of the process and the formal working groups that form part of it.

Yet, a number of paradoxes remain. For if the Bologna process has rapidly acquired a certain standing, its organizational basis, compared to the Commission on the one hand and the member states and other Bologna countries on the other, remains fragile. There is no permanent secretariat of any size or scale. Nor did the signatory states embark upon building up a (semi-)permanent administration with an executive capacity to support the pursuit of the process. Moreover, organizing the biennial ministerial meeting falls to the country where the meeting is to be held. Clearly, whilst the Bologna process provides the setting for the countries committed, the Commission, and other major stakeholders to take stock of how far Europe's universities are moving towards a "new architecture," it is evident by no means who retains the guiding hand.

Nor is it implementation alone that stands as a moving target. The continued adding by successive Ministerial Conferences of further dimensions to the original six objectives means that both the agenda and the range of issues at the political and inter-governmental levels are themselves targets both moving and multiplying as they move. In short, we have two very different perspectives on Bologna: first, the high profile and, from the standpoint of issues injected into the Bologna process, the rapid evolution of the political agenda; second, when attention is turned to the grounded realities of implementation, the difficulties of grasping where precisely we are. This is caused, amongst other things, by the grossly inadequate methodology that accompanying progress reports, including the EUA trend reports,[121] display.

This implies that the Bologna process advances at various speeds. The purchase we might have of the dynamics of Bologna depends intimately upon which level of analysis one focuses. There is a "high speed track," represented by the statements of intent and the continuous adding of new items by each succeeding Ministerial Conference. However, one gets a less complacent vision of progress achieved when attention turns to implementation, which moves at a very different pace, as most of the progress reports admit, albeit reluctantly.

Analyzing and understanding the Bologna process would be relatively simple if it advanced only at *two* different speeds. Self-evidently this is not so. For if attention is turned to the state of play in individual university systems – irrespective of the particular perspective – the impression one retains is one of great variation and diversity in the implementation of the Bologna Declaration, an impression that emerges, for example, in the passing of legislation, the intention of institutions and their leaders (EUA 2003; Neave 2005), not to mention the percentage of all students in a given university system enrolled in the Bachelor/Master degree structure. It is possible – and indeed is indulged with enthusiasm, for example, in the work carried out under

---

[121] For an overview of all progress reports published until June 2005, see the Bologna-Bergen website (Main Documents): http://www.bologna-bergen2005.no

the auspices of the European University Association (EUA) – to hail every shift as a success. However, that the EUA played a central role in the signing of the original Declaration, that it now engaged in observing and admiring the consequences of its own handiwork places grave doubts as to the plausibility of such a monitoring exercise.

Even so, to view Bologna less as a statement of intent but rather in terms of what has been achieved, fulfills a purpose no less important. It serves to moderate the more exaggerated goals which Ministerial enthusiasm has heaped upon Europe's universities. When Bologna is examined from the perspective of the individual university – and only recently has this been tackled by the European University Association (EUA 2006) – the stage of implementation stands in sobering contrast to the speed at which the political agenda moves. In the wine of Ministerial ambition, implementation of the Bologna process puts much water.

Thus, it is not entirely surprising that from very early on in the dynamic of the Bologna process, a gap emerged between "*le pays politique*" arraigned around the Bologna process at intergovernment level and "*le pays reel*" that is, the grounded response at institutional level (Neave 2004a). The intentions of the former are not always reflected in the capacities – or perhaps the willingness – of the latter to move at the same pace. In short, the gap between the political agenda and institutional take-up, far from closing is, on the contrary, widening.

Yet, this is not the only aspect that portrays the Bologna process as a moving target. There is another one which entails moving on from that fundamental principle which in the educational domain hitherto determined the relationship between member state and Commission. It involves a fundamental shift in the grounding principle which, from the very outset, determined the relations between member states and the Commission. The practice long established first within the EC and later the EU held that university policy was wholly the affair of the individual member state (Neave 1987). However, negotiating the "roadmap" of the University in Europe has itself moved on from "mutual adjustment" to intergovernment negotiations (Scharpf 2001). In the domain of university policy, the Bologna process is, in effect, the main vehicle that brings about this shift, shaping and consolidated it. Formally the Bologna process functions as a major intergovernmental arena. The question remains how far and how fast its current status may evolve further. How far will the process be assimilated into the Commission's ambit? Another way of looking at this is to revert to Scharpf's typology. Is higher education policy in Europe destined to move on from intergovernmental negotiations towards "hierarchical direction?" Hierarchical direction sees competences hitherto sited at national level, centralized at the European level, carried forward by supranational actors with the *participation* and support of member state governments.

THE CORRECTIVE LENS OF HISTORY

At this point, it is worthwhile setting the Bologna process against an historic backdrop. Even if we rely on the least intelligent of criteria – that of sheer geographical coverage – it is clear that the Bologna process figures amongst the most significant reforms to have taken place in the 900 odd years of the history of the University in Europe. Even when confined to the basic six objectives the Bologna process remains significant for the sheer variety in the different systems ostensibly willing to be committed to a single purpose, not to mention their apparent willingness to subscribe to the schedule fixed in the Declaration (Tomusk 2006). Both these features have no precedent in the long history of Europe's universities. Leaving aside for the moment the dimensions of competitiveness and attractiveness, it may be argued that the remaining principles of employability, readability (of diplomas), transparency and comparability that form what is now taken to be the basic minimum of the Bologna agenda, have less claims to historic significance and originality *per se*. Indeed, the historically minded might also point out that the medieval *quadrivium* of music, arithmetic, geometry and astronomy together with the Faculties of medicine, law civil and canon and theology (Frijhoff 1992: 1254) upheld remarkably similar principles in Europe of the early Middle Ages.

If we take this latter interpretation into account, namely that it is less the principles stated in the Bologna Declaration so much as their geographical coverage which gives Bologna its special nature, we obtain a very different perspective on what may truly be said to constitute the exceptional nature of the process. The early medieval University rested in principle on a single system of individual certification to teach (*jus ubique docendi*) which was in the gift of a single authority to wit, the Pope. It also depended on the same source for what today would be termed "accreditation," namely the recognition of institutions as qualified to dispense the *studium generale* (Cobban 1992). Furthermore, the early universities shared a high degree of similitude in both curriculum and, to use a further anachronism, a homogeneity in the levels of certification. This implies that there are precedents, however remote, to these aspects of the Bologna process. Put another way, from this very particular historic perspective, the significance of Bologna resides less in the basic principles to which authorities set their hands in June 1999. Rather, it resides in an "ideograph," that is, an implicit referring back to an earlier age, intending to show that the radicalism of what is proposed indeed has a historic precedent (Neave 2001: 10).

THE UNIQUE ASPECTS OF BOLOGNA

However, as a policy process Bologna has other dimensions that are of relevance. These involve some important omissions or oversights which emerge in three details. First the imposition of datelines for its completion by 2010 – with the operational definition of completion being the proposed template for study duration across the signatory systems. It is not the principle of setting a schedule that may be contestable. More daring was the assumption that a bare decade would be sufficient for the Bologna principles to be embedded at institutional level. Remarkably, no prior assessment was made into the capacity of national systems to adapt to these principles, still less whether the dateline set was realistic.

Second was the absence of any special budget, allowance and allocation to sustain universities in their transition from their tried and tested study programs to the

Bachelor/Master format, and to offset the forcible re-adjustment within the curriculum to accommodate the change in the modal study duration at undergraduate level in Western Europe from 5 to 3 years.

Finally, there stands the total absence of prior consultation with the university world's equivalent of the social partners. The failure to consult the social partners prior to moving on to the Declaration itself is more than a glaring omission. It may well be the prime feature which, in the pattern of negotiation the agenda for European integration, sets the university dimension aside from its counterparts, for example, in the areas of social affairs or health policy. That the Bologna process should drag on for six years without any formal representation for the one Estate on which implementation ultimately depended – namely academia – is also remarkable (Neave 2005), given that the student Estate, represented by ESIB, the National Unions of Students in Europe, was recognized and consulted almost from the beginning.

These three weaknesses raise a number of subsidiary issues that take on a more enduring importance as Bologna moved on from a Declaration to a process, from being a tactic to clear a political logjam between Commission and some of Europe's universities, to becoming the coping stone in a broader venture (Neave 2003: 157).

From the perspective of changing policy agendas the Bologna Declaration represents a significant shift in the discourse that was underlying the interpretation of higher education as a nationally sensitive policy area. As with the broader Lisbon agenda and the Council of Ministers' meetings after the Lisbon summit in 2000 (see chapter 8), so with the signing of the Bologna Declaration in 1999: Ministers responsible for higher education stopped to celebrate the divergence and diversity of their university systems and started to come together for discussing common challenges and interests.

Apparently, the EU member states that signed the Declaration were prepared to yield on the principle of harmonization, at least in an intergovernmental setting. After the Lisbon 2000 summit the Commission, for its part, gave way on its interpretation that the University should be conceived wholly and solely in terms of vocational training, which formed the basis of its university policy since the passing of the Gravier Judgement in 1986. This quid pro quo emerges in the text of the Bologna Declaration itself, which asserted that the central purpose of the University lay less in economic than in cultural terms. Even though the virtues of competition were not played down, they were nevertheless restated in a broader and somewhat more ambiguous notion of "cultural viability," which from a perspective external to Europe, was presented in terms of the **cultural** attractiveness of "European" higher education on a world market.

Compared to the combined economic and social focus of the Lisbon 2000 agenda, the Bologna Declaration thus marked a different, cultural focus in university policy. Briefly stated, the Bologna Declaration's text included no direct reference to the economic paradigm and thus subordinated it to the central vision of Europe as a cultural entity. The Declaration clearly emphasized the University's central role in developing cultural dimensions in Europe (European Ministers Responsible for Education

1999). Seen within this context, the Bologna Declaration and thus the first phase of the Bologna process, were build more upon the Magna Charta Universitatum (1988), the joint declaration of European universities, than on earlier Commission's communications, such as the "Memorandum on Higher Education" (Commission 1991), the "Teaching and Learning: towards the learning society" White Paper (Commission 1995a), and the so-called Delors White Paper (Commission 1993).

The contrast between the two modes of discourse – between the Commission which, from the early 1990s took on an increasingly utilitarian, technocratic mindset, and the Bologna Declaration which (re-)stated the primacy of the cultural dimension, may, at one level, reflect the long drawn out tension between member states and Commission that marked the mid 1990s (Wit and Verhoeven 2001). The cultural discourse was then an expression, upheld by the member states, of cultural diversity as a permanent condition, permanently to be defended. Economic utilitarianism, for its part, reflected the Commission's notion that diversity served merely as a prior condition to convergence and an integrated market. Beneath these two very different constructs is the struggle inherent in the transition of higher education policy at European level from highlighting educational diversity to embracing joint education interests, which constitutes a very specific form of Scharpf's notion of intergovernmental negotiations (Scharpf 2001).

THE SOURCES OF A NEW SENSITIVITY

That certain member states revealed a new sensitivity should be seen less in terms of their having second thoughts about the basic principles of Bologna, about a common architecture, still less doubts about the drive towards a European Higher Education Area (EHEA) or a European Research Area (ERA). Rather tension appears to lie in two different domains. The first, an old source of friction that often surfaced in the mid 1990s over the control of the finance and selection in the ERASMUS program (Wit and Verhoeven 2001) – namely in whether setting the pace of European integration with respect to the University, should be the responsibility of individual member states or the Commission.

However, there is a second element which specifically related to the dynamic of the Bologna agenda itself. Should the Bologna process permeate into such areas as curricular content, teaching methods and last but not least, into organizational autonomy as part of the necessary adaptation of the University in Europe to external competition? How far should the Bologna process extend beyond the public domain of higher education and infiltrate to its private domain, and thus redefine its core values and tasks? From a short-term perspective, this issue raises an interesting point, that is, whether it does not reflect a certain disquiet amongst some national authorities over the implications of cross-frontier mobility for social cohesion within host countries.[122]

---

[122] This theme was debated as part of the run up to the Bergen Meeting of May 2005 four months earlier (27–28 January 2005) in a seminar at the Sorbonne. The theme of the seminar was: "The social

SOCIAL DIMENSION OF THE BOLOGNA PROCESS

Social cohesion has for long been one of the tasks of education in general and higher education more specifically so (Neave 2006b). Indeed, the reforms at the beginning of the nineteenth century that established the two basic variations of the modern European University – the Humboldtian and the Napoleonic – had, amongst other purposes, the very deliberate task of promoting social cohesion. This is scarcely surprising given the situation both countries then faced – the collapse of the social order of the first after the battle of Jena (Nybom 2003) – and seating a dynasty on firmer footing in the case of the second (Verger 1986). Yet, neither in the text of the Bologna Declaration nor until the Berlin meeting of Ministers in 2003 was hardly any formal attention paid either to the social dimension or to the key dimension of social cohesion. What changed this situation? What led the European Ministers responsible for Higher Education (2003) in their Berlin Communiqué to reaffirm "the importance of the social dimension of the Bologna process"? What lay beneath the subsequent debates, conferences and publications dedicated to this theme? Whilst we do not claim that the motives can be limited to two possible explanations, nevertheless there are two that merit further exploration.

The first has to do with the fact that only in 2004 higher education, and thus the Bologna process, were "formally" linked to the Commission's education work programme (Council and Commission 2004). Neither the Sorbonne nor the Bologna Declaration formally involved the Commission. Indeed, at the Sorbonne meeting the Commission was not even invited as observer. Thus the drawing up of an intergovernmental Declaration on Higher Education can be interpreted as an effort by those EU member states involved to "re-patriate" the initiative for higher education policy at the European level back to the national, and in some aspects, institutional level. Earlier moves by the Commission to profit from the momentum that had build up in the aftermath of the very real success of especially the mobility programs, by creating a European level policy arena, failed. Thus, the proposals for European level policy making in higher education presented in the Memorandum on Higher Education (Commission 1991), were rejected by the member states (Petit 2002). The mid-1990s were a time when tensions between the Commission and the member states ran high on the subject of higher education. These tensions found a real echo in both the Sorbonne and the Bologna Declaration, in the language used as well as in their programmatic foci. Far from subscribing to the economic role of the University, which the 1991 Memorandum and the Delors White Paper both advanced, the signatories "reaffirmed" the cultural basis of the European University, thus renewing in a number of respects the spirit of the 1988 Magna Charta declaration.

As is discussed at more length in chapter 8, the initiatives that followed upon the acceptance of the member states at the Lisbon 2000 summit that in the area of education joint interests of the member states should override the traditional national

---

dimension of the European Higher Education Area and world-wide competition" (http://www.bologna-bergen2005.no/EN/Bol_sem/Seminars/050127-28Sorbonne.HTM).

sensitivities, did not at first extend to higher education. The momentum that had accumulated around the Bologna process, its emphasis on the cultural primacy of the University, and the unpleasing memories of the relations during the mid-1990s were apparently a deterrent sufficiently strong for the Commission to not interfere directly in university policy. However, given the main aims of the Lisbon agenda and the University's role in it as the "Knowledge Institution" it is no surprise that the separated intergovernmental and supranational university policies and visions came to be linked.

In this respect a gradual adaptation of the Bologna process' main focus can be observed, amongst other things, in the text of the Prague and Berlin Communiqués (European Ministers responsible for Higher Education 2001, 2003). If the Prague Communiqué still emphasized the cultural role of the University, it also invoked the link between lifelong learning and the future competitiveness of the European economy. In addition it noted that "The quality of higher education and research is and should be an important determinant of Europe's international attractiveness and competitiveness" (European Ministers responsible for Higher Education 2001: 3). While this statement by the Ministers established no direct link between University and economy, the text of the Berlin Communiqué included for the first time in the short history of Bologna process direct references to the economic role of the University. It also stressed the need to take the conclusions of the Lisbon and Barcelona Councils into account in the Bologna process (European Ministers responsible for Higher Education 2003: 2). As is discussed in more detail in chapter 8, as a consequence, the Bologna process and the Lisbon strategy (as well as the Copenhagen process) were linked closely through the "Education and Training 2010" work programme[123] of the Commission (Council and Commission 2004). Thus, implicitly the main aims of the Lisbon strategy, strengthening economic competitiveness and stimulating social cohesion, have become central to the Bologna process as well.

Second, the current interest in the implications the Bologna process has for higher education's role in promoting social cohesion relates to the issue of funding European students to study elsewhere in the EU. This second set of arguments underlines the complexity of the European integration efforts in higher education. They also show that the "stylized visions" introduced in chapter 2 (Table 1) provide an important analytical framework, but are unable to capture all facets involved in the complexities of this "social experiment."

The concept of social cohesion can be operationalized around very different criteria, which may include the disparities between modes of student financing and the

---

[123] On this matter the "Education and Training 2010" website of the Commission indicates that "Education and Training 2010 integrates all actions in the fields of education and training at European level, including vocational education and training (the 'Copenhagen process'). As well, the Bologna process, initiated in 1999 is crucial in the development of the European Higher Education Area. Both contribute actively to the achievement of the Lisbon objectives and are therefore closely linked to the 'Education and Training 2010' work programme." (http://ec.europa.eu/education/policies/2010/et_2010_en.html; visited 25 October 2006).

differences in portability.[124] The differences between member states in ways of student financing, and hence portability are considerable. More surprising is that such differences should be seen as posing obstacles to "social cohesion" (Vossensteyn 2004). It may well be that such a diagnostic term is not meant to be understood as it stands. If so, it opens the door to further questions, for example, concerning the particular type of governance required to ensure cohesion defined solely in terms of student finance, the actor(s) who shall exercise it, and the type and the range of "solutions" that may be envisaged to this end. The core issue turns around whether such solutions are to be set in unitary terms – one size fits all –, or whether they are to perpetuate the notion of national diversity by defending the continuation of national practice.

A Broader Understanding

Once "social cohesion" is interpreted in the narrow terms of financing students when abroad, it risks re-kindling the conflict over the distribution of power between Commission and member states, quite apart from the issue by whom and how student mobility is to be sustained in the near future. Who is to pay what, for whom, how and how long? Nor does the issue stop there. If, for a moment, we assume that "social cohesion" is in reality a stalking horse for issues of co-ordination, a question of far broader import for policies of European integration targetted on the University can be raised. It is this: "where are we to set the limits to conceiving differences as obstacles, for example, for realizing (some of) the Bologna aims?" If differences in national practice are an obstacle, and we have spent the last two centuries seeking in every way possible to mark ourselves off from our neighbors by our differences, where is the process of "removing obstacles" to stop?

However, social cohesion only comes into question with the imminent prospect of social instability or its likelihood. In Europe a number of feline phrases are currently going the rounds that give voice to this anxiety, though it has to be said that they are not identified with the Bologna process as such, even though Bologna might be used to amplify our awareness of them. Within the nation state, marginalization and exclusion fall into the category of those forces in society that weaken the social fabric. Or, as another possibility, as forces that work in favor of new definitions of collective identity that do not lend themselves easily to accommodation within existing institutional or social structures. Notorious poverty or a shared sense of what Gary Runciman termed "Relative Deprivation" may serve to accelerate and precipitate such tensions (Runciman 1966).

That the Bologna process has opened up the social dimension (European Ministers responsible for Education 2005) serves to underline that factors of disparity, which determine and accompany differences in the quality of life within the nation state, are now shared across them. Such disparities, whether socially or geographically sited,

---

[124] "Portability" refers to the right to use a study grant awarded in one country to support studies in a second – in short, whether students can "take their grant with them" to support themselves during periods spent in study abroad.

are not new. Indeed, higher education policy – at least in Western Europe – has from the mid-1960s onwards been engaged in seeking to remedy them. This has been done either through policies of institutional distribution or through various measures to strengthen the influence of regional authorities in the affairs of academia, beginning in Sweden with the 1977 reforms, and spreading into Spain with the Organic Law of 1983, Belgium with the federalization of the Kingdom in 1988, and Britain with the regionalization of the higher education funding base in 1992. Others are certainly not backward in this sphere. The "fit" between the location of universities and regions of notorious deprivation is not always close. Nevertheless, the use of the University to spur regional development, if not always regional identity, remains an enduring trend during the past four decades (Kyvik 2004).

SOCIAL COHESION AND THE UNIVERSITY: A BRIEF EXCURSION ACROSS HISTORY[125]

In linking social cohesion to the University, two key questions are posed. "Is its purpose to achieve even closer harmony, architecture or common practice?" Or "Is social cohesion evoked simply because the thrust of social and technological change is dissolving the established mechanisms of social stability?" What evidence has come from the domain of the University, and how does that relate to the Bologna process?

Competition, meritocracy, value and worth, are among the abiding values of higher education (Rothblatt 2006). But their continuing and vital role in determining who goes to higher education can be made to serve vastly different social objectives and thus very different interpretations of social cohesion. The historic and identifying feature of the European University, contrary to its US counterpart, has been its continuous close alignment with public service, construed in terms of the services of the State (chapter 4). The historical origins of this engagement to the collectivity, not unnaturally, vary from country to country. They may be traced back to the Josephine reforms at the end of the eighteenth century in Austria, were reaffirmed in the Memorandum of Wilhelm von Humboldt on the future of Berlin University in 1806 and, for France were re-stated in the form of the Imperial University (Neave 2001). The University acting on behalf of the nation supplied the talent that in turn fed what Dahl termed "the value allocating bodies in society" – the church, the law, the education system, national administration, occasionally the military, and, not least, the tax system (Dahl 1966). These ties were made closer by what in some countries is termed the civil effect of university education, namely that certain degrees were held to be valid to compete for a place in public service and for a place in what economists qualify as "the fixed price labour market" (Kerr 1986).

Clearly, in Europe the first major break in the saga of the elite University took place with the drive towards massification from the mid 1960s onward. Its rationale remained fully within the post-war settlement which involved the nation assuming

---

[125] This section as well as the following ones is to a large extent based on Neave (2006b).

new responsibilities and thus taking over new dimensions that underpinned social cohesion in the form of the welfare state – with high aspirations in areas such as health care, unemployment and child benefits, pensions, and not least the right first to secondary education and later to higher education. Key to this was the recognition that education determined life chances. Higher education took on an active and re-distributive role as indeed the welfare state itself performed. Education and the University by extension were seen as a public instrument for the aspired re-distribution of wealth through investing in social mobility and above all, through public investment in the younger generation.

Seen from this perspective, the first stage in Western Europe's drive towards massification stood as an unprecedented act of social solidarity and very explicitly so in its focus on "first generation students." The fundamental assumption that underpinned this interpretation of social cohesion rested on the conviction that social mobility and raising the general level of education amongst the population was an issue of collective responsibility. It extended into higher education the basic tenets of the welfare state in the broad domain of social security. In this, three aspects remained constant. First the principle of merit itself. Second that mobilization of society around technological and social change was primed by the public sector – a social counterpart of Keynesian theory in economics. Third that the pace of economic change was dependent on the capacity of the higher levels of the labour force to remain updated in the area of relevant competencies and skills on the basis of the intellectual baggage it had once acquired in the University.

In effect, the factors that undermined this particular model of the University's part in social cohesion are also to be found along these three dimensions, especially in the relationship between social cohesion and economic development. Is social cohesion a condition of economic development? Or, on the contrary, is economic development a condition of social cohesion? The fundamental assumption that lay beneath the "welfare state" model of university policy inclined towards the former, namely that social solidarity was a prior condition to economic development, a view which received operational definition by placing priority on equality of opportunity, often expressed in terms of "social justice." If we accept this interpretation of social cohesion, we have to ask ourselves: What were the elements of dissolution as can be observed, for example, in the Lisbon agenda, that assumes economic development to be a condition for social cohesion?

Erosion of a Model of Social Cohesion: The Welfare State

The usual explanation given for the demise of the "welfare state" model of social cohesion with respect to the University is astounding in its simplicity – namely, that the nations of Europe could not afford to fund the mass University in the same lavish manner as they had its elite predecessor. None will disagree concerning the part cost played. But there is another explanation, and whilst both are inextricably linked to the process of massification itself, the second is important on its own account. Social demand for university education not only outstripped the ability – or, as the theory of fiscal stress suggests (Vossensteyn 2003) – the willingness of governments and their citizens to pay (an interesting example of de-solidarization). It also outstripped the capacity of the public sector to absorb the increase in qualified output from university education. Precisely when this historic watershed was reached is not greatly important. There is evidence aplenty to suggest that the latter part of the 1970s – with variations between countries – provides a reasonable marker. There are other pointers as well, not least of them being the refocusing of university policy and research away from access to output, occupational change and the increasingly problematic ties of the University with the labour market.

Such a refocusing went hand in glove with a root and branch revision in re-thinking the place of the public sector and, more to the point, the economic condition of the nation, a revision which, in its more extreme forms set about defining the economy as the prime lever in social cohesion. This, in essence, is precisely what is meant by the twin credos of "marketization" and "privatization." In other words, the relationship between social cohesion and economic development which, in the welfare state inter-pretation of the University, saw social cohesion as the path that led on to economic fortune, was thus reversed. Economic development was thus the prior condition to social stability, if not to social cohesion.

Effects Upon the University

Placing the emphasis upon the market as the prime condition of social cohesion has had weighty consequences indeed for the European University – as the unprecedented 20 years saga that lies behind us of reform in purpose, administration, governance, authority, funding and intake capacity of the University all bear witness. This is not to say that the place of the University is any the less central to society. Indeed, the very idea of a knowledge economy and within it, the strategic place of higher education, affords it even greater significance as the prime supplier of trained human capital and capital expressed through ideas and innovation (Kogan 2006; Maassen 2006). Even so, the University occupies a very different position precisely because social cohesion is held to be conditional upon the economy rather than the other way round.

Our tendency in the area of policy research on the University has been both to conceive and to analyze these reforms individually and separately. Each is, after all, a highly complex affair. There is, however, an excellent case to be made for trying to weld them into a whole and to re-contextualize them within the framework of the consequences they have for the notion of social cohesion. The first thing to note is that inverting the relationship between the economy and social cohesion places the latter as a sub set of a particular ideology that is variously described as "economic liberalism" or in certain quarters, "ultra-liberalism" which has a certain kinship with supply-side economic theory. It is, amongst other things, claimed to be the guiding Mantra behind the process of globalization (Marginson 2004), even though this claim has also in the field of higher education been driven more by a certain form of ideological conviction than being substantiated through empirically founded analyses.

The interpretations that may be placed upon this ideology are many. For its adepts, the market provides the freedom for individual initiative and as such, a necessary cor-rective to the restraining influence of the state. Individual freedom and enterprise, thus liberated, drive the economy forward, create jobs, satisfy consumers and contribute to the wealth of individuals inside the nation (Neave 2003). The central credos of neo-liberalism turn around individual performance, efficiency and above all competition which, aggregated up, ensures national prosperity. Placed in an organizational setting, its institutional form of reference is the business enterprise and the world of corporate practice.

There are two features well worth noting that accompany the permeation of this doctrine into society. This first is that the nation state itself assumes the status of the local context and very particularly so in the case of multi-national firms. But the firm does not simply exist in the nation or across nations. Nor is it simply the prime operant of "globalization." Economic liberalism, since it cannot entirely eliminate the value allocating bodies without putting itself in danger, in effect adds one more to those bodies that operated within the nation state: it adds "The Firm." If one wishes evidence for this statement, one has only to consider how far current-day reform of the University turns to "business practice" as the yardstick of its successful modernization (see chapters 1 and 6). And whilst practices are not always the same thing as "values," nevertheless the influence of what is held to be "good business practice" exercises upon universities – whether entrepreneurial (Clark 1998) or innovating – suggests that institutional centrality of the firm, which characterizes economic liberalism in its relationship to society, is indeed every bit as comparable in its pervasiveness and its norm-shaping power as earlier bodies of value allocation. Indeed, business efficiency becomes a value in itself.

However, there is a second difference and it, too, has direct bearing upon the notion of social cohesion just as it does in the relationship of the University to social cohesion. The relationship of a firm with other enterprises may carry obligations. But in essence, it is contractual, formal, written and based on a utilitarian notion of securing services, advantages or advancing opportunities – most of which are time specific and conditional – that is, there are objectives to be attained as part of the exchange, the attainment of which determines the fulfillment of the contract. And indeed, it is precisely this type of contractual, targeted and conditional relationship that now governs the ties between the University and the public. As is discussed in detail in chapters 1 and 9, this contractual relationship is very different from the traditional "pact" between the University and society. The University is no longer perceived in terms of collective identity, as a repository and as hander down of the national genius or, for that matter as the crowning example of national unity, all of which are forms of cohesion expressed through notions of continuity and commonality pursued across generations.

One can, of course, point out that this nineteenth century vision of the University had already been severely mangled in the heady days of May 1968 and its aftermath that spread across Western Europe. Very certainly, the advent of participant democracy (chapter 5), of group interests inside the groves of Academe, (Groof et al. 1998) antedated the arrival of neo-liberalism and the advent of New Public Management (Pollitt 1990). Nor is it out of place to note that even the welfare state model of social cohesion defined and measured how far the University had met its mission of social cohesion in terms of groups defined by social background or relative disadvantage.

If anything, the drive into higher education from the mid 1980s through to the mid 1990s, put a final touch to the fragmentation of the student Estate, extending its range of ambition. Most significant of all, it brought to an end the concept of students as part of an organic collective order – the student Estate as opposed to the academic Estate. In keeping with the tenets of neo-liberalism, the status of students was individualized, in the sense that they became "consumers."

Towards the Stakeholder Society

In Europe few systems have gone as far down the path as the UK in shaping the University as a "consumer service." However, that the student qua consumer is today a common-place, is much more than a shift in analogy and symbolism. The shift from collective "student estate" to individual "consumer" is in itself a very sensitive indicator for some of the basic changes taking place in the meaning of the concept of social cohesion within the University. What separates the "student qua consumer" from the student as member of a one-time privileged order is not just that the notion of "privilege" has disappeared and with it the sense of obligation to public service that implicitly accompanied student funding under the welfare state. It is the shift towards the individual assuming responsibility for investment in him- or her-self. As enrolment fees are introduced across Europe and repayable loans replace grants or indirect subsidy, so the cohesion symbolized by inter-generational investment transmutes into an instrumentality representing individual competition as well as individual accommodation to rapid economic change. With it also changes the notion of the State both in its relations with higher education and vis a vis the individual student. For whilst one may argue that a certain element of solidarity has not entirely vanished and is visible in the form of publicly provided loans, they constitute very much a short term conditional solidarity. Student funding systems become stakeholders in the student, just as students in turn, for the period of their studies, become stakeholders in the University: the former for the repayment of the loans, the latter for that training which will furnish him – or her – with the operational competencies and skills to ensure "employability" and thus permit the repayment of that loan. Seen from this angle, loans are not so much an act of solidarity – though means-testing permits a nicer rationing of the amount of solidarity to be afforded – so much as a lien upon the individual and as a spur for the individual to be "performing" if the debt is rapidly to be discharged.

The individualization of student status, the fragmentation and diversity in ability and social origin have radical consequences for the University. Whilst the notion of the "Stakeholder University" is more evident in English speaking systems – especially Australia, the UK and the USA – certain dimensions of the Stakeholder University are becoming generic to the University elsewhere in the world, and are also visible in the Bologna process. The first of these features is the re-formulation of the idea underlying the University as an expression of national culture and instead characterizing it as a service and training institution the purpose of which is predominantly defined in terms of serving one particular interest within the nation, namely the firm and the development of one over-riding priority – the embedding of entrepreneurial culture as its central referent.

Of relevance here is that the University as an expression of national culture has primarily been linked to education. This is also clearly visible in the text of the Bologna Declaration that emphasizes the central role of universities in developing European cultural dimensions (European Ministers of Education 1999). However important the cultural dimension is, universities have also been regarded throughout their history as important carriers of European humanism (chapter 3) and they have played a core role in the development and maintenance of the European civil society. On the other hand, the research and science function of the University has a stronger universal component.

Re-socialising the University

There are many pointers to this re-alignment, both in the terms some higher education institutions use to distinguish themselves from the historic University and in terms of the skills which they claim to engender amongst their students. Evidence of the former emerges, of course, in such self-descriptions by individual universities as "Entrepreneurial," "Responsive," "Innovative" or "Service-enterprise" (Neave 2004b). From a European perspective, such descriptors are a good pointer to the detachment of the University from public service. They also point to an amazing reduction in its central purpose, which, if more precise and for that reason more capable of being operationalized, is but the servicing of one interest in society. Such descriptors thus stand as a fundamental re-alignment in the dialectical relationship between the University and society which calls for the University to adapt to external change – a far cry from its civilizing mission within the nation state that once it had.

The second feature is rather more subtle. It involves an equally marked shift in what may be seen as the University's role in socialization. This has narrowed from the broader definition in terms of broad social obligation, professional skills and ethics to concentrate on the technical and operational skills and attitudes that accompany performance in the private sector – to wit, the much quoted trilogy of flexibility, adaptability and performance. Certainly, few systems have gone so far as the United Kingdom which, in the mid 1990s, sought to inject an "enterprise culture" into academe in the shape of the "Enterprise in Higher Education Initiative" project (Kogan 2005). By the same token, few universities in Europe will deny their engagement to this new and more focused edition of socialization presented under the guise of "professionalization."

There remains, however, a third dimension and that is the pace of change itself. That the University has entered a phase where, if the growing literature on the matter is to be believed, change is held to be continuous as new occupations are created – above all in the area of Information and Communication Technology (ICT). This is why such a premium is placed upon responsiveness in universities, adaptability amongst their students, and flexibility in both.

Taken together, these three features of the contemporary University pose a number of very crucial questions about the viability of the cohesion they appear to endorse. The first of these is whether the transformation of the University into a University of interests is not itself a dissolvent of collective solidarity. This is not to say that conflict of interests is absent from academia and that all is sweetness and light. Even so, the individualization of the student status, the notion that the purpose of the University is to optimalise individual choice as a means for the individual to ensure his/her own "employability," poses another highly uncomfortable question. That question is whether the University may be said to be symbolic of any kind of unity – regional, national or for that matter, European – let alone of solidarity and cohesion. That the governing ethic of the contemporary University is one of competition serves merely to underline the issue.

The Ambiguous Nature of Competition

Competition may indeed secure brilliant students and lavish sources of revenue. But it cannot, by definition, do so for all. Competition discriminates – in the original meaning of the word; or it differentiates. Just as the massification of higher education posed the issue of public service versus private advantage, so the drive towards universal higher education – which 30 years ago Trow (1974) set at a 40% enrolment rate for the appropriate age group – raises another highly delicate problem – namely, that of exclusion. Many systems of higher education in Europe have already gone beyond the threshold of "universal" higher education - with France in the lead as it was in passing the tipping point to mass higher education in the early 1970s.

Exclusion takes two forms. The first being the consequence of massification. When the number of people having a university degree is growing, its value will subsequently diminish. Certainly, advantages – and very substantial ones at that – are still to be had by participating in the University: as discussed throughout this chapter these concern social, political, cultural as well as economic advantages. But, by the same token, as more students enroll in the University, so the penalties for those who do not, increase. The problem of downward substitution – that is, those better qualified replace those less qualified in jobs once identified with the latter, an outcome of the diploma spiral – may not be as great as many feared (Teichler 1998). However, the perception that this process stands in the wings is most assuredly present and with it the very real possibility that, even if the University does not generate exclusion through its graduates replacing secondary school leavers in the central labour market, thereby forcing the latter into the peripheral labour market, the belief that it does, is present, powerful and highly detrimental to the public image of the University. There is no greater threat to the University than for it to be seen wholly and exclusively as a competitive arena, above all by those who, for one reason or another, cannot – or will not – come in from the cold. And whilst it may be argued that compensatory opportunities are present in the form of lifelong education and training, one cannot ignore the fact that for the most part, those who take up these opportunities are largely those who have already been hearty consumers of the University's services.

CONCLUSION

The real question the Bologna process poses is how far in advancing both an economic and social dimension a balance may be struck between the principles of individual opportunity and those of collective advantage. From the standpoint of political philosophy, this is a very old dilemma and one which, when extended beyond Europe, is no less evident in the relationship Europe seeks to have with the rest of the world. It is also explicit in the narrower terms of "social cohesion" as it applies to the different modes of financing those who study abroad. As we have argued, this particular instance is but one manifestation of a broader and deeper-seated dilemma.

In truth, the dilemma that confronts both Bologna and the EHEA is how to reconcile Adam Smith with Thomas Hobbes. Each in his way was concerned with the place of competition in the social construct. For Smith, competition was the driving force of human society and individual initiative. For Hobbes, competition was most certainly an innate human trait. It was not, however, positive (Oakshott 1972). On the contrary, competition was the brutish comportment of man in the state of nature, prior to the social contract, when "Every man's hand was turned against his neighbour," and where the lot of Mankind was "poor, solitary, nasty, brutish and short." For Hobbes, in competition lay the heart of mayhem and civil strife. These two contrary imaginings extend to the place of the state as a very real restraint upon individual adventurousness in the case of the father of Economics or as a restraint upon the bestial excesses of Man's otherwise natural instincts in the case of Hobbes as advocate for the rule of Leviathan.

That competition can be subject to so different interpretations is quintessential to the current challenges that confront us in the construction of the European Higher Education Area. We are facing the same dilemma about the degree of solidarity that forms the basis on which social cohesion in its deepest sense reposes. Yet very precisely, this dilemma is in-built to the Bologna Declaration itself. It emerges in the notion that relations between university systems inside the European Union are to rest on the principle of cooperation and that competition – in the form of our civilized attractiveness – shall shape our dealings with the world at large. As a statement of intent, it is a fine and splendid thing. We agree to reserve Adam Smith for "external use only," and we hope that Thomas Hobbes will serve us well on the home front.

The European dilemma is how far the gospel according to Adam Smith should be seen as "the way, the truth and the life," just as it is how far we see it desirable to abandon Leviathan and with it the social cohesion Leviathan regulated and shaped – in higher education, not least. The problem can be stated conversely, of course. How far is Europe prepared to accept a possible further weakening of social cohesion by utterly embracing the unpredictable acts of Adam Smith's more ardent pupils who in their organized expression may just as well be Leviathan dressed in corporate clothing?

These are delicate issues for whilst their resolution lies at the heart of building the European Higher Education Area, they also re-shape the social and institutional fabric in general. Yet, if Europe is to generate any citizen cohesion – apart from that expressed in the administrative, legislative and formalistic domains – it is important to ensure that interests external to Europe do not confine the European identity to that construction from which we are just emerging, namely a "Common Market," populated not by citizens but by consumers. Yet, the translation of consumers to citizens depends precisely on creating a sense of solidarity. Whether that sense of solidarity without which social cohesion remains a technocratic code word, is to permeate from above or grow up from below is very certainly a task that deserves our engagement, if only to find ways by which Mr Smith and Mr Hobbes may be reconciled.

CHAPTER 8

THE LISBON PROCESS: A SUPRANATIONAL POLICY PERSPECTIVE

INSTITUTIONALIZING THE OPEN METHOD OF COORDINATION

Åse Gornitzka

INTRODUCTION

While national Ministers of Education across Europe were joining the Bologna process and were addressing common structural issues in European higher education outside the setting of the EU, the heads of state of the European Union met in Lisbon in 2000 and agreed to embark on a strategy to make the European Union the most competitive and dynamic knowledge based economy in the world by 2010. With the launching of the Lisbon Strategy the University came to the centre of attention within the EU. In the Lisbon Strategy the University, as part of education and research systems in Europe, was envisioned as a core institution of "the Europe of knowledge." Unlike the Bologna process – a European level process unique to the higher education sector – the Lisbon process directed the attention to education and research much more broadly in making them means to reach the ambition of socially and environmentally sustainable economic growth.

The Lisbon Strategy signaled that this requires the EU to venture into nationally sensitive policy areas and areas with institutionally entrenched diversity. The Lisbon 2000 summit announced a method that could make this plausible. The Open Method of Coordination (OMC) offered the member states and the EU institutions a template for coordinating public policies within the EU that in principle would not upset the balance between the nation states and the supranational level. When the Lisbon Council launched the OMC it was portrayed as a mode of governance based on setting common objectives, establishing indicators and benchmarks for comparing best practices and performance, and translating the common objectives into national and regional policies. In principle it is a mode of governance that assumes that coordination can happen across levels of governance without transferring legal competencies and budgetary means to the European level. For European research and education systems it brings to the forefront essential questions that concern the possible repositioning of levels of governance and shifts in means of governance. From the perspective of the study of political organization, the introduction of the OMC can also be seen as an instance of political innovation that brought a new template for organizing political space in the EU. In this chapter the adoption process of the

P. Maassen and J. P. Olsen (eds.), University Dynamics and European Integration, 155–178.
© 2007 *Springer.*

OMC as organizational practice within the EUs education and research policy is the main theme.

We address the issue of what the Lisbon Strategy and the method that it carries have implied for European level governance approaches to research and education policy, the two core policies areas that frame the European University. Has the application of the OMC created a new political space in these two policy domains? Did this application lead to the institutionalization of an organizational innovation? What forces shaped the inception of the OMC as organizational practices in the two policy areas? Which factors maintained, changed and moulded them?

We expect that the way in which the Lisbon Strategy and the subsequent implementation processes have been addressed as European education and research policy processes can unveil key elements in the dynamics of European integration relevant to European research and education, as well as change and stability in the policy spheres and actor constellations that currently operate within these spheres at the European level.

The actors in this story are the European institutions and their interrelationships, the member states' governments and their national administrations, transnational actors, but also actors that represent different institutional spheres. In the implementation of the Lisbon Strategy different institutional spheres met and were confronted with each other and the dynamics of such encounters came to the surface. Furthermore, the way in which EU institutions, member states and other actors responded to calls for innovation provided by the OMC template, should be understood as conditioned by existing institutional arrangements within the two policy arenas.

The University as a key European institution with two basic functions is in policy terms placed in the middle of two policy domains that are marked by different institutional structures and traditions. As policy domains at the supranational level the actor constellations and approaches to European integration are evidence of the differences between European integration with respect to the research function of the University compared to its educational function. This chapter will argue that these differences can also be divulged as the EU is embarking on its path to realize its ambition of becoming the most competitive knowledge economy in the world by 2010.

ANALYTICAL PERSPECTIVE

The exploration of how the OMC concept spread and became practice within the two political domains of research and education policy presented here might be seen as the micro level account of political innovation and institutional resilience at the European level. Focusing on the micro-processes that are in operation when new organizational forms proliferate and take root within such a cosmos, this chapter explores how diffusion patterns are affected by the existing institutional arrangements and established practices. This raises what has been described as the paradox of institutional theory of how actors that operate within established institutional settings manage to change the very institutional arrangements that constitute them (Holm 1995). In the context of this chapter this translates into the following question: Faced with a new template for organizing political space such as OMC, how do actors respond?

Theoretically it is possible to assume that actors in a policy domain can ignore or reject new templates. Also a response to new templates will represent no or little spur for institutional change if actors construct symbols of application by re-labelling or subsuming the template into existing procedures and arenas. If this would be the situation in our cases, we will find processes that are empty or that are referred to as OMC, yet without these representing a novel political space.

If new templates are adopted, they can still be subject to different trajectories of institutionalization. The institutionalization of a political space can be seen as the process by which it emerges and evolves towards having a "widely shared system of rules and procedures to define who actors are, how they make sense of each other's actions, and what types of actions are possible" (Stone Sweet et al. 2001: 12). Institutionalization of political space would see the development of formal structure, conventions for handling everyday "business" and cultural dimensions such as norms, values and identities within an organization (cf. Bulmer and Burch 1998: 604). Following Olsen (2001b), institutionalization of political space implies establishing rules and repertoires of standard operating procedures attaching capabilities and resources to it. Further institutionalization would carry with it that practices and procedures come to be seen as appropriate and legitimate. This speaks to how enduring and autonomous organizational practices become. In our case the more the OMC as political space is being institutionalized the more one should be able to observe the following: (1) Actors developing standards of acceptable conduct, impersonal roles, rules and standard operating procedures downloaded from the template of OMC; (2) Development of organizational capabilities in as far as resources, such as staff and budgets, are assigned to uphold the OMC processes as a distinct political space; (3) The practices and procedures of the OMC are valued "beyond the task at hand," that is, that they acquire a self-legitimated and taken for granted character, where their existence is not continuously questioned or subject to cost-benefit calculation.

No a priori assumption of an even, steady and linear development towards full institutionalization is made here. Rather the possibility of non-institutionalization, de-institutionalization or partial institutionalization is taken seriously. Non-institutionalization includes cases where OMC practices are adopted but quickly abandoned following a faddish pattern of diffusion (Abrahamson 1991; Strang and Macy 2001). Also an organizational template and innovation can be subject to transformation during the process of adoption (March and Olsen 1989: 62–64) and often cannot be reproduced reliably from idea to practice in a uniform manner across different institutional contexts (March 1999b). Such a transformation includes institutionalization of parts and not the entire template. This is particularly likely when an item of diffusion is a theoretical construct and idea rather than a hands-on and specific object with complete and unambiguous practical references (Strang and Meyer 1993: 499), as is the case with the OMC template.

POTENTIAL DYNAMICS OF INCEPTION AND INSTITUTIONALIZATION
OF NEW POLITICAL SPACE

The central assumption explored in this chapter is that the way in which an organizational template is picked up and processed in a political order depends on the nature
of existing institutionalized practices. Such a link would be a gateway for gaining
insight into the dynamics of a policy domain at the European level also beyond the
case of the OMC. The more elaborated and dominating the extant official structure,
the more likely that a new function and new activities will be absorbed by it in preference to the creation of new structures (Meyer et al. 1997). If that is the case, we
would expect the speed and depth with which the OMC as a practice is established to
depend on the density of institutionalized practices in the policy domain. In order to
investigate such an assumption we will have to demonstrate that the policy domains
under study are indeed varying in terms of institutional saturation. Furthermore it
is not only a question of "thickness," but also of the nature of these institutional
arrangements relative to the template for organizing political space offered by the
OMC. To what extent does the template of the OMC represent a radical departure from
existing practices and the nature of existing political arenas within these two policy
domains?

The argument above underlines the stickiness of institutions and their less than
readiness to respond to impetus for innovation. However, institutional theory suggests
both inter- and intra-institutional dynamics through which change and innovation
occur (March and Olsen 2006b). Institutions exist within a larger institutional setting
and order – as is indeed the case with EU institutions. The point here is that innovations and change can occur in the interface between different orders of institutions
(Holm 1995) and when the balance between partly autonomous Institutional spheres
is disturbed (cf. chapter 1). This can refer to balance between levels of governance
(such as between EU institutions) and institutional spheres that run along sectoral
lines. Friction may occur when different institutional spheres collide with each other
thereby triggering institutional change (Olsen 2001b). Such interrelationships are
highly relevant for the study of diffusion of organizational templates. Coercive spread
implies imposition of organizational templates where institutional resilience to change
or institutional inertia is trumped by hierarchy or by specific financial conditionality
(DiMaggio and Powell 1991; Bulmer and Padgett 2004: 107–109). Such diffusion can
also rely on the hegemonic status of one societal sphere over others (see chapter one).

Inherent tensions *within* a political arena can be conductive to innovation. As
argued by March and Olsen (1989) there is no intrinsic need to assume that institutions
represent perfect equilibriums and unambiguous and consistent frames for action in
complex institutional settings. Also, political actors can reach the limits of existing
procedures (Stone Sweet et al. 2001: 10–11), and can consequently be ripe for change
and engage in search for other ways of organizing political space. *"Critical moments"*
and system failure can provide opportunities for significant change (March and Olsen
1989). Such change may be induced by *skilled actions* of entrepreneurs that "create
or manipulate frames that make sense of institutional or policy problems and offer

persuasive solutions" (Stone Sweet et al. 2001:12). We can thus expect to observe entrepreneurs that give voice to the translation of the OMC template and that are able to define crises and breakdowns and use them as opportunities to promote the template in the established order.[126]

OMC IN CONTEXT: THE LISBON 2000 SUMMIT AND THE KNOWLEDGE ECONOMY PARADIGM

At the Lisbon 2000 summit several partially interconnected developments seem to have crossed each other, including setting the agenda for the EU as an economic and as a social project, and rethinking governance issues in the European Union, hereunder the official sanctioning and labelling of the OMC. The Lisbon Summit did not carve the attributes of the OMC in stone, it identified at least four core markers of the OMC template that are contained by the following key concepts: benchmarks, indicators, peer review of policy, and iterated procedures (European Council 2000: §37). Yet, all of these elements are not necessarily carried into the processes that, following the Lisbon Summit, were referred to as OMC processes.

The Lisbon Summit announced OMC processes both in research and education. As such they are both among the "old" Lisbon OMCs. However, the Summit did not invent the EU's involvement in education and research. Both areas have long traditions as policy areas for the EU.

There have been two fluctuating tendencies in the history of research policy – between the intergovernmental means of cooperation[127] and Community action with the Joint Research Centres organized as part of the Commission (JRCs), and the Framework Programs from 1984 (Guzetti 1995). The research policy of the EU has gradually evolved to become a very dense area of activities covering a sizable share of the Community budget and a large DG for Research. The supranational executive and the set of committees and working groups in this policy area have strong established procedures for formulating, shaping and executing the RTD programs. They are primarily a "Framework Program machinery." The Council structure has most of its political energy attached to decisions about the level of funding and profile of the RTD Framework Programs. EU R&D policy has historically been fashioned as distributive policy anchored in the elaborate rules for the Framework Program procedures in the Treaty. The Treaty of Amsterdam, article 165, also allows for a

---

[126] The account of the development of OMC practises draws on document analysis and 15 semi-structured interviews conducted during 2005–2006 with people who have been involved in these processes at the European level. Second, I have analyzed the many reports and publications that have been produced by working groups and by the Commission. Third, I have consulted official documentary records from the EU Consilium for Minutes from Council and Council Committee meetings (especially CREST). Finally I have used notes and minutes from meetings, and e-mail messages, etc. that are not publicly available, but that I have been given access to by the interviewees.

[127] Notably institutions such as CERN, EMBL, ESA and intergovernmental programs, especially EUREKA and COST.

coordination of national and European research policies, but in practice this element of European research policies has been overshadowed by the distributive policies of the Framework Programs (Banchoff 2002).

The legal status of European policy is weaker in the area of education than in the research area. Education was first enshrined in the Treaties in 1992. Yet the article on education explicitly rules out "the harmonisation of the laws and regulations of the member states" (The Treaty of Amsterdam §149). Education has a more tense and hesitant history of European level activities than research (Wit and Verhoeven 2001). There is considerable national sensitivity attached to system diversity of European education, especially when education is seen in its socialising, cultural function, rather than in its social and economic role. Nevertheless, there has been a gradual institutionalization of the policy area (Beukel 2001), marked by policy entrepreneurship at the European level (Corbett 2005). The educational programs of the EU are quoted regularly among the major successes of the EU, even though financially they are not in the same league as, for example, the Framework Programs. In addition the education programs have a much more decentralized implementation structure compared to the Framework Programs and the allocation of funds is for the main part not decided on a competitive basis by the Commission.

The launching of the Lisbon strategy as political embodiment of a European knowledge economy policy implied a sharpened focus on knowledge policy areas such as education and research. All European summits from Lisbon 2000 and onwards have underlined the contribution of research and education to setting up the European knowledge economy, and becoming "... *the most competitive and dynamic knowledge-based economy in the world capable of sustainable economic growth with more and better jobs and greater social cohesion.*"

As an expression of an underlying educational and research policy paradigm, the Lisbon Summit did at least three things. First it reasserted the role of R&D for economic competitiveness and growth. Second it underlined the role of education as a core labor market factor as well as a factor in social cohesion. Third it asked for a focus on *common* concerns and priorities (European Council 2000: §27), as opposed to taking as a point of departure the "celebration" of national diversity of education and research systems. The Lisbon triangle of employment, growth and social cohesion saw research as a major cornerstone of the Lisbon strategy, and education as a key element (Kok 2004a, b) in social policy, labor market policy and overall economic policy. The Lisbon agenda can be seen as the embodiment of a common model of socio-economic development, or a "world script" (Meyer 2000), with an emphasis on science-based innovation as the engine of economic development and education as a necessary investment in human capital. This script is contained in core political buzzwords such as "knowledge-based economy" and "the New Economy." The Lisbon strategy provides a practical-political expression of the way in which education and research as policy areas are defined and framed within a knowledge economy discourse. Yet this political expression is moulded and redefined continuously.

As an overall political project, the Lisbon strategy is open for various interpretations, and there are ongoing attempts to define what it represents (see, e.g. the reactions to the Work group report: Kok 2004a, EUobserver 3/11/04[128]). Several have suggested that the Lisbon strategy is embedded in neo-liberal ideology (Radaelli 2003; Chalmers and Lodge 2003).

It is also possible to read it as a marriage between a neo-liberal ideology and a social welfare model (Zängle 2004). At least it can be interpreted as an attempt of "horizontal integration," that is, linking the social and economic aspects of European integration (Borras and Jacobsson 2004: 186; Olsen 2004b: 4). There are some core assumptions concerning the primary factors that affect economic competitiveness and the kind of economic environment Europe is faced with. The European Council described the situation as a challenge stemming from globalization and a knowledge-based economy where education and research policy reform, along with employment and competition policy, are at the core of what is seen as the required "quantum shift" (European Council 2000). Yet, the Lisbon 2000 summit represents more an agenda than a full-fledged "theory of competitiveness and social cohesion." As such this agenda reflects the vagueness that is presumably necessary for reaching consensus on some overarching common goals for the member states.

The ideas that found their way into the text of the Lisbon conclusions have a long history. The OECD must be seen as a core international site where the idea of the knowledge economy has been pushed (cf. especially OECD 1996) and that has been conductive to identifying and quantifying "the New Economy" (Godin 2004). In Europe these ideas have been developed in interaction with a scientific and political agenda (cf. Rodrigues 2002). Also before the Lisbon Summit such concepts have been visible on the EU agenda as their ideational heritage can be traced back to at least to the early 1990s. A core reference in this respect is Delors' 1993 White Paper on Competitiveness, Growth and Employment. But also education has been a longstanding item on the agenda of the European Roundtable of Industrialists (ERT) (e.g. "Reshaping Europe" from 1991). For instance, the ERT's education policy group published reports, such as *Education for Europeans – Towards the Learning Society* (ERT 1995), that were reported to have been "enthusiastically acclaimed by the Commission" (Richardson 2000: 20).

To realize the ambitions agreed upon in Lisbon, the role of education and training is considered to be crucial. It is assumed that without a high quality education and training system it is impossible to make the transition towards a knowledge society and to further develop the knowledge economy. For reaching the Lisbon ambitions not only a "radical transformation of the European economy" is required, but also a "challenging programme for the modernization of social welfare and education systems" (European Council 2000: §1 and §2).

---

[128] http://euobserver.com/?iad=1768&sid=9.

MAKING OMC INTO PRACTICE: TWO TRAJECTORIES

Education Policy – "a method for us"

Following the agreement upon the general Lisbon strategy a mandate was given to the Education Council to discuss what was referred to as the concrete future objectives for the education systems. The European institutions in the policy domain interpreted the signals from the Lisbon Council as the go-ahead for establishing a program for the "modernization of European education systems" and what at a later stage became the "Education and Training 2010" program (E&T). In the view of the Commission the Lisbon conclusions represented a landmark for the EU's involvement in education: "Never before had the European Council acknowledged to this extent the role played by education and training systems in the economic and social strategy and the future of the Union" (Commission 2003c: 3). Consequently it was the outcome of the meeting of the European heads of state that gave the initial push towards a modernization program for European education systems. Two years later at the Barcelona European Council they reiterated this ambition by stating that European education systems should become a world quality reference by 2010.

In the meantime the member states' ministers of education agreed on three very broad strategic goals for European education and training systems: to improve the quality and effectiveness of education and training systems in the EU; to facilitate access to education and training; and to "open up education and training systems to the wider world" (cf. Stockholm European Council March 2001). They were refined in 13 associated objectives adopted at the Education Ministers' Council meeting in 2002 that covered the various types and levels of education and training (formal, non-formal and informal) rooted in a broad definition of lifelong learning. Commission expert groups started working on a wide range of issues, such as teacher training, basic skills, ICT and efficiency in education, language learning, and access. This implied a shift in the attention towards primary and secondary levels of education, in contrast to the higher education and vocational training emphasis that characterised the European programs of the pre-Lisbon period.

In May 2003, the Education Council selected five benchmarks for the improvement of education and training systems in Europe up to 2010.[129] Of these five "Increase in the number of graduates in maths and sciences" is the only one that addresses European universities directly.[130] These benchmarks were established only after long negotiations in the Council, and they clearly touched upon issues of national sensitivity as benchmarks were seen as setting a glaring light on national performance. The Ministers could, for instance, not agree on setting a benchmark for investments in education, as suggested by the Commission (Commission 2002d). The status of a European benchmark was also a touchy subject and in its conclusions the Education

---

[129] Council Conclusions of 5 May 2003 on "Reference Levels of European Average Performance in Education and Training (Benchmarks)" (OJ C 134, 7 June 2003).

[130] The other four refer to dropout rates in secondary education, increasing education attainment, better reading skills, and adult participation in lifelong learning,

Council underlined that these benchmarks were not concrete targets for individual countries to be reached by 2010, but "reference levels of European average performance." Yet, compared to the hesitation with respect to cooperation 10–15 years earlier, the political will to issue a common position had changed among European Ministers of Education.[131] The question was no longer if national policies *should* be coordinated but *how* they could be. The efforts were bundled into one package and being referred to as "OMC."

Initially the OMC process in education materialised as what was referred to as the "objectives process" and the work organization set up around the 13 objectives, but from early 2004 on other parallel processes were added to include the EU and its member states work with the Bologna process and the Copenhagen process[132] in the area of vocational training. From then on the OMC process in education was referred to as "Education and Training 2010" covering European cooperation in education and training as an integrated policy framework, which implied that higher education reform became a core object of the OMC process.

The absence of higher education from the OMC process in the beginning is explained through the non-EU Bologna process' "capture" of the higher education reform agenda in Europe. Although the OMC education had in this way left higher education to the Bologna process (see chapter 7), the Commission had prepared its higher education policy position through the work on the Communication "The Role of the Universities in a Europe of Knowledge" (Commission 2003a). As the Commission was increasingly linked to the Bologna process, the Lisbon agenda was explicitly linked to the accomplishments towards the European Higher Education Area.[133] So from 2004 higher education (and vocational training) joined the modernization program for European education that operated with OMC at its heart.

What Kind of Political Space?

An organizational apparatus was set up as part of the OMC process at the European level and Directorate-General for Education and Culture (DG EAC) had a core role in orchestrating the process. The role of the DG EAC was central, especially in the day-to-day running of these processes, and clearer in this OMC process, compared to other sectors. However, the DG did not operate as a free OMC agent – the OMC process was anchored in the continuous formal support of the Education Council.

---

[131] "Ministers of Education had not been willing to make any type of Community decision – even the non-binding instruments used in education" (Hywel Ceri Jones, former Director in DG Education quoted in Corbett 2005: 132).

[132] Based on the Copenhagen Declaration from 2002, the Copenhagen process was set up to mirror the Bologna Process in the area of vocational education and training (VET) primarily for establishing "common currency" for qualifications and currency, common criteria and principles for quality in VET, common principles for validation of non-formal and informal learning. Contrary to the Bologna process this is an EU process where the Commission from the start has been a driving force backed by two core EU agencies in the area (CEDEFOP and ETF).

[133] This is very clearly expressed in the Commission's position paper for the 2003 Berlin meeting of "Bologna Ministers of Education" (Commission 2003d).

The way in which the OMC has been practiced in this sector brought the Commission close to national administrations in some of the sub-policy areas. The national experts serving on the OMC working groups were predominantly drawn from national Ministries of Education; only a few were from national agencies or expert/academic communities. Social partners and stakeholders from about 30 different European level organizations/associations[134] were also represented, and in some cases the secretariats of international organizations, most notably the OECD and the Council of Europe. All in all, in the first years of OMC education close to 500 experts participated in working groups; through the OMC practices they were brought together in iterative interactions at the European level.

The quantified aspects of the OMC process have been most deeply institutionalized. In 2002 a *Standing Group on Indicators and Benchmarks (SGIB)* was established to advice the Commission on the use of existing indicators and the development of new ones. After its establishment the SGIB has had internal acceptance by most of the member states' representatives, with a rather high level of attendance and also external recognition. The quantification is also an area that has been subject to skilled action from one unit within the DG EAC that has persistently pushed the need for quantitative indicators in OMC education. The focus should be on quantitative rather than qualitative indicators because of the demand for "strong policy relevant messages."[135] With the OMC, considerations surrounding statistical and indicator work were brought into an overt political setting. The significance attached to indicators was confirmed by the establishment of a centre (CRELL) as part of a Commission JRC in Italy in 2005 in order to support the EU's indicator development in the area of lifelong learning. This can be directly attributed to the OMC process. Furthermore, in 2005 the Education Council decided on new indicators in language learning and the following year the legal basis for EUROSTAT's education statistics was strengthened. With the instigation of OMC education, the EU entered an already established indicators' and statistical order, that encompassed national European and international cooperation in the production of educational statistics and indicators. Through the OMC process the EU was strengthened as a "centre of calculation," especially relative to the indicators the OECD provides in education.

In November 2003 the Commission came with a main assessing document that contained a serious and rather pessimistic picture of the progress made towards reaching the goals set for Education and Training systems in Europe (Commission 2003c). This document called, amongst other things, for member states to submit a consolidated report on all the actions taken to increase "the impact and efficiency of the OMC" (Commission 2003c: 17). The joint report of the Council and the Commission also contained similar references to the need for a more coordinated reporting in order to monitor progress and strengthen co-operation (Council and Commission 2004). The first four years of the process the OMC in education was very far from developing

---

[134] European level associations such as UNICE, ETUCE/Education International, European School Heads Association, European Parent's Association and the European University Association (EUA).
[135] SGIB minutes from 3rd July 2002, first meeting: p. 5.

a routinized *national reporting system* similar to, for example, the National Action Plans of the European Employment Strategy. However, in 2005 all national Ministries of Education produced national progress reports on the implementation of the Education and Training 2010 program. This was envisioned as the first in a system of biennial national reporting. The reports followed a standard set up by the DG EAC. The E&T national progress reports devoted a substantial part to higher education and especially to how the Bologna Declaration was implemented in national policies. These documents and the Commission analyses of them signaled quite clearly how the national and European accomplishments towards establishing the European Higher Education Area were cashed as part of the education sector's delivery for Lisbon.

The organization and practices for *policy learning* and *peer reviewing* have lived in a tensile balance between institutionalization, experimentation and disintegration. At the European level the organized learning through peer review and exchange of good practice of the OMC was intended to find a home in the thematic working groups. Some of the reports included examples of good practices from various national settings. Referring to the OMC legitimised the work done by these groups. However, the thematic working groups did not immediately grasp what it meant to "do the OMC." The DG representatives were crucial in determining the content and working procedures of the OMC groups. Yet, especially in the beginning the national participants who were sent to Brussels for working group meetings described the experience as sitting there with the OMC "landing in their lap" or being part of political "extreme sport," not knowing what you were in for and where the work was heading. The viability of the working groups, and what later turned into "learning clusters,"[136] was predominantly determined by the informal assessment made by the DG EAC. For the thematic working groups "doing the OMC" 5 years after its instigation was partly still an experiment within its wider concept. This has in particular to do with the ambiguities of practicing organized policy learning and peer reviewing.

Key Conditions for Constructing Political Space Around the Concept of OMC

The Commission's Directorate-General for Education and Culture (DG EAC) had been very attentive to the message of the Lisbon Council and especially the messages given on the "new method": "It was **immediately** in the education field understood that this concerned us – 'this is a method for us'."[137] The DG EAC paid full attention to the Lisbon 2000 summit and with the resonance the message got in the DG EAC, there was a ready translator of the OMC concept. And on a more practical note, the Commission also found a budget line in the SOCRATES program to finance the OMC activities at the European level.

---

[136] In 2005 the OMC structure was partly reorganized with the thematic working groups resurfacing as learning cluster whose predominant working methodology is so-called Peer Learning Activities, that includes site visits of good practice and in situ peer reviewing. The standing group on indicators and benchmarks was not affected by this reorganization.

[137] Interview December 2005.

Furthermore, the Lisbon Summit provided a "fitting" diagnosis of Europe – she was lagging behind her competitors in the transition to the knowledge economy. The DG EAC in its follow up activities to the Lisbon strategy used a dramatic language to accentuate the need for common action to modernize European education – it "hinges on urgent reform." The modernization of European education became linked to an overhaul of Europe envisaged in the Lisbon strategy. Similarly the DG EAC had watched the European Employment Strategy moving very close to the traditional educational policy area as an element of labour market policy. The Education ministers became aware that the interests and perspectives of the labour market policy sector, and its institutions were, through the EES, impinging on the core areas of educational domain, especially in the area of lifelong learning (Pochet 2005: 47). Also, European Ministers of Education had for some time been dissatisfied with the procedures and practices of cooperation – especially how the rotating presidencies biennially ruptured the policy agenda in the Council configuration. Consequently the launching of the OMC happened at a time when the education sector was in a situation of institutional defense (collision with the EES), with institutional self-assertion (having a rightful place in the Lisbon strategy), and EU institutions, that is, the Education Council and the DG EAC, being dissatisfied with their working procedure. To top it off – the education sector was defined as being in a performance crisis.

OMC Education Taking and Learning its Place

For the role of (higher) education in the Lisbon process the *Bologna process as political arena* has been a site of inspiration, competition and support. Just prior to the Lisbon 2000 summit the same ministers had been signing the agreement to establish a European Higher Education Area within 2010, an unprecedented experiment in European integration outside the EU. The development of the EHEA related directly to fundamental and sensitive issues, such as the structure of higher education systems and quality assurance, including the recognition of qualifications and degrees. The Lisbon process in education both feeds and feeds on the Bologna process. Even though the Commission has strengthened its role in the Bologna process, the Lisbon process and E&T, the Commission is acting as the orchestrating node and ideational centre. The rationale of the Education and Training 2010 program lies in its link to a greater order of the EU's Lisbon strategy and anchorage in the larger political order of the EU. This gives this process a different frame compared to the Bologna process. Competition between the two processes is also evidenced especially in the way the issue of the European Qualifications Framework (EQF) has been a bone of contention – the Bologna process has promoted a qualifications framework specifically tailored to fit higher education whereas the EU has promoted the EQF for a much broader conception of educational qualifications.

Within the EU institutions the OMC process seems to appropriate existing cooperative structures found within this policy domain (such as the education programs). In addition it generates new activities in other areas and policy development where the DG EAC can draw on the work done within the framework of the OMC. For example, the new generation of programs prepared for the period from 2007 will be more closely integrated with the overall objectives of the EU. It is clearly the ambition to integrate the EU's traditional incentive based educational programs with the coordination process that the Lisbon strategy has activated and also to use legal means in the Lisbon related reforms.[138] Also important initiatives coming from the Commission in the education sector – the development of a European Qualifications Framework, initiatives in the area of European quality assurance and accreditation of higher education, and most recently the initiative to establish the European Institute of Technology – have been actively liked to and argued on the basis of the Lisbon process and the Education and Training 2010 program. Most notably when the Bologna process and the Copenhagen process were latched on the Education and Training 2010 program, it became evident how much the OMC process had become a magnet for policy initiatives that the Commission had been working on prior to the Lisbon process as well as those that were spurred by it.

COORDINATING RESEARCH POLICIES

The Lisbon conclusions encouraged "the development of an open method of coordination for benchmarking national research and development policies" (European Council: Lisbon conclusions §13). It packed the use of the OMC into the ambition of developing a European Research Area (ERA)[139] that in turn was framed as part of the instruments of the 2010-Lisbon target. In the area of research the OMC is set in a complex web of various efforts and means of co-ordination within the framework of the ERA.[140] Identifying the OMC process in research is not a straightforward task as several processes especially linked to the ERA activities are referred to as "OMC." In the year following the Lisbon Council, the Commission worked on several versions of OMC processes related to research (Commission 2000c), including what was later referred to as "o.m.c. light" (CREST 2003a: 2) and "activities that contain elements of omc" (CREST 2003b: 7). A benchmarking exercise of national research policies was launched already in 2000 with the European Research Area as framework for "voluntary policy co-ordination," and to pave the way for the application of OMC to R&D policy, even though this exercise was probably more inspired by the EU's attempts of developing benchmarking technology in the 1990s than directly inspired by the OMC template (Bruno et al. 2006: 527). The benchmarking exercise that lasted until January 2003 included a High level group especially directed at

---

[138] For instance, the directive that was adopted on the recognition of professional qualifications was seen as part of the "legislative roadmap" of the Lisbon strategy (European Parliament and Council 2005)

[139] The Commission paved the way for the ERA through its Communication "Towards a European Research Area" of 18 January 2000 (Commission 2000a). The Council made the official resolution "on the Creation of a European Research and Innovation Area" 15 June 2000. The Draft Constitutional Treaty also included a direct reference to the ERA.

[140] This comprises the Community Framework programs (including Networks of Excellence and Integrated projects), technology platforms, coordination of national research council programs (ERA-NET) and the establishment of a European Research Council (see Kuhlmann and Edler 2003; Gronback 2003).

indicators collection and development in human resources in RTD, scientific productivity, RTD investment and indicators for RTD impact on economic competitiveness
and employment, altogether a list of 20 indicators, of which 5 had to be developed
(see Commission 2000c: 12–15). The Directorate-General for Research also established working groups for the analysis of national policies in the same thematic areas.
These groups were of a very different nature than found in the OMC education. The
groups comprised some of the top *academic* expertise in the area of research and
innovation policy and thus the benchmarking managed to enlist certain segments of
the European academic community, but not the member states' sector ministries.

Meanwhile, the heads of state agreed in their Barcelona European Council in 2002
on the very ambitious goal of increasing investments in R&D to 3% of EU GDP,
from the 2000-level of 1.9%, with private sector investment representing 2/3 of this
investment. That was the first time a commitment was made to a quantitative objective
for research at such a high level (Caracostas 2003: 36) and officially all member states
have identified their national R&D target for 2010 or beyond as part of their Lisbon
Reform Program (cf. Competitiveness Council 2006: 18). The investment target could
also be measured by the existing, well-established R&D indicator for investment as
a percentage of GDP. Such an ambition would, if realized, have strong consequences
for the funding of European universities as well as for the national R&D investments.

The Commission started working out the plans for how this objective could be realized, but procedures for how to apply the OMC were weakly described (Commission
2002b). The Commission staff working paper "Investing in Research – an Action Plan
for Europe"), proposed "open processes of co-ordination" for R&D investment and
for human resources in science and technology as two among the many new actions
outlined (Commission 2003d: 8–9). Soon after that, the Competitiveness Council[141]
accentuated the need to push the use of the OMC forward and invited COREPER to
"examine the concrete use of an open method of coordination" (Council 2002: 4).
The result was that the Scientific and Technical Research Committee (CREST) was
charged with a key role in the organization of the "3%-OMC process." From then on
the OMC became a permanent item of the monthly CREST meetings.

Given the mandate and composition of CREST the orchestration of the OMC was
thus placed not in the hands of the Commission, even though the DG Research has
the chairmanship of this committee, but in this permanent, *advisory* committee that
comprises member states' representatives at the level of senior civil servants from
national research ministries. Especially in the beginning of the OMC for the 3%
target the Commission's representatives were important in defining the themes and
the methodology of OMC. Yet, they clearly stated that the 3% OMC was to be seen
as an operation driven by the member states where the Commission is "offering
assistance as a facilitator" (CREST 2003c: 8), The OMC process evolved into a test
case for the role and function of this committee on a more general level (CREST
2004a: 4). After all, the coordination of national research policies was part of the

---

[141] Further underlining of the role of research for economic competitiveness could be read from the decision
to change the configuration of the Council in 2002 to a Competitiveness Council consisting of the previous
Internal Market, Industry and Research Councils.

official mandate of this committee (CREST 1995). In this respect the application of the OMC revitalized a function of CREST to which its 30 years of existence has not produced much result (Guzetti 1995). The Commission did not take on an orchestrating role in the OMC procedures, and the burden of keeping this OMC organization alive was left to the member states' representatives in CREST. Consequently redefining and reorganizing the OMC process has been in the hands of the member states.

In fall 2003 CREST appointed five expert groups[142] to work on tasks related to the 3% target and whose chairperson reported to CREST.[143] Each subject area was headed by CREST members from national ministries that volunteered to take the lead in the organization of CREST's expert groups, that is, this OMC process had (at best) part time staff of national administrators assigned to these processes. The OMC for the 3% objective had a different participatory structure compared to the Commission's "Benchmarking R&D" process: the academic experts had practically all been replaced with representatives from member states' ministries or implementing level such as national agencies, research councils, technological transfer offices, and so on. The Commission moved more backstage. Somewhat to the surprise of CREST-members DG Research also instigated parallel activities within the 6th Framework Program (FP6-RTD-OMC-NET),[144] under the label "OMC" (CREST 2005a:9). They were presented as the Commission's "bottom-up" supplement to the OMC process run by CREST. The DG Research continued to organize other areas for "mutual learning" and also monitor the ERA development amongst other through R&D indicators (ERA key figures/ERA STI), ERAWATCH, and scoreboards.

In addition to the different role of the Commission in this process, the *participatory structure* in this OMC process is narrower compared to the OMC education. Especially the transnational or international level organizations and other stakeholders have barely been present in the working organization of the 3%-OMC practices (cf. Conference on OMC and CREST 2006: 307th meeting: 4). The lack of regional representation is obvious (see Kaiser and Prange 2005), but that also applies to the OMC education.

Experimentation and Institutionalization

The first years of the OMC for the 3%-target did not follow clear procedures and that left those participating in the process in a state of role confusion.[145] CREST revised the OMC's operational set-up (CREST 2004b and 2005) to deal with the "teething

---

[142] These expert groups worked on the following themes: national policies for public research spending and mix of national research policy measures, public research organizations and their links to industry, fiscal measures to support R&D, and intellectual property rights and policy to strengthen the research links of small and medium-sized companies.

[143] All expert groups produced their final report to CREST in June 2004 and all of them clearly identified their work as part of the OMC 3% Action Plan.

[144] SEC (2005) 1253.

[145] One expert group stated this outright referring to the ambiguities associated with the application of the OMC itself[...] "In particular in the beginning it was unclear if (a) the Expert Group was asked to formulate real recommendations and for whom, (b) if quantitative or qualitative data should be tackled,

problems."[146] A main disturbance of this OMC process was the practical work load it placed on national administrations that were put under pressure to produce and deliver information to working groups (CREST 2004b: 11). This is a rather prosaic element in the dynamics of institutionalization – yet an aspect consistent with an institutional account. When the OMC reporting requirements were disturbing daily bureaucratic lives, the concept of OMC was resisted, not because of ill will or resistance to the idea of European policy coordination, but as a result of reporting fatigue of national ministries and agencies. There were several unsettled issues within this process. When CREST entered a second cycle it aimed at creating a "clearer and lighter model" for the OMC process, implying voluntariness and a less capacity demanding process (CREST 2004b: 11 and CREST 2005a and 2005: 3–5). A contested element was the extent to which recommendation should be issued by CREST and how specific it would be (CREST 2004d: 11). The OMC expert groups also identified this as a problem of context dependency of good practice (CREST 2004c 295th meeting: 3). Also in this OMC process peer learning and best/good practice methodology is the least well-established part of the OMC. Collecting data and information was deemed as useful to gain an overview of policy measures taken in the member states, yet a *review* of policies was made difficult by the practical workload (CREST 2004c 295th meeting). CREST has been hesitant in giving country-specific recommendations in their overall report from OMC.

On the other hand, the overall idea of having an OMC for the 3%-target seems uncontested and legitimate. There is agreement within CREST, and thus the representatives of the member states' research ministries that continuing the OMC process is a worthwhile endeavor. The attention to OMC research has not dwindled; there are signs of rekindling and rethinking of the OMC research, as demonstrated when the Commission organized a conference on "Improving research policies in Europe through the OMC" under Austrian Presidency (Brussels 18 May 2006). Even though the thematic agenda of the OMC for the 3% target has been shifting, having an OMC process has become an institutionalized part of the CREST agenda.

OMC Research and its Place in a Larger Order

The CREST organization of the OMC 3% investment target had several unspecified interfaces to ongoing activities in the coordination of research policies. This concerned Commission led activities, such as the ERAWATCH (cf. CREST 2004c 295th meeting: 3), or OMC as a Framework Program project. CREST's role in the coordination of research policies has also been affected by the general reorganization of the Lisbon strategy after the new Commission took office in 2005 – the discussion here is how CREST and its OMC activities can be part of the overall Lisbon National Reform Plan and general national reporting for the Lisbon strategy and how that should be organized (CREST 2006: 5–6). The OMC as practice(s) in the research

---

and (c) if new or existing R&D indicators should be used" (CREST expert group on SME and research (final report June 2004: 14).

[146] Report from the CREST expert group on SME and Research (Final report June 2004: 14).

sector has become a recognised method for working towards what has been identified as a common goal for increasing investments in R&D, yet in this sector it is
one element in a much broader setting and cannot be seen as the mainframe of the
European approach to research policy comparable to the way the OMC process has
evolved in the education sector.

First of all it is the broad ERA concept that is the overall ordering frame, and this
concept with its diverse set of instruments can be accomplished largely without the
interference of national policy makers, if research institutes, universities and industrial
actors engage in the kind of network based cross-border collaboration beyond the
national reach that is envisioned by the ERA instruments (Edler 2003: 118). Also
the investment target which has been seen as primarily in the sphere of the national
governance level, is worked at from many different angles, some of which have
elements of the OMC template, and some not. In the communication "More Research
and Innovation, A Common Approach" (Commission 2005c) the position of the OMC
is spelled out – the methodology of the OMC is one element of the research policy of
EU, but the display of the battery of approaches envisaged in this action plan clearly
indicates how legal integration (state aid regulation, intellectual property rights, the
directive for third country researchers) and funding mechanisms at the Community
level are the heartbeat of the EU approach to research as a policy domain. The OMC
template's focus on policy learning and improved national level policies is but one,
yet not neglected, element of this battery of Community level measures.

CROSS SECTORAL COMPARISONS: EXPLAINING COMMUNALITIES
AND DIFFERENCES IN OMC AS PRACTICE

Institutional Saturation and the Construction of New Political Space

In research and education as policy domains the OMC as a template for organizing
European co-operation has made an impact. The OMC processes are not phantom
processes in either of the cases, yet they have followed different trajectories for
developing the OMC template into practice. These differences are consistent with
our initial contention on the role of what we termed institutional saturation in a policy
domain with respect to shaping the responses to the call for innovation.

Research policy at the European level is filled with complex sets of standard operating procedures, established rules for participation and decision-making that all
together constitute a machinery for distributive policy in the shape of the Framework
Programs. In the research policy domain the OMC elements are spread across many
activities and there OMC seems more important for giving a label to procedures
that were already there than for tailoring new political arenas and establishing new
standard operating procedures. In the research policy domain, actors did not ignore
or reject the idea of OMC, but the OMC has not been the magnet that has attracted
and enrolled other coordination processes. The latter has been the role assigned to the
OMC in the education sector. OMC practices have been spread across and experimented with in different sub-arenas. This does not imply that the OMC is unimportant

to the research sector – especially CREST is now engaging in new working methods and activities in the name of OMC. Nor does it imply that EUs research policy has been at a standstill since the Lisbon 2000 summit. The former Commissioner Busquin's initiative to establish the ERA has seemingly triggered a number of innovations especially *within* the coming 7th Framework Program. Also the attempts of building a European institution for the funding of basic research represents a significant change in the EU research policy domain, but this can hardly be attributed to the application of the OMC template.

Even though the education policy domain was far from institutionally empty, there were certain conditions that were conductive to the embrace of OMC as a template for change. Ministers of Education and DG EAC who were frustrated over their working methods and were already experimenting with changing established cooperation procedures formed one main element in leaving a space open that could be filled by the OMC. In the education sector, the concept of OMC has opened up a distinct new political space and has been turned into practice, and there are signs of an institutionalization of the kind of political space that carries the label "OMC." Actors within this policy domain have developed shared rules of procedure for what it means to practice the OMC, what kind of actors are to be involved and what kind of actions are acceptable and appropriate within this setting. So far it has attracted attention and energy. Permanent staff within the DG EAC has been assigned to keeping the OMC alive, reporting procedures have been established at least between the EU institutions and there is a budget item for which it is acceptable to finance OMC activities. National Ministries send their civil servants to Brussels in order to participate in activities that are legitimised to themselves and to outsiders by the reference to OMC. Not all elements that are possible to download from the template of the OMC as coined in Lisbon show signs of durability, autonomy and "taken for grantedness." OMC education does not represent full blown institutionalization of the entire OMC concept. Yet, OMC education represents one package and one program, and the OMC practices can be identified as new and autonomous political space that did not exist prior to 2000. It has enabled the European agenda to move in areas of education that did not have an established history of cooperation and coordination at the European level. The OMC template has implied so far a radical change in European level involvement in the education policy domain.

Inter-sectoral Communalities

OMC in education is not a replica of what has been going on in other sectors, research policy included. It does not have identical participatory structures, OMC's reporting procedures are not identical and the anchor is different (DG Research versus CREST). Nonetheless, *common* to the post-Lisbon Summit development for both the research and education sector is how policy makers emphasise common challenges in these sectors and a common diagnosis of the predicament of the European knowledge economy. Concomitantly, there is a stronger legitimacy for using quantified objectives as a point of departure for European cooperation in these policy domains, as can be read from the Council's and European Council's decisions on benchmarks and common goals and the predominance of statistical and indicator work. The monitoring of education systems' performance in Europe through quantitative indicators is the most institutionalized practice within OMC education and shows the signs of a new activity in the EU's education policy domain, with stable and accepted procedures and practices. There is some evidence of external domain contestations, especially with respect to alternative venues of international indicator development. However, it does not seem to be at immediate risk of de-institutionalization with both a strengthened legal basis for EUROSTAT's educational statistics and the establishment of a centre within the Commission's JRC system. On the research side the picture is murkier – not that R&D indicators are less established – but it is less clear if the quantified approach to European integration is something that is downloaded from the OMC as a template, or whether the OMC confirmed the EU's role in R&D indicators. Also the EU's relationship with the OECD's R&D indicator work was settled already before the Lisbon process rejuvenated its political saliency (cf. Godin 2002, 2004).

Similarly, there is a common underlining of the need for "mutual policy learning." Although, OMC research and OMC education have not organized such learning exercises in the same way, it is quite striking that the ambiguities of undertaking peer review, and defining criteria of best practice are common to both sectors – on the whole it seems that defining rules and standard operating procedures for the organization of policy learning is in both policy domains problematic. The European organization of policy learning is in a much less stable position than the reliance on R&D and education quantified indicators, as EU institutions are testing out different organizational solutions and measures. That member states' research and education policies should benefit from mutual learning is taken for granted as appropriate; how to do it is not.

Inter-institutional Tensions and Dynamics of Change

Dynamics of inception and institutionalization of OMC as political space should also be understood in terms of "interaction and collisions among competing institutional structure, norms, rules, identities and practices" (March and Olsen 2006b: 14). In the case of OMC education this took the shape of an inter-sectoral collision of ideas. This has came to the fore especially when in the EES education policy was defined and understood as an appendix to labor market policy and European coordination efforts in this area. The "collision" that contributed to creating new political space in the case of OMC education was between the cognitive and normative understanding of "education and learning" as part of the institutional sphere of labour market policy, rather than as education policy. Education ministers and the DG EAC headed the defense of the sectoral logics by the opportunity provided by the concept of the OMC. Such a collision meant a collision over appropriate "rules of engagement" for employment policy versus the education sector, since under the employment article European recommendations with respect to this policy area can be issued to member states, whereas for education this would be stepping over the remits of the Treaty. On the other hand the interaction with the larger political order of the European Union must be seen as a very important factor for the education sector making the most of the OMC template. In education the OMC became the arena that actively linked this policy domain to the larger European agenda. The way the OMC was put into practice also reflected the institutional defense, not so much of its distinctiveness, but of the sector's rightful place in European integration. The expansion and dispersion of the education agenda in Europe is sought to be coordinated within this organizational setup and as part of a translation of the Lisbon agenda. The OMC became an acceptable and recognised procedure and a signal of appropriate behaviour.

Similar triggers of change and construction of new political space could not be seen in the research policy arena with respect to the application of the OMC. For research policy there was no apparent institutional collision present – the research policy paradigm was already well embedded in a competitiveness/innovation oriented understanding and an understanding of the so-called European paradox, that is, the conjecture that EU member states play a leading global role in terms of top-level scientific output, but lag behind in the ability of converting this strength into wealth-generating innovations.[147] The ideas promoted in the OMC research were very much geared towards better extracting the University's potential for industrial innovation and contribution to economic growth in Europe. Institutionally also the research sector is embedded directly in internal market and industrial affaires as the member states' Research Ministers in the Competitiveness Council co-legislate on these matters (Davies 2004). Certainly, a fierce sectoral defense was going on in the EU budget negotiations concerning the proposed major increase in the R&D budget to the detriment of the agricultural subsidies. But in the Lisbon strategy's research policy has been linked to innovation and had an undisputed place as a core element in competitiveness. The normative and ideational underpinnings of the EU's existing research policy and policy instruments were not radically challenged by the Lisbon agenda in this respect.[148] A more overt collision of the understanding of the University's research function and its links to the European level we see in the discussions concerning the European Research Council – where the role of University as site of basic research is much more the subject of competing visions.

Yet, we need to acknowledge that the responses found in the research sector should not be regarded as a case of complete institutional inertia. Consider, for example, the hierarchical order within the EU institutions, and especially the hierarchical legitimacy of the European Summit *vis-à-vis* the Council sectoral configurations and with

---

[147] An earlier version (Commission 1995b, 7) of this *European paradox* claimed that "the limited capacity to convert scientific progress into marketable products and services is not due to a lack of resources devoted to R&D. From a European perspective this innovation deficit originates primarily from a limited coherence of R&D and innovation policies conducted at the regional, and European levels" (Kaiser 2003: 290). Apparently, the Commission's interpretation of the causes underlying the "innovation deficit" has shifted from a lack of policy coherence in a multi-governance system (Commission 1995b), to an underperformance of European universities (Figel 2006; Commission 2006b).

[148] There are on the other hand some indications of inter-institutional tension between the DG research and the DG enterprise that has had as a consequence a demarcation of innovation versus research policy. The term European Research and Innovation Area has been tried out but "lost" against the term European Research Area (Edler 2003: 123).

respect to the sector DGs. The "Lisbon coining of the OMC" represents some measure of a hierarchically legitimated source of diffusion that seems to have carried some weight in defining it as appropriate to have at least a minimum of practices that could represent the sector's "OMC." There has been a definite proliferation of the use of the OMC also within the research sector and that may indicate the value attached to the OMC as symbol and signal of appropriate behaviour, and as seen here such symbols are not necessarily merely ceremonial, but can develop a life of their own. There are no indications suggesting that EU institutions coerced the implementation of OMC practices – although the advisory body of CREST might have felt some pressure of social sanction had it failed to respond to the call for organizing the OMC for the 3%-target.

External Shocks and Institutional Change

The Lisbon Summit and the hyping of the OMC concept came at a moment that succinctly defined the performance of education and research systems in Europe as in a critical situation. The Common European level diagnosed a *gap* in the sense that research and education were lagging behind in the transition to the knowledge economy in comparison to its competitors, the lag was identified in terms of investment deficits in research and "human resources," brain drain to the USA, and low performance of basic skills in many European countries. Through the Lisbon Summit the overall performance crisis was publicly announced. This diagnosis underpinned the whole of the Lisbon strategy and the method that was launched to make probable the success of "Lisbon." The Lisbon strategy's ambition was presented as an exceptional challenge demanding exceptional measures. When European research and education systems are lagging behind in the knowledge-based economy, one would need to boost coordination in a way that does not get entangled in the traditional turf fights between the national and supranational level, was the argument. The two policy domains show varying responses to the identification of dire straits. The diagnosis was just as profiled for European research systems (underinvestment in R&D and the failure of European universities to deliver their research potential and the "European paradox") as for the European education systems. This gap would become broader when the new member states were to be counted as belonging to the Europe of Knowledge.

Actors in the education policy domain have persistently promoted this diagnosis and a language of urgency permeates the Commission's documents of the Education and Training 2010 program. In education policy the crisis was not identified as massive failure of existing EU institutions, as education still was a national prerogative, but it was turned into a common challenge. The OMC concept's set-up that compared the performance of European education systems with each other and the USA especially undercut the traditional cooperation modus among Education ministers who would come together and celebrate the uniqueness and assets of their respective education systems. In the case of research policy this diagnosis was not the spur of an autonomous "OMC-space," but was captured by the urgency with which the ERA concept was promoted, implying that the OMC became practice as an "added touch" to existing policy arenas and a boost to policy measures at the European level that could be argued as excellence and innovation enhancing.

Robustness and Autonomy of the OMC as Practice

Acknowledging that the use of the OMC has served as an enabling device for European integration efforts in an area where the EU's legal basis for policy coordination was weakest, one should be quick to add that the enabling of the EU in education also was dependent on the legitimation not only of a method but of a world view. The discourse of the knowledge economy permitted the EU to legitimately take a stronger interest in the knowledge sector and to set concrete and quantifiable targets for collective achievements in relevant policy areas. It may be hard to separate the introduction of the OMC from the activities that were generated by the specific political ambition that was agreed upon in Lisbon 2000. It has, for instance, been argued that if the overall Lisbon ambition fails it might disrepute the OMC as a viable new approach to governance in the EU and imply an ideological crisis of the idea of new governance (Zängle 2004: 13). In the case of education the legitimacy for further coordination of educational policy in Europe might suffer from it, as some sort of guilt by association. Education as an object of policy coordination might be more at risk to the possible failure or fatigue and consequent loss of legitimacy in the Lisbon process.

Some of the core actors in this process see the embrace of the OMC not only as an enabling action of the EU in education, but as an opportunity for the education sector to prove itself as a "high performing" sector within the European integration project. Doing well as a sector, that is, contributing to the success of the Lisbon strategy, would establish education in its rightful place according to a sector logic that links national ministries, European institutions and stakeholder organizations in education. What has been observed, however, is that in non-economic sectors there has been a gradual decoupling of the Lisbon strategy from its instrument, the OMC (Laffan and Shaw 2005) which supports the argument that the method and the strategy of Lisbon are not symbiotic. When political space has internal defenders then the external attacks are less likely to lead to de-institutionalization. So far OMC education has had its full-time staff defenders at the European level. The policy framework for European research policy has had other strong institutional pillars to rest on.

CONCLUSIONS

This chapter represents a brief part of the long-term development of European level action in the areas of education and research. It has explored how small parts of the European political space emerged and evolved. It has focussed on the establishment of rules, practices and organizational capabilities that came under the name of OMC in two policy domains at the European level triggered by the Lisbon process. It is a story of which the end has not yet been written – as it is not clear yet whether the political arenas will be sustained over time. Nonetheless, so far these are not empty processes: they are definitively in the making and under construction. These two cases juxtaposed indicate how existing institutional orders impact on dynamics of change (cf. March and Olsen 2006: 16). Dynamics of change as seen from inside these processes is not consistent with environmental determinism nor is it an example of how actors by way of design or political imposition construct new political space unencumbered by the frictions of existing institutional arrangements.

If we grant that the OMC represents potentially a novel element in European integration, then the study of how it evolved in practice can tell us how political institutions change and how they innovate, and what characterizes the dynamics of change inside the small pockets of policy areas. In practice the OMC processes evolve in ways that deflect from and reflect existing webs of procedures and governance modes at the European level. In education policy the existing practices were traditionally less dense and the application of the OMC has implied that new political space has been added to the existing ones. In research policy the OMC processes are lighter and more at the margins.

The two policy domains have responded to the introduction of OMC – but in different ways. The research policy domain has experimented in search for an appropriate set-up and has dispersed the OMC process into several different settings and modes of operation. Here the OMC template has largely been blended with existing procedures and has been used for diverse sets of purposes. Elements of the OMC template have been used to support and strengthen the role of benchmarking, quantitative indicators and monitoring of national performance, and the use of the OMC as a working procedure has been a channel for the common ambitions of increasing R&D investments in Europe. These are not insignificant aspects of the European approach to research policy, but the existing procedures in this policy domain were already well developed in the shape of the Framework Programs and the concept of ERA, implying that the OMC in the research policy domain has had many different and already institutionalized elements to build on.

The education policy domain, on the other hand, has erected new political space based on the OMC template as the centrepiece of the European approach to education, and this has so far lived on and entered an (incremental) process of partial institutionalization. The OMC process has been framed as the European program for modernizing education systems, and this process and the larger Lisbon processes within which it has been embedded have acted as a magnet for other initiatives. The OMC in education has implied a strengthening of the European dimension in national Ministries of Education through their participation in working groups and national reporting. These actors met on a regular basis with the DG EAC and representatives of interest groups and European stakeholder associations. The Commission has through the OMC established a significant extension of its capacity for policy making. National governments still hold the legislative power and the funding levers for their education systems, but we have made the argument that with the OMC as practiced in education a political space of ideational convergence has emerged, at least in terms of the setting of the agenda and the development of quantitative indicators that compare performance. How this percolated into national agendas and what the policy transfer effects are at the national level remain unspecified.

The Lisbon strategy contains loud demands for reform of a wide range of social institutions. This process and the method that dovetailed it have announced particularly strong demands for radical reform of the European University. These demands have been uttered directly towards the University as a research institution that in particular needs to step up its interaction with industry, and as an institution for lifelong learning. Also importantly the processes instantiated with the help of the OMC show how European level processes may affect the University indirectly and as part of a much larger policy framework that mixes innovation policy, economic policy, labour market and employment policy, training policies, and so on. This chapter has shown how the dynamics of policy sectors have different starting points at the EU level. Overarching political processes that have ambitions of grand scale horizontal policy coordination, such as the EU's Lisbon strategy, cannot be properly understood unless the histories and traditions of political organization within different policy areas are taken into account.

PART 4

A RESEARCH AGENDA

CHAPTER 9

"EUROPE OF KNOWLEDGE": SEARCH FOR A NEW PACT

Åse Gornitzka, Peter Maassen, Johan P. Olsen, and Bjørn Stensaker

A BRIEF RECAPITULATION

The general aim of this volume is to contribute to an improved analytical framework and empirical basis for understanding the processes, determinants, and consequences of change in the University, as a key institution of modern society. We take a general interest in how the University is organized and governed, how it operates and performs, and how it develops over time. The more delimited research question explored is: How has the dynamics of the European University been affected by European integration, cooperation and policy making?

Improving our understanding of the relationships between the dynamics of change in the European University and European integration requires that we address a number of core questions concerning the dynamics of each of them, as well as their interrelations. These issues were introduced in chapter 1 and can be summarized as three challenges:

1. To map actual changes in the European University: how much, and what kinds of, change have there been in its organization and governance? Have the ways in which the University is organized, governed and funded been revolutionized or modified, or has rhetoric changed more than practice? Have the core activities of research and teaching been affected and is there a performance crisis? Has there been a single pervasive trend when it comes to institutional development and performance?

2. To map the long-term build-up and development of European-level institutions, actors and policies with possible significance for the European University. What have been the most relevant European-level factors, including supranational, intergovernmental, and transnational deliberate attempts to influence the University? What other European-level institutions, actions and developments, not aimed specifically at affecting the University, have eventually had an impact?

3. To explore what have been the relationships between (1) and (2). There are sufficient indications that governance levels as well as modes of public governance relevant to policy processes, administrative and academic activities in higher education and research have to some degree been integrated, suggesting that European elements can in practice hardly be separated anymore from the national ones. This implies that for understanding some core dynamics of institutional change in the University it is important to address European integration as a possible key explanatory factor. This acknowledgement, in turn, fuels the call for seeing present day attempts

181

P. Maassen and J. P. Olsen (eds.), University Dynamics and European Integration, 181–214.
© 2007 *Springer.*

to establish European areas for research and higher education as linked to the broader process of European integration.

Yet, not all actors, processes, and forces that affect the University orbit around European cooperation. Which factors, then, explain university dynamics, and what is the relative importance of European level institutions, actors, and policies? Furthermore, compared to other processes of change, what has been the relative importance of deliberate institutional design and reform in university transformations? What has, for example, been the significance of the deliberate attempts to "modernize" European universities in the framework of the construction of "a Europe of knowledge," a European Research Area, and a European Higher Education Area, with the intention to make the University an instrument in the transition to the "knowledge economy," a "knowledge society," and a "learning society"?

In chapter 1 we observed that there are major knowledge gaps in the European policy debates on the University and that weak and ambiguous data are often used to legitimize strong conclusions concerning the need for urgent and radical reforms. We also observed the lack of a generally accepted analytical framework and a sound data-basis for interpreting and explaining the dynamics of the European University. University studies have to a large extent been disconnected from more general studies and knowledge on European integration processes. There are excellent studies on the Europeanization of higher education (e.g. Witte 2006). However, they have usually treated higher education as an isolated phenomenon – isolated from the dynamics of science and research policies at the national and European level, as well as from the overall European integration processes.

After presenting some preliminary theoretical ideas about institutional change, two approaches were used to explore possible ways of filling some of the observed gaps. In part II we presented and elaborated four stylized visions – Weberian "ideal models" – highlighting alternative (typical) characteristics of the University's constitutive logic, criteria of assessment, reasons for autonomy, and processes of change. Each of the four visions turned out to be useful for capturing important aspects of university dynamics. Yet, it also became clear that universities and their dynamics are too complex to conform to interpretations based solely upon a single stylized vision.

Therefore, rather than starting out with an analytical framework, part III confronted the empirical complexity of European cooperative efforts with respect to the university sector, as observed in the Bologna and Lisbon processes. However, while the study of such processes unveils key elements in the dynamics of European integration and cooperation for the transformation of the University, we also observed that it can be problematic to study any single process in isolation. Bologna and Lisbon have illustrated that at least under some conditions reform processes interact and become intertwined, as several partially interconnected developments cross each other (chapters 7 and 8).

Many of the questions raised in chapter 1 remain unanswered and instead of making an attempt to summarize the findings of the Volume, this chapter, *first*, discusses five lessons that can be drawn on the basis of the previous chapters and the general literature. The lessons are presented as possible starting points for developing analytical frameworks capturing historical and contemporary university dynamics. *Then*, four themes for an empirical research agenda are suggested as following from the stylized visions and the empirical processes that we have presented and analyzed in the previous chapters.

FIVE LESSONS

How then to move on from the current situation? How can we improve our understanding of the nature of the transformations that have taken place in European universities? That is, how can we comprehend the processes through which change in university organization and governance has taken place, the effects on university performance and development, and the determinants of change, in particular the significance of European integration and cooperation?

Given our observations in the previous chapters – the almost continuous demands for comprehensive reforms; the search for new legitimate ways and means to govern universities and the layering of piecemeal changes over decades; strong commitments to institutional solutions yet without much evidence of how precisely each of them affects academic performance; competing diagnoses and visions for the future University in spite of a dominant functional language; the multi-institutional setting in which university change and reform are taking place and their close relationship to societal developments in general; the tendency to believe in simple causal structures in spite of an increasing complexity in terms of actors, forces and events across levels of governance, institutional spheres, and policy areas – given all this, the main argument in the following is that we have to go:

- Beyond routine, incremental change and reform, and conceptualize current dynamics as *search for a new pact* between the University and its environments.
- Beyond a dominant concern for substantive performance and explore the possible independent importance of the *legitimacy* of institutions in the assessment and justification of existing arrangements, reforms and change.
- Beyond functionalism and analyze change as processes of *contestation*.
- Beyond a single-institution framework and take into account *inter-institutional tensions and collisions*.
- Beyond explanations based upon environmental determinism or strategic choice and consider the more *complex ecology of processes and determinants* in which the European University is currently embedded.

Search for a New Pact

Under some conditions change and reform take place routinely and incrementally within a fairly stable institutional framework. Under other conditions institutional frameworks are themselves changing as the shared understandings underlying the political and social order are questioned and possibly modified or replaced.

However, it is often difficult to say exactly under what conditions radical or revolutionary change is taking place or is likely to take place (chapter 3). Apparent revolutionary events, such as the democratization of the University during the 1960s and 1970s (chapter 5), may in a longer perspective turn out to have less transformative impacts than those taking part in, or observing the events believed. Neither is it unimaginable that the same observation will be made in the future concerning the impact of the market vision (chapter 6). On the other hand, consistent incremental change may over time transform the university system in fundamental ways.

A main argument in this Volume, nevertheless, is that the University is in a "critical period" with a potential for a major rebalancing of internal and external relations of authority, power and responsibility in university governance. Behind labels such as "a Europe of knowledge" there is a search for a new pact between the University, political authorities and society at large. A "pact" is a fairly long-term cultural commitment to and from the University, as an institution with its own foundational rules of appropriate practices, causal and normative beliefs, and resources, yet validated by the political and social system in which the University is embedded. A pact, then, is different from a contract based on continuous strategic calculation of expected value by public authorities, organized external groups, university employees, and students – all regularly monitoring and assessing the University on the basis of its usefulness for their self-interest, and acting accordingly.

The University is in search of a new pact and a legitimate position in the political and societal order at the same time as Europe in general is in search of a new order (Olsen 2007). The two sets of processes are related, so that the University's search for a new pact is part of the more general transformations in the European order. The current dynamics, therefore, raise core questions: What kind of University for what kind of society? What do the University and society expect from each other? How is the University assumed to fit into a democratic polity and society (chapter 2)? Like other institutions under re-examination the University has had to re-think its rationale, identity and foundations, its ethos, codes of behavior and primary allegiances and loyalties. There has been a need to explain and justify foundational institutional principles and rules and, for example, to give policy makers and citizens good reasons for accepting university autonomy and individual academic freedom.

The four other lessons are closely linked to this interpretation of the ongoing dynamics of change in the European University as a search for a new foundational pact.

Legitimacy

Organized cooperative efforts and reform proposals are usually explained and justified by their assumed beneficial consequences. Focus is upon how change in organization and governance can be expected to improve substantive performance directly or indirectly. An example of the latter is when organizational change is assumed to improve an organization's ability to learn and adapt to shifting environments, which in turn is seen to produce desired substantive consequences.

While expected consequences under many conditions are used as the main criteria of assessment, actors may nevertheless have preferences over institutional arrangements, and not only across policy outcomes. In such cases characteristics of institutions and forms of governance are seen to have an inherent value, that is, institutional properties are not (solely) assessed in terms of their contribution to immediate substantive benefits.

Under some conditions, and the search for a new pact is likely to be an example, reform impacts upon institutions are also considered more important than impacts upon substantive policies and outcomes. Assessments and justifications of institutional arrangements and reforms then focus upon what are seen as legitimate institutional arrangements in the relevant culture. Evaluations are based upon the institutions' intrinsic, not instrumental values. They are primarily deontological rather than consequential (Olsen 1997).

The European Union has committed itself to institutional arrangements such as democracy, the rule of law, human rights and a market economy. Nevertheless, in the Union, as well as in other European cooperative efforts, predicted and desired consequences in terms of improved substantive benefits, together with increased institutional learning and adaptability as tools for improved performance, have been predominant. The raison d'être of European integration has been portrayed as the Union's supreme ability to meet (some of) the needs of European citizens and solve problems that each member state cannot solve equally well by itself. The Commission has repeatedly emphasized that "Europe needs results" and much of the university reform discourse has also been organized around assumptions about "performance crises," Europe "lagging behind," and the University's inadequate ability to learn and adapt to its environments.

Policy debates, for example, usually do not acknowledge the importance of the specific institutional history, characteristics and context of the European University. This can be illustrated by a recent Communication of the European Commission on the modernization agenda for universities which declares that "Universities should be funded more for what they do than for what they are" (Commission 2006b: 7). Here the Commission portrays Universities as organizations without a long history and an identity with intrinsic value. The University is seen as operating in an institutional vacuum and can be basically stimulated from the outside to become more effective if only the right measures, for example, an introduction of performance-based funding, are taken.

However, while it has been commonplace to see expected and desired substantive consequences as the most important motive behind university reform, many actors have also seen organizational structures and processes as having inherent value or dangers. They have supported or opposed different institutional arrangements on the basis of fairly enduring general beliefs, stereotypes or ideologies, rather than on the basis of documented substantive outcomes. Different actors have expressed general trust in, or scepticism to, majority rule, internal and external interest representation, market competition, and academic autonomy and freedom (chatper 2). They have done so, not on the basis of continuous feedback about the benign or disastrous substantive consequences of each arrangement, but rather on a basis of long-term commitments to the appropriateness and legitimacy of specific institutional principles, rules, practices, and reform procedures.

While trust in the University and willingness to give it organizational autonomy is likely to be influenced by the University's substantive performance and how existing autonomy is actually used, it will often be difficult to know exactly *which* reforms will work and *how* they will affect performance. For example, in a world where many factors are changing simultaneously it will be difficult to disentangle exactly what has been the impact of a specific modification of the University's internal organization and system of governance. It will especially be difficult to foresee and control precisely the long-term consequences of organizational reform for the type and quality of research and education. Therefore, we expect it to be easier to deliberately change formal organizational arrangements, rules and budgets than to influence academic performance and achieve pre-specified, substantive results by changing university organization and systems of governance.

A possible implication is that the longer and more uncertain the causal chains between university organization and performance, and the more uncertain the existing knowledge about the substantive consequences of proposed organizational reforms, the more likely it is that reforms will be assessed on the basis of long-term commitments to competing institutional arrangements rather than on continuous calculation of the substantive benefits following from organizational change. There may, however, be tensions and conflicts whether assessments and justifications are made on the basis of the inherent value of institutional arrangements or in terms of substantive benefits.

Contestation

As already argued, the most typical language used to explain and justify organized cooperation is functional. Focus is upon how joint efforts produce desirable substantive results and added value. Key words are modernization, problem-solving, improvement, expertise, effectiveness, and efficiency. Under some conditions it is also true that Pareto improvement takes place as a functional superior alternative, leaving some better off and nobody worse off, is discovered through analysis, design or accident and then peacefully replaces a functionally inferior solution. For example, in democracies public deliberation about reform schemes are supposed to contribute to a reasoned popular consent, as collective problem-solving produces renewed trust in an existing pact, reinterpretation and modification of that pact, or a consensual development of a new one.

Under other conditions reform and change are strongly disputed. Typically, the search for a new pact raises many "why-questions" as well as "how-questions," that is, foundational questions about the values, norms, interests, and power underlying the system, and not only questions concerning functional performance, effectiveness, efficiency and improvement. There are competing values, norms, interests and world-views. It is easy to identify losers as well as winners, and there is contestation and threats of withdrawal of support for the existing institutional order. Such situations tend to activate a variety of issues to which there rarely are technically superior, durable and agreed-upon solutions. Contestation, coalition-building and conflict resolution, therefore, are likely to be central aspects of reforms.

The language of university reform, like that of European integration in general, has primarily been functional. For example, in policy documents from the European Union a core assumption has been that there is an agreed-upon agenda for university reform. It has also been commonplace to argue that it is undisputable how things work and how they could be made to work better (chapter 1).

However, the previous chapters have shown that university reform tends to involve contestation and that especially issues of education, identity-building and the socialization of the young have turned out to be national sensitive policy areas. There have been competing visions of how the University should be organized, governed, funded and changed, and attempts to purify a single vision have historically mobilized countervailing forces in defense of other visions. The definition and monitoring of performance and quality has to a considerable extent been moved out of the universities. A result has been that the boundaries between universities and society have been blurred and there have been tensions and contestation over who can legitimately define criteria of success, social relevance and academic quality, processes sometimes creating new links and alliances.

As suggested in chapter 1, university dynamics are rarely driven by stable, consistent and agreed-upon preference functions. Attempts to create an agreement on a limited number of operational reform objectives have rarely succeeded. Actors have often been pursuing many and conflicting policy objectives or they have been acting according to competing norms. Apparent consensus on overarching goals have required a considerable degree of vagueness, "softer" methods of governance such as the Open Method of Coordination (OMC) rather than legal measures, as well as uncertain implementation (chapter 8). The different objectives defended by competing groups have operated as independent constraints (Cyert and March 1963) in processes aimed at discovering or defining viable reform options.

Furthermore, there have been competing diagnoses of how well European universities perform according to different criteria of success as well as competing interpretations of which factors determine university performance. There has also been disagreement about who should pay for what – public authorities, students and their families, industry and other users of research and education. These contestations have involved organized groups and individuals. They have also involved tensions and collisions between institutions founded on values, norms, interests, and world-views that are not always easily reconcilable.

Institutional Collisions

Under some conditions reform and change are regulated by a single and fairly stable institutional framework: institutional rules and practices, causal and normative beliefs that explain and justify the institution, and stable resource allocations. Under other conditions there are frictions and collisions between competing institutional actors who are carriers of different behavioral logics, traditions and resources (March and Olsen 1989, 2007; Orren and Skowronek 2004).

Historically the University has had both a transnational and a local dimension. Yet in Europe the territorial state has for a long time been the main framework for university policy making, functioning, and development. There have been tensions and conflicts between institutions and policy sectors, but conflict resolution has primarily taken place within the overarching framework of the sovereign territorial state. In comparison, new visions for the future of the University seem currently to have their origin at the European, more than at the national level. There is European-level institution-building creating an increase in organized capacity for action – policy making as well as research and education. There is also a growing underbrush of organizations, including new ones, such as the European University Association (EUA), the European Association of Institutions in Higher Education (EURASHE), the European Centre for Strategic Management of Universities (ESMU), and ESIB, the National Unions of Students in Europe.

These are processes taking place in the interface of levels of governance, institutional spheres, and policy sectors, with frequent frictions and collisions between institutions that are carriers of different national University, state, and state-society traditions. Consequently, not only the University but also national research and educational policy establishments have been challenged and have had to re-think and re-learn their place in a larger political and social order, including the power relationships between key institutions.

In such situations – where the European University is involved in a search for a new pact and there are contestations over visions for the future – university dynamics cannot be understood by studying universities, or any other single institution, in isolation. Analyzing only institution- or sector-specific conditions leaves us, at best, with a one-eyed understanding of how universities function and develop. Neither the competitive market nor any other stylized vision has completely replaced all others visions. Each vision and their underlying institutional arrangements still have their supporters, and they are also likely to do so in the future, even if the support may wax and wane and the balance among the visions change. Understanding university dynamics, therefore, requires attention to the interface between the institutional arrangements upon which the various visions are based.

At the European, as well as the national level, the University has several policy anchorages that complicate the study of how inter-institutional processes affect its dynamics. For instance, so far policy making at the European level concerning the University as a research organization and an educational organization have been coordinated separately, implying that the institutional embeddedness of these two policy areas differs (chapter 8). The education-research separation is also upheld through practices outside universities, for example, as evaluation of education and research are made separately. There are countervailing processes – the new forms of institutional accreditation emerging in Europe are, for instance, blurring the distinction between the two areas. Disconnections, furthermore, should not necessarily be interpreted as a lamentable lack of horizontal policy coordination, but rather be seen as expressions of how policy sectors and their institutional traditions have been organized at the European level. The disconnections also provide starting-points for studies of how reconnection of policy-fields and institutional spheres may take place. For instance, the EHEA has met the ERA when the former started to take an interest in research education and doctoral students, as also expressed in the 2005 Bologna meeting of Education Ministers in Bergen, and the agenda for the 2007 London ministerial meeting.

Unquestionably, the University has developed into a key institution that impacts most aspects of democratic societies, and research and education have come higher up on the European agenda and are now getting a sizable share of the Community budget. However, all this does not imply that research and educational institutions and policy making have become more autonomous. Neither does it mean that this sector has become more powerful as a core premise-giver to other policy sectors.

Rather, a more prominent place on the political agenda has come together with demands that research and education have to become better integrated with the overall objectives of the Union. Universities have in particular faced strong demands for better contributions to furthering the European knowledge economy and making Europe the most competitive and dynamic knowledge-based economy in the world. Generally, more participants, problems and solutions have been mobilized in university reform policies. Research and higher education policies have developed an increasing interdependence with a variety of policy sectors and sector-external concerns have become increasingly important both directly and indirectly.

Arguably, the education and research sector has become a net receiver of external premises as policy makers have to a lesser degree treated the University as a unique institution, for example, by importing organizational patterns, governance systems, management techniques, and funding arrangements inspired by private business and competitive markets. The University has been "prey to" general shifts in public governance, maybe not so much as a result of a distrust in the efficiency of the universities to run their own affairs per se, but rather as a consequence of the shift from input control to performance control of public institutions, based upon the general belief that public institutions perform better when they are in competition with each other and private sector organizations.

Furthermore, European level developments have impacted the European University indirectly and as a side effect. In the same way as European hospitals' basic activities have been affected by European market regulating instruments, such as the working time directives and the directive on professional qualifications (Greer 2006), the University's basic functions have felt the effects of "Europe" in areas such as intellectual property rights, and state aid rules, while they have also been affected by instruments and initiatives that have been explicitly designed to aid the construction of the European Research Area or the European Higher Education Area.

In sum, change and reform processes have to be analyzed as part of larger interinstitutional transformations, in a European rather than a national context. Students of university dynamics have to attend to institutional collisions and possible alien invasions from other institutional spheres. They also have to attend to the possibility that the search for a new pact involves a complex ecology of processes and determinants.

A Complex Ecology of Processes and Determinants

Under some circumstances change is determined by environmental processes of competitive selection. Under other circumstances change is the product of strategic choices of leaders and managers, that is, change reflects the will, understandings, and power of an identifiable group of actors. Both explanatory frames are prominent in the academic study of institutional and organizational dynamics. Change, nevertheless, routinely involves a much larger repertoire of standard processes and in contemporary settings change often takes place in a complex ecology of actors, processes and determinants (March 1981; Brunsson and Olsen 1998).

European policy makers often use the environmental determinism and strategic choice frameworks to describe or prescribe the dynamics of change in the European University. The preceding chapters, in contrast, have observed that European (and global) competition in research and education is far from perfect and that competitive environments are likely to influence, but not determine university dynamics (chapter 6). Likewise, several chapters have shown that there are many actors and forces across levels of governance, policy sectors and institutional spheres and that no single actor or coherent group of actors is likely to perfectly control reform processes and their outcomes. Hence, we should not expect a straight causal line from European integration, or from the intentions of identifiable actors, to university performance and development.

Furthermore, the preceding chapters have documented that university change and reform can be triggered and influenced by many factors and that change processes follow many different trajectories. University developments are also strongly embedded in institutional arrangements and traditions and there are path dependencies. The fifth lesson of this Volume, then, is that while environmental determinism/competitive selection and strategic choice are possible explanatory frames, contemporary transformations cannot be predicted or understood solely in terms of these two interpretative frames.

An institutional approach, in particular, emphasizes the possible robustness and resilience of well-entrenched institutions against changing environments and deliberate reform efforts (March and Olsen 1989; 2006 a, b). Institutions provide elements of order. Therefore making sense of university dynamics requires that we take into account the density and types of institutionalized rules and practices in which the University is embedded, as well as the origins and histories of the University and other relevant institutions. Properties of such institutional configurations and traditions are, for example, likely to influence the degree to which the University will be able to counteract deliberate efforts of institutional imperialism and other invasions of alien premises, and also the University's ability to re-examine its foundational identity and its pact with society (chapter 2).

One implication of an institutional perspective is that we, in order to explain how much and what changes have taken place in the European University, have to go beyond environmental determinism. Yet we have to take into account that current transformations are part of a broader political and societal transformation and that change takes place in a specific historical and cultural context. This is a context where the relationships between the University, political authorities, and society are redefined, and where the significance of European integration efforts for higher education and research is linked to the larger transformations and the conditions set by them.

The differentiation of universities and systems of research and higher education in Europe is closely connected to the nationalization of these policy areas and the integration of research and higher education institutions in the service of the territorial state. Consequently, the state traditions encompass different understandings of how to control domestic institutions (Hood et al. 2004: 4), such as the University, and of how to instill a national order on the higher education systems and the basic activities of the University.

Less variation between national university systems and more variations within the university system of a single country (among other things) can be seen as an indicator of European integration (Egeberg 2006c). While the germs of such developments can be observed, there is still considerable variation within European research and higher education systems both in terms of the strength and autonomy of the University and the strength and autonomy of the state and its constituent parts relevant to this sector (Gornitzka and Maassen 2000b; Maassen 2006).

The European level of governance has become more important, but it has far from replaced other levels of governance. The role of the government as the grand conductor making sure that the included actors stick to a common "script" is less visible now than 15–20 years ago, and this has been interpreted as the abdication of government to the market, through the deregulation of national legal and regulatory frameworks, and the decentralization of decision-making authority. However, the territorial state cannot be assumed to be static in face of European-level dynamics and arguably the state has repositioned itself, rather than abdicated (chapters 7 and 8). Changing state traditions and state-society traditions continue to affect how universities are impacted by European integration.

National governmental ambitions with respect to the universities are, for example, present and alive and express themselves through the continued and renewed governmental grip on core levers of control (Hood et al. 2004: 75–130). In Western Europe the funding of universities is still dominantly public (Lepori et al. 2005) and the legal frameworks have been changed but not emptied. University reforms continue to a large extent to be orchestrated by governments within a national context, with a firm foundation in national policy processes and legal frameworks.

Therefore, it is no surprise that the general observation in the literature on European integration – that national institutions have made a difference and that there has been "domestic adaptation with national colors" (Risse et al. 2001: 1) – turns out to be relevant also for the European University as an entrenched and endurable institution. European decisions and forces are interacting with nation state, state-society, and state-society-university arrangements and traditions, and obviously significant national, policy-sector, institutional, and disciplinary idiosyncrasies have so far outlived European integration.

Making sense of university dynamics and of changes in these dynamics will, furthermore, require attention to shifts not only between the nation state and the European level, but also from and to the other relevant levels of governance. In some countries the challenge to national systemic control comes from the regional level. In other countries the nation states have had a different point of origin in terms of governmental control over higher education systems and institutions, and they have actually increased their control ambitions over parts of the universities' basic activities. There are also variations in the extent to which external regulation and control over academic activities have come to be accepted as natural and legitimate (Salter and Tapper 2000).

However, the University has prior to and parallel to European-level developments undergone changes that have opened higher education and research to the transformation implied in the construction of "a Europe of knowledge." We have seen how the four visions of the University are rooted in different societal and political conditions. Understanding the changes related to the Humboldtian vision is impossible without understanding the political and societal conditions within which it arose (chapter 3). The hierarchical vision of the University is crucially linked to changes in the conception of the nation state and its role in society. We have also observed how national development and reform of a system of universities is linked to the functions and means of governance of the modern welfare state (chapter 4) and that national institutional traditions have shaped the systemic diversity that are present today in the university landscape. The rise of the democratic vision is related to processes promoting representative democracy in society at large as well as work-place democracy (chapter 5), while the current dominance of the market vision has to be linked to changing conceptions about the role of government in steering society and specifically in Europe the strong political focus on the problems of the continent to compete in the global higher education and research markets (chapter 6).

Neither can reform processes be understood without appreciation of their various points of origin. For instance, how the Lisbon process has proceeded with respect to the University within the stage set by the European Research Area is highly dependent on the path EU institutions had taken prior to the more recent events in research policy cooperation (chapter 8). In those cases where the University was seen as part of the education sector and an instrument of lifelong learning policy, the policy process has a very different point of origin and has followed a different trajectory. Studies of university dynamics, therefore, can benefit from knowledge about how institutional arrangements and trajectories may impair or reinforce environmental change. Such studies can also benefit from knowledge about how institutions constrain and enable actors differently.

The general literature, as well as the previous chapters, also suggests that studies of fairly institution-free worlds can add valuable insights. For example, it is commonplace to observe that excessive institutional segmentation tends to make it difficult to achieve coordination, coherence, and consistency across levels of governance, policy sectors, and institutional spheres. It has been somewhat less common to observe that loosely structured contexts and contexts with institutional competition and no institutional hierarchy and overarching authority, may have similar effects. Under the latter conditions, reform processes may be connected ad-hoc through temporal sorting and "garbage can" processes. That is, actors, problems, solutions, and choice opportunities are connected due to their simultaneous arrival and presence, rather than due to their causal connections (Cohen et al. 1972; March and Olsen 1989).

The European context of university reform has some such properties. There are weakly developed institutions in some areas and competing institutions in other areas. Like elsewhere, "garbage can"-processes have been seen as "pathological" – as producing undesired results and requiring agreed-upon principles and rules of coordination. There have been repeated calls for eliminating existing incoherence and inconsistencies and providing better integration across levels of governance, policy sectors and institutional spheres. For example, according to the Commission there is a need to boost coordination, and demands for urgent and radical university reform have to a large extent been triggered by assumed performance crises which at least partly have been seen to be caused by the lack of European coordination, coherence, and consistency.

As part of an attempt to understand strategic leadership or management efforts to provide better coordination and integration in loosely structured contexts, we consider three dimensions of "integration": interdependence, consistency and coherence, and structural connectedness (March 1999b: 134). Often reform processes are triggered by the discovery that the degree of integration varies along these three dimensions (Olsen 2001b).

Typically it is, *first*, claimed that there is interdependence in terms of significant causal effects across levels of governance, policy sectors and institutional spheres. *Second*, it is observed that there is a lack of consistency and coherence, that is, that actions and beliefs do not fit together from the point of view of shared policy objectives and standards of success. *Third*, the lack of consistency and coherence, and possibly a perceived performance crisis, is attributed to a lack of structural interconnectedness, that is, missing or weak common institutional arrangements and organized networks.

Attempts at policy integration take place both within a specific level of governance or policy sector and between levels of governance and policy sectors (Ugland and Veggeland 2006). However, it has often proved difficult for leaders and managers to achieve coordination, not only across highly segmented institutional spheres but also in loosely coupled systems characterized by temporal sorting of actors, problems, solutions and choice opportunity. One challenge, then, is to explore the conditions under which such coordination is possible, that is, the conditions under which decision-makers have the will, understanding, and control, needed for coordination. Another challenge is to explore the conditions under which a tightly coordinated University and university system are likely to produce better academic results, in terms of research and education, than a more loosely coupled University or university system.

MAKING SENSE OF AN EMERGING PACT: FOUR PRIORITY AREAS FOR FUTURE RESEARCH

As observed in chapter 2, many of the challenges the European University now faces are due to the University's success. Reformers typically start out with the new potential importance of the University – the importance for individual life chances and well-being and importance in terms of national or European economic, technological, and military competitiveness and power, and strengthened social cohesion. Reformers argue that the University has to be reformed in order to fully realize this potential and live up to society's expectations. In brief their claim is that without reform the University will be marginalized, while the result of the suggested reforms will be a renaissance: the University will be more important than ever before.

Opposition to reform plans typically starts out with an institutional rather than an instrumental perspective. The University is an academic institution with an identity of its own. Reform plans now threaten this identity. Left to itself, the University has a potential for self-renewal, as it has shown throughout history. In brief, the claim of the reform opposition is that reforms will destroy the identity of one of society's key institutions and disintegrate the University. Left to itself, the University will be able to cope with shifting frameworks yet keep its foundational identity.

There are tensions within both the instrumental and the institutional view. The first includes what and whose goals the University should be an instrument for. The latter includes tensions between the requirements of big science and disciplines where individual work is more common and costs are low.

Nevertheless, to make sense of a possible new (emerging) pact, we have to understand the interface between the instrumental and the institutional conception of Universities and the tension and conflicts generated in this interface. In particular, we need to understand the rebalancing required if political, economic and social importance and academic institutional identity is to be reconciled.

The research challenge is to identify the conditions under which various reforms will lead to improved performance and not to the decay of a key societal institution, as well as the conditions under which self-governance will lead to renewal and further development and not to stagnation and marginalization. However, we acknowledge that there is no ready-made theory that can help us identify such conditions and capture the complexity observed in the preceding chapters. The diagnoses and predictions of both those generating reform plans and those defending the traditional university identity also underestimate current differentiations among universities and countries and probable developmental trends. The fact that the European level has become more important furthermore makes it even more difficult to identify the cumulative long-term effects of the poorly understood and conceptualized, on-going piecemeal changes in university organization and governance.

To get beyond this situation and the cognitive and normative dominance in current debates of the stylized instrumental and institutional interpretations, detailed empirical observations of actual patterns of organization and governance, as well as performance are needed. Here we give priority to the following four research themes:

1. European-level ideas and capabilities. The European level is where new ideas and strategies are produced; and there is a growing capability for both governance and research at the European level.
2. European ambitions meet national realities. We need to avoid the interpretation that the national level just adapts to the European level; research needs to capture the interaction between the two levels of governance and also do justice to the loosely-coupled nature of the relationships.
3. Consequences for the University. Research is needed to examine the impact of the interactions between European level ambitions, national and institutional realities; this goes for the University's organization and governance, but even more so for the possible penetration of these interactions into core academic work processes.
4. Beyond Europe. To study university dynamics implies understanding the University as a universal institution. In this endeavor we cannot limit ourselves to intra-European processes; we aim at comparing the dynamics of the European University to the change processes the institution is undergoing in other contexts, in the first place the USA.

EUROPEAN LEVEL IDEAS AND CAPABILITIES

Chapter 1 poses the question of how far European integration efforts have penetrated into the University's core activities, and placed this question within a theoretical approach to institutions and institutional change. Such a focus cannot be pursued unless we understand the institutional makeup of the European dimension in higher education and research, and the dynamics of European institution building in these policy areas. Studying European integration and the transformation of the University implies studying the development of political institutions and administrative capacity relevant to the "Europe of Knowledge." For more than 50 years the University has featured on the European agenda and there are established institutional arrangements for European cooperation relevant to the way in which higher education and research operate. Yet these arrangements are in many respects still in the making, and actors and institutions involved are, if not negotiating, then at least looking to position themselves in a changing institutional order (chapters 7 and 8).

In addition to the market order of the EU, there is already an established European administrative order. Administrative capacity has been built up also in research and higher education to host the European dimension, linking the European executive, national, and sub-national levels of administration in these sectors. With the gradual build-up of the Commission services and its functional differentiation into a DG for

Research and a DG for Education, a permanent, and partly autonomous, administrative capacity has been established, organized according to sectoral lines. The two distinct, basic University functions of teaching-learning and research are retrieved in the political-administrative organization of the "knowledge sectors" the European level and to some extent at the national level. At the European level this split should be seen in light of the history of European integration and the international dimension of the two policy areas. Research policy issues have for several decades been the object of international and European coordination. Education as a policy area has traditionally been more contained by national borders and presented as nationally sensitive. The institutional horizontal split in research versus education has had important implications for the dynamics of integration even though they address in essence the same object of integration (chapter 8).

Common to both sectors is that their respective DGs have become a platform for networking administrations across Europe. The Commission services rely heavily on the networks that connect the supranational level to the other levels of governance, as seen in the elaborate structure of committees and expert groups organized by the Commission.[149] These are networks for European policy making, for affecting national policies, for information exchange and for the implementation of European policies and programs at the sub-national level. These networks both bypass and include the national governmental level. National ministerial administrations are key participants, but administrative networks also link national agencies and intermediary bodies, universities and research groups to each other and to the European level.

Of particular interest to us is that intermediary bodies, such as funding and quality assessment agencies, have experienced a changing role in the governance of national higher education and research systems. In some countries they traditionally served as buffering organizations to soften the impact of government on universities. For example, in the UK these bodies were explicitly changed to act as agencies of national ministries and to protect the interest of government rather than the universities in the coordination of higher education (Meek 2002; Kogan and Hanney 2000: 142–179).

Another example concerns national research councils, that even before adding a European dimension, exemplified "multi-hatted" national agencies, balancing the interests of the research community, government and industry, as well as other interested parties in their coordination function. Research councils have gained agency autonomy also in order to pursue new functions, such as formulating and identifying "strategic" research, science forecasting, or research evaluations.

The nature and role of these types of national agencies have not been systematically studied with reference to their connection to the European level and their role in European level coordination of higher education and research. One possible hypothesis is that the European level institutional build-up not only changed the

---

[149] The Commission's register of expert groups listed over 80 expert groups under the DG Education and Culture and over 120 for DG research in 2006. http://ec.europa.eu/transparency/regexpert/search.cfm

multi-level administration of research and higher education by adding another layer, but that European integration also pushed the establishment and homogenization of national agencies in Europe and promoted national agency autonomy (Egeberg 2006a: 10).

Multi-level administrative networks also incorporate transnational actors, such as disciplinary associations, expertise networks, and European level stakeholder associations, that in themselves might already challenge the cohesion of national systems of research and higher education. As the DGs divide their work primarily according to sectoral lines, both the DG EAC and the DG Research represent access points for interest groups in the sector (Egeberg 2006b: 42). Such interest groups and European transnational organizations have institutionalized their participation in research as well as education, and some of them are are also sustained by European funding and support.

Links to sub-national actors and the European level do not exclusively run via the European associations and expertise networks. Administrative networks also include direct connections between the European Commission and individual universities and research groups. Evaluations of national participation in European programs have shown that they have spurred the establishment of administrative capacity within the universities that connects directly to the European level (e.g. Nuffic 2003; Pirrie et al. 2003; Vabø and Smeby 2003; Godø 2004). What we do not know is how stable these connections are and how they connect to other structures that make up university and national governance arrangements.

Investigating the dynamics of such networks is essential in order to understand European integration in these policy areas. The connections are a core part of both the European Research Area and the coordination of higher education activities in Europe. Multiple administrative networks challenge the conception of clear loci of control over research and higher education systems in Europe. A simple mapping of the structure of such networks would in itself be a major accomplishment as a step towards understanding the role they play in administrating the "Europe of Knowledge" – that is, the kind of means of governance they employ (see below). Studying such networks would give insight into the links that are forged between multiple levels of governance in Europe and how they handle various, in some respects, competing University traditions and perceptions of the role of research and higher education in contemporary society.

To start with, what kind of challenge – if any – to national systemic cohesion do the networks represent? They can be expected to represent varying challenges to the role of the nation state in higher education versus its role in the research sector. We could expect the restructuring of Europe as a research area to take place with less of a pivotal role of national ministerial level administration than in the case of the European Higher Education Area. Furthermore, what are the consequences of participation in such administrative structures across Europe? Do ways of thinking, identities and practices remain mainly nationally structured or do they become aligned with those developed in European networks, thus disconnecting from the operations of national or sub-national administrations?

Current administrative networks appear to be the sum of connections that over time have dovetailed the absorption of activities at the European level, rather than being the result of grand designs or reform by the Commission or national institutions. If that is the case then processes underlying the institutionalization of such connections have been incremental. Yet it does not necessarily follow that this will be the dynamics of capacity building at European level in the future. Rather we would expect that networks established across the Europe of Knowledge are important for paving the way for more sudden leap-frog developments in European integration. Traditionally the legitimation for creating new institutions at this level has not been strong. We know from the study of the early history of the European Community that building a supranational institution to emulate the University met with national resistance (Corbett 2005). Nevertheless, currently there are two major attempts of institution building, the establishment of the European Research Council (ERC) and the proposal for a European Institute of Technology (EIT), unfolding at the European level. Both speak directly to core aspects of the University as an institution and its work organization. The EIT is a proposal for common capacity building at the European level: building an academic institution with (semi)permanent staff, resources and a different kind of research organization than the model for European research collaboration embedded in the R&D Framework Program. Creating a common University organization that combines teaching and research is an innovation in the European context with respect to traditional ways of thinking about and organizing research. That is an unfolding experiment in research organization comparable to previous attempts in the earlier history of European integration. For example, what became The European University Institute in Florence was a diluted version of the vision of a European Community University proposed in 1955–1957 (Corbett 2005). Likewise the ERC indicates a different role for the European Union in basic research to be added to its traditional R&D policy focus.

    Why do such institution building attempts merit a place on the research agenda? Institution building for research and higher education at the European level touches upon the principles of organization and funding, the perception of the role of the University, and the underlying vision of the University and academic research and the evaluations and assessments of higher education and research. These are rooted in national and institutional traditions, in different professional and disciplinary traditions, and they are framed by interests of actors. These meet and might collide in the process of crafting common institutions. Norms of assessment and the legitimacy of models for organizing and funding research and higher education that may be taken for granted within such traditions and other levels of governance, will have to be justified and argued at the European level. Some actors will succeed in having their interests, ideas and values taken up as the basis for the common European institutions while others will not. Latent tensions between different visions of the University and of the European level in research and higher education are likely to become manifest during the process. Both the proposal for the European Institute of Technology and the European Research Council are breaches with the dominant pattern of European cooperation in these areas, suggesting that a different kind of dynamic will come into play than an incremental one, a phenomenon certainly deserving to be studied in some detail.

EUROPEAN ASPIRATIONS MEET NATIONAL REALITIES

What happens when emerging European aspirations and institutions enter national higher education and research systems that traditionally have known a high level of system integration through national laws, regulations and funding? As national systemic borders are perforated nation states' ability to keep national University systems coherent is challenged, suggesting a process of "de-bordering" taking place (Bartolini 2005; Kohler-Koch 2005). Such de-bordering is not without tensions and the extent of and how de-bordering takes place will be conditioned by diverse national and, as we return to later, institutional realities.

Tensions between the levels of governance, closure and opening of institutional spheres and policy areas speak to changes in the relative strength of *who* controls research and higher education, and *from where* such control is exercised. Associated with these shifts are changes in *how* control is exercised and the dynamics of policy change with respect to the University. The University has prior to, and parallel to, European developments undergone changes that may have opened national research and higher education systems to transformations foreseen in the construction of a "Europe of Knowledge." At the national level, several studies have pointed to the shifts in governance that concern the University (Goedegebuure et al. 1993; Gornitzka and Maassen 2000b; Kogan et al. 2000; Maassen 2006), yet without an unequivocally unidirectional development towards one type of control mechanism and governance arrangement to the detriment of another. However, the study of governance in higher education has not included the systematic effect of the entry and institutionalization of the European level in a multi-level system of governance.

The European ambitions for redesigning the European University have been attached to various sets of levers of control that operate in interaction with the existing practices and means of coordination within universities and at the national and sub-national levels. The perforation of national systemic borders by the attempts to establish a European Research Area and a European Higher Education Area opens the territory also for the investigation of the effects and effectiveness of different means of control, from incentive based competition, standardization and ideational based modes of governance, to legal means of integration. How strongly European integration efforts will affect national systems depends on what holds these together (Kohler-Koch 2005).

Laying Down the Law

As argued by Katzenstein (2005), European integration is unique in that it is more rooted in legal integration than any process of regional cooperation anywhere in the world. Yet, according to the Treaties, the European level has had limited legal recourse in the higher education and research sectors, more limited for the former than the latter (Shaw 1999; Guzzetti 1995; Banchoff 2003; de Elera 2006). National legal frameworks are still a basic component of what defines national borders of higher education and research systems. Yet, the impact of Europe on national higher education and research systems has come in the shape of legal integration. This concerns the interface the University and the "knowledge sectors" have with other institutional spheres that have consequences for the control over/regulation with respect to knowledge.

This is most prevalently evidenced in the interface of market and labor market regulations, where EU legislation regulates areas, such as staff working conditions, through the "service directive," and regulation concerning the use of biotechnology. EU directives in these fields assert (indirect) control over the basic functions of the University or over how the European University as a work organization can operate. EU regulations concerning the mutual recognition of qualifications and diplomas exemplify European regulation of academic knowledge, and the directive on mutual recognition of professional qualifications provides the framework for national rules that regulate how formal education can be converted into professional practice. In the latter case the University, its academic communities, and professional associations are the end implementers of an EU directive.

There are transformations of national legal frameworks that clearly have a European dimension yet are not cases of national transpositions of EU directives. The legal implications of boundary redrawing are already visible in higher education as the structural convergence of higher education systems are at the core of the EHEA. The national implementation of the Bologna process requires in practice revisions of national legal frameworks (chapter 7). There are also legal side effects ensuing from university participation in EU education programs. These are not instances where the national legal and regulatory order is penetrated by the legal system developed at the European level, but where such changes are implications of European integration.

The case of joint Master degree programs selected by the EC's Erasmus Mundus initiative, is a telling example of this. These programs operate in a grey zone between national legal frameworks and European level integration ambitions. National participation in the establishment of a joint Master degree program and the issuing of joint diplomas have de facto implied regulation changes at national level and changes in local rules. This is a consequence of an indirect pressure on national regulations from the institutions that are participating in this scheme. Pressure on national regulations and policies stems from the European Commission, but also from transnational actors, notably the European University Association (EUA) that actively promotes the development of joint degree programs, amongst other things, as part of its participation in the Bologna process.

Concurrently, during the last 10–15 years governments across Europe have revised their own legal frameworks that regulated their higher education systems. This offers cases for investigating core questions. What does change in the legal framework tell us about the role of law in the governance of the European University and in its different core activities? How is the European dimension reflected in changes in national University law? Is the legal framework for national systemic integration affected by the ambitions to create European systemic integration, under the overarching norm of no European harmonization?

The search for a new pact may also be evidenced in such legal changes. The role of legal means of control over universities has traditionally varied across national systems: where some systems have relied on strong, detailed legal frameworks for regulating the operations of the University and for systemic integration, in other systems we have seen for some time now the reliance on framework laws. One hypothesis in this respect would be that the occurrence or adjustment to European integration is dependent on a loosening of the legal grip that national governments have over the University.

We can also expect differentiated effects according to what kind of University activity is subject to national law: teaching provisions compared to research. Traditionally, these areas have been subject to different legal regimes. Accordingly, we could hypothesize that the implementation of ERA is less dependent on changes in the national legal framework and thus less dependent on national law makers being alert to the European agenda.

Spreading the Idea

The literature on a new mode of governance has triggered an interest in the question of how policy coordination can be achieved without "hard law." Several dynamics have been seen as taking the place of the disciplinary and coordinating force of hard law and economic sanctions. The assumed dynamics of integration without law rest with the expected coordinating capacity of the convergence of ideas (Dehousse 2002: 15; Radaelli 2004). The power of definitions and framing of policy is visible in its effects on participation patterns and governance approaches (Ugland 2002).

The loud calls for radical reform of the University seem to form an overarching, converging idea in the European policy arenas. The simple question of how the expectation of reform and change of the University is executed would demand the unveiling of the chain connecting European developments and integration efforts to University dynamics. Although changes in policy theories in research and higher education policy seem to have been incremental rather than to come in the shape of sudden, paradigmatic shifts, the history of European integration in research as in higher education is also the story of *contested* ideas. The definition of both means and goals of research and higher education have been subject to controversy, for instance, with respect to the Framework Programs and in the ideas of ERA (Banchoff 2003) or when the Commission's Memorandum on Higher Education (Commission 1991) was severely opposed by the member states on grounds of its obvious economic tilt (Petit 2002: 17–18). Such contestations have come to the fore in the attempts to subordinate research to the goals of innovation policy or higher education to labor market policy.

Ideational shifts are important to examine also because of their implications for the national sensitivity of policy areas and thus the propensity for transfer of legal competencies to the supranational level and the implications for types of governance across levels. Higher education, especially when framed as vocational training, has in the 30+ years of EU involvement in education been less nationally sensitive than compulsory education, and education defined as economic policy has been less nationally sensitive than when defined as part of the cultural policy areas.

Issues of definition are not once and for all settled and politically neutral, and carry considerable tensions and implications concerning the actors that will have a legitimate say in control over knowledge. These contestations run along party political, national, sectoral lines, as well as between levels of governance. They can be seen in the everyday interactions that take place in the many policy arenas and sub-arenas at the European level and interactions across levels of governance.

Current integration processes in these sectors revolve around organizing information exchange and common European surveillance, be it through formal information networks, initiatives such as ERAWATCH or statistical integration. The role of ideas in the de-bordering of the European University is striking in the prehistory of EHEA and ERA (see chapters 7 and 8). Policy ideas concerning the European University that were until recently "unthinkable," have become ideas "whose time has come" (Corbett 2005); in the context of the Bologna process, the European Research Area and the Lisbon strategy process their desirability seems to be taken for granted.

Against this view one can argue that when the "real" means of control are absent, pushing ideas formulated as common understanding or common European ambitions is a bland, toothless substitute. However, the transformation from unthinkable to what is commonly accepted relies on the presence of institutional carriers of ideas and organizational capacity in the shape of supranational executive networks of policy making that can store, develop and spread such ideas. Changes in the organization of policy making, for instance, inform us about changes in underlying ideas of research and higher education policy; how these are framed and how some sectoral aspects are organized to be coordinated while others are organizationally separated (Steunenberg 2002; Egeberg 2006b). This can be illustrated by pointing to the change in the Council configuration from a separate Research Council to a Competitiveness Council, or when the Commission reorganizes its portfolios (Guzzetti 1995; Corbett 2005; Spencer and Stevens 2006).

Likewise the processes that explicitly organize common European agenda setting, policy learning and transfer can accelerate ideational shifts. This should be framed as a research question for critically examining the impact on European policies that are based on a cognitive logic (Knill 2001: 221), that is, changing the beliefs of actors at national and sub-national levels, under the following main condition. The spreading of ideas, agendas, ambitions occur through organized networks and institutions. Ideas and normative understanding underlying the modernization of the European University are not "free-flowing" *zeitgeists* but are promulgated by institutions that carry some version of University visions elaborated in this Volume. Further they are also subject to competing interpretations, as well as to learning.

A sober understanding of such means of European integration needs to take into account the parallel or interactive development and interpretations of ideas that take place in national reform processes. This is a question of the processes and actors that define the frame and agenda for the modernization of the European University. The transformative effect of such framing is largely dependent on whether ideas match and confirm domestic understandings or the extent to which they run counter to them. Arguably, the effect of European ideas depends on the national contingencies and circumstances as when European commonly defined ambitions can be used to push and legitimate national reform agendas. The evidence of such effects are starting to surface in the literature on the domestic adaptation to the Bologna Declaration (Gornitzka 2006; Witte 2006), but can also be expected to operate when ambitions of research investments, policies for bridging the gap between University and industry and so on, are spread throughout Europe.

Setting the Standards

Ideas can harden into explicit standards elaborated in European processes and agreed on by EU institutions. Standards can be seen as a form of regulation that produces order as an alternative or supplement to hierarchies and market coordination (Brunsson and Jacobsson 2000). Standards are particularly amenable in areas of social interaction where states or other sub-national actors have regulatory autonomy (Kerwer 2005), as is the case with respect to the European University. With the development within the University and in its environment a strong focus should be directed on how European standards are formulated, how they function across levels of governance, and across diverse national and institutional settings. Standards are certainly not a new invention in the higher education sector, with its auditing and accreditation structures and procedures. Peer review and collegial control according to academic standards and the assessment of quality have been an integral part of the research and teaching and learning process. Setting of standards at the national level, for example, concerning common national curricula, is not alien to the University.

The element that separates the latest developments from the institutional traditions in this area is that standards (especially in the area of quality assurance) have been formalized and moved out of the academic arena into an administrative or political-administrative sphere. National agencies organize the production and use of standards of assessment and accreditation. Such standards are being defined in interactions across levels of governance and the development of a European level of governance, including its organization and means of coordination. Few other areas are able to demonstrate so amply how European cooperation in interaction with other international developments affects how control over knowledge is being exercised.

There is a strong European element in the rise and spread of quality assurance regimes that has been firmly put on the agenda by the Bologna process. Yet there are domain contestations as to what arenas and what standard sets should become institutionalized and what kinds of organizational solutions to setting and using quality assessment standards should be supported. For example, the proposal of the European Commission to develop institutional arrangements at a European level in the area of quality assessment, assurance and certification has not been accepted – instead the embryonic compromise is the network of national agencies and a register of accreditation agencies organized at the European level.

The development and use of quality assessment standards in Europe is thus a potentially rich case for studying the linkages of various actors, that is, national governments, national agencies, private agencies, universities and academic associations, educational experts, and transnational and international organizations that are involved in the development of such standards. This includes the relative impact of European standards and the issue how standards become effective. Likewise the intergovernmental arena (the Bologna process is the prime example) has in particular resorted to development of standards for assessments that are argued on the basis of "compatibility" and that directly addressed the core aspects of University functions. On the research policy side, European standards have been developed and recommended for use on essential academic staff issues across Europe, as set in the European Charter for Researchers and Code of Conduct for the Recruitment of Researchers (Commission 2003b).

Very little is known about how such standards are dealt with at different levels of governance and among different actors in the university sector, and also what national or institutional conditions work as filters for or insulation against the penetration of European standards in local practices. There is very little systematic investigation of whether the growing volume of European standards promulgated with intensity at European arenas can best be seen as symbolic standards affirming European common values and ideas, as European or national policy instruments for auditing and oversight or as standards developed as market information to make cross border and cross systemic interaction possible.

This means primarily that the role of standards has to be investigated in the context of the use and development of standards nationally, especially at the level of national agencies. National and European standards could be developed parallel with each other where the latter amplifies the former, or it could be that European standards come in addition to national ones or that national regulation produces a "double whammy" of formalized rules (Hood et al. 2004: 16). If European standards are directly presented to the University, as in case of market information standards, then we expect new standardized rules without the reduction of state rules. When European standards hit the University via the changes in the national sets of rules, then such a double whammy pattern does not necessarily follow, as might be expected in academic staff issues. On the other hand, European standards might represent a formalization of control of academic practices, as is likely in the case of quality assurance and accreditation.

Similarly *quantified standards* are being developed and used as an alternative to hard law. These are fashioned as systemic performance indicators. In terms of ideational based control, indicators are significant because they black-box certain world views. Once a statistical category is established, the priority given to longitudinal comparison makes it hard to change. We can assume that such quantified standards play varying roles in multi-level governance. At the European level such numerical information is important in a dual function. According to a naming-shaming logic, national governments and their national system will accelerate their efforts to conform to common goals through reputational control. On the other hand numerical

standards mobilize bias (Sverdrup 2006: 105) and thus become a means of conceptual and idea-based convergence. At national and institutional levels, information on
good performance (i.e. increasingly set in the form of European harmonized, statistical categories) is converted into authoritative resource rewards and penalties (Kogan
2005: 17), at least in some national systems. There is a good case here to be made
for studying the parallel or interactive development of quantified information-based
systems of governance at the European, national, sub-national and even possibly
University level.

We would expect to see differentiated effects of standardization as a means of
control in this sector. A likely assumption is that in areas where there has been relatively little rule-based interaction between national governments and the universities,
and where consequently there are few institutionally entrenched practices and perspective. European set standards will penetrate more easily compared to areas that
is covered by well-established regulative frameworks. If administrative capacity is
built up around European standards the national take up of European standards will
be easier.

We suggest that national agencies, such as research councils or quality assessment
agencies, are the core institutions to study. They represent the government apparatus
that is set to effectuate standards. And to the extent that these agencies are connected to
European level and other national agencies, they could serve as channels for spreading
the application of European standards.

Paying the Price

The ubiquity of numerical information and European numerical integration (Sverdrup
2006: 105) can also be linked to the changes in the funding mechanism. Quantification
of knowledge on university and system performance is linked to the shift in the
perspective on the University. If universities are expected to produce on demand and
get paid on delivery (Fuller 2003) and governments are to fund the University more
according to "what they do" than for "what they are," then information of what they
do is a prerequisite.

Concerning the funding basis of the University, in a number of countries attempts
have been made to redistribute the public funds for education on the basis of performance or other non-traditional criteria. However, for various reasons the end-effects
are not always according to intended redistribution. Usually the recommendations
with respect to new funding mechanisms have been "modified" by institutional representatives, especially from the institutions that threatened to lose funds in the intended
redistribution. An exception in this is formed by the UK where the part of the university budget that is covered by the public governmental grant is in general lower
than on the continent (Lepori et al. 2005), and the universities are promoted to further
generate their own funds from a variety of external sources (e.g. sponsorship, tuition
fees, and donations).

The extent to which students and their parents should be paying the price is in some
systems one of the most contested issues. Concerning tuition fees a wide variety of
trends, initiatives and developments can be observed throughout the EU. National

governments do not allow the universities to determine the level of the tuition fees they can charge for their programs themselves, if they can charge a tuition fee at all. Organizational autonomy with respect to the level of the tuition fee only exists in some cases, such as Denmark, the Netherlands and the UK where the universities are expected to use special tuition fee levels for non-European students, allowing the universities to charge the costs of their education to (specific groups of) non-EU students. Clearly, the funding issue is at the core of lowering the national systemic borders and establishing new boundaries around Europe. The European Court of Justice's decision on fee payments – the so-called Gravier Judgment – has been one key element in the development of European education policy and continues to be so.

As indicated, there is evidence suggesting that changes in the share of public funding of the European University have been modest over the last decade, at least from an international comparative perspective. Although there are exceptions, for example, in the UK where the state is no longer the primary funder of all higher education institutions, stability rather than change can be said to characterize the sector in a European perspective. In general the last decade has not resulted in a decrease in the available resources for higher education institutions. One can witness a decrease in the share of governmental appropriations and an increase in grants and contracts, but this shift has not substantially altered the distribution of the institutions' funding pies (CHINC 2006).

However, even if the share of public funding has been rather stable, there is evidence that the form of funding has been changing more. Over the last decade more emphasis has been given to interdisciplinary and applied research as well as commercialized research and patenting (CHINC 2006). So competition between universities, and between the universities and other entities, has become a stronger element of the control regime of European universities. Likewise, changes in level of funding and funding mechanism might affect the diversity and stratification of higher education institutions across Europe.

Changes in funding patterns of a key social institution are not trivial matters. Who pays for the University is a question of redistribution of resources. At the European level we see it in, for example, the battles over the level and profile of the Framework Programs. The justification for seeing this as part of a research agenda sketched out here, rests on the assumption that it conditions the dynamics of European integration in this sector.

First, European integration directly affects the University, since the European Union is a modest but strategically important funder that generates additional R&D efforts and additional funding (Godø 2004: 99–101) and is involved in funding student/staff mobility. Much of the EU research policy since the first R&D programs has relied on incentives for cooperation across borders within Europe. Attempts to connect national research programs (ERA-NET) embody the European ambition to couple and align national research funding within the EU/EEA area. The issue of funding is linked to how the University can operate in a European Research Area or for that matter European Higher Education Area (EHEA) as in a European "knowledge market."

Whether this means that European universities are becoming more closely related to and dependent upon external stakeholders is an issue of study that remains to be examined. Also there is significant differentiation within and between higher education institutions when it comes to operating in a European research and higher education market. Given, for example, the nature and size of the various thematic priority areas in the EUs Framework Programs, it is obvious that traditional research universities and within them faculties, departments and research centers in specific disciplines, such as medicine, informatics, natural sciences and engineering, clearly are in a more advantageous position in this compared to, for example, teacher training colleges. De-bordering of national systems is likely to create losers and winners.

Another question is to investigate what kind of (new) relationships are emerging as a consequence of the growing importance of the Lisbon strategy's social and economic issues underlying the university research agendas. Given the competition in the emerging applied and "strategic" research market, one trend that is becoming more visible is the search for "excellence" and new ways to organize and promote research. It is likely that the price to be paid in this area will include internal restructuring of universities, new forms of research governance, and more comparable performance measures and indicators.

CONSEQUENCES FOR THE UNIVERSITY

For the European University the aspirations voiced at the European level, national level and by other constituents of the European University address essential questions concerning its core activities. These aspirations are related first and foremost to the quality of the European University. The reform agendas and policy aspirations towards the University are driven, amongst other things, by the expected contribution of universities to the "knowledge economy" and the perceived "lagging behind" of the European University in comparison with universities in other parts of the world. The perceived "under-performance" of the University forms the rationale behind deliberate attempts to reform the European University. These reform attempts, and other potential impacts of European integration processes, travel through several layers of governance, and operate through different means of control. Just as we have argued that such effects are conditioned by various national realities we see the potential impact of European integration on the University as conditioned by institutional realities and characteristics of the University's internal dynamics.

One such characteristic concerns autonomy. The University as institution and as an object of public policy is veiled in many layers of autonomy. The research and education sectors are in many national systems marked by norms of self-regulation. Relative academic autonomy and academic freedom, the sanctity of the class room and the lecture hall, organizational and disciplinary autonomy, educational organizations as loosely coupled systems, are all elements in what constitutes a challenge for hierarchical control in this sector. As public institutions universities are both state dependent and independent; both positions are argued on the basis of the nature of function the University performs. The traditional interpretation has allowed a higher degree of discretion for the University and the academics than for other public organizations that are subject to direct national lines of command to a national authority such as the military, tax authorities or social security services (Kogan and Hanney 2000: 22–24), and the means of control over University conduct are less directly hierarchical and more based on competition and mutuality than in many other public policy areas (Hood et al. 2004).

The degrees of academic and institutional autonomy of the University vary across systems, over time and over different activities of the University. As duly noted in this volume, variations in autonomy are linked to the kind of vision that forms the basis for University governance arrangements. Yet the point to be made here is that the study of the impact of European integration on University dynamics will represent the study of integration under conditions of comparatively high sub-national actor autonomy. This makes such a study amenable to cross-sector comparisons in areas were such conditions are less present.

The core functions related first to the teaching and learning activities, and second to the research endeavors of the University, are characterized by different kinds of dynamics. Teaching and learning as the basic activities of the University are strongly embedded in the organization of the University. As an educational institution it is an entity whose practices are subject to a, mainly nationally determined, regime of formal rules that regulate access of students, teaching requirements, curricular development and program provisions. In this regime especially the structure of teaching provisions (study plan), what is taught (curriculum development, program innovation), and how teaching and learning are assessed (quality assessment of teaching, credit assessment, recognition of qualifications) have an (emerging) European dimension.

Studies of curriculum change suggest that the very concept of learning within the University is changing – away from the idea that universities should teach students traditional academic competencies and occupational or professional skills, towards a "learning to learn paradigm" that consists of new competencies and skills closely associated with the essential characteristics of the knowledge society (Bleiklie 2005). This might be seen not so much as a new conceptualization but rather as a reactivation of some of the core ideas contained by the Humboldtian vision (chapter 3).

Nevertheless, this "new learning paradigm" has been a core ideational frame of reference for European education policy. Also more limited, deliberate attempts of European systemic curriculum integration at the level of academic disciplines can be observed, for example, the "European Core Curriculum" (Bache 2006) and the EU-funded "Tuning Project," are addressing conditions to make an internal "knowledge market" work, as well as for European identity building. If professional, educational and disciplinary competencies and identifications are being defined in European terms rather than in national terms, that should be taken as a sign that a de-nationalization of the European University is accompanied by European re-bordering.

The point of interest here is whether shifts in ideas, changes in degree structures and European curricular alignments, and criteria of assessment challenge existing knowledge regimes and the national or institutional boundaries that uphold national systemic integration as well as the institutional identity of the University. How much of a challenge such changes represent we would expect to be dependent on the strength of national integration, and on internal governance arrangements that regulate the teaching/learning as well as disciplinary differences.

From previous studies we know that European universities in the 1980s and 1990s tended to protect their traditional degree programs. External demands for new teaching provisions led, for instance, to new structures outside the core organization or they were dealt with in separate, marginal pockets of the core organization thereby combining adaptation and continuity (Gornitzka and Maassen 2003). Such a pattern of change might not be sustainable in a situation of a confluence of change processes that mix national reform efforts with European intergovernmental and transnational cooperation.

The research function of the University is less embedded in the individual university organization than the teaching function. It has the academic discipline as one of its main basic sources of academic belief (Clark 1983) and is therefore less reliant on the University qua formal organization, and less contained by organizational and national borders. Analysis of academic research has taken the structure and nature of academic disciplines as the locus of the dynamics of science and has assumed that the cognitive and social structures of academic disciplines are the main determinants for the dynamics of university research (Becher 1989).

There is evidence of patterns of change in research practices that suggest a lowering of boundaries between the University and its environment. There are increased university research collaborations with industry, and with other types of research organizations. Increasingly university researchers also collaborate and co-publish with researchers across national borders in all geographical directions, but especially within Europe (cf. e.g. Gulbrandsen and Smeby 2005; Smeby and Trondal 2005; RCN 2005). Some report, especially in the context of the US University, a shift in the norms of academia that can be associated with the funding and organization of research (Guston and Kenniston 1994; Slaughter and Leslie 1997). Other studies have reported normative resilience among academics even under new organizational and funding arrangements (Mathisen 1994; Gulbrandsen and Langfeldt 2005; Marton 2005). The literature on University Triple Helix (Etzkovitz and Leydesdorff 1997) and "mode I versus II" (Gibbons et al. 1994; Novotny et al. 2001) suggests that this amounts to a *fundamental* change in the nature of knowledge production, from a disciplinary to a trans-disciplinary mode, blurring the boundaries between the University and other actors in the research process. It is still debatable whether this conceptual shift rests upon a substantial transformation of research practices or represents advances in the theoretical understanding of the dynamics of research.

Changes in the University's basic activities of academic research, and teaching and learning, as well as in institutional organization, governance and funding pointed to in this volume, present the contours of the circumstances under which European integration encounters the University. The loss or weakening of the boundaries of the

University, be it national borders or borders towards industry, is not just a question of changes in the material conditions of the University but of the University's identity. The long history of institutionalized cross-border identity and the universality of the University are not obviously compatible with European re-bordering and a distinct European mission for the University.

The reform agenda for the University that is promoted at the European level, the Bologna process, the supranational direct instruments of the ERA concept and the OMC address most of these changes, as do side-effects and indirect effects of European integration processes in other areas. Yet, there are no foregone conclusions to be made as to how strong a role European integration is playing with respect to the dynamics of the University, other than that we expect that current patterns of change and characteristics of University dynamics create varying conditions for the impact of European integration on the basic activities and the work organization of the University.

Notwithstanding the different points of origin and the different trajectories that have ensued, the EU's research and higher education policy are addressing the same key societal institution. That allows us to test assumptions of differentiated effects of European integration even within the same unit of study, according to differences (1) in the nature and traditions of European institutions and at national level in research policy versus higher education, and (2) differences in governance and means and degrees of control over teaching/learning as opposed research. One overall working hypothesis is that given these differing conditions for integration, the dynamics of European integration with respect to teaching and learning would be more intergovernmental, state-led and regulatory based than in the case of academic research. As such this can be expected to be de-bordering under government control (Kohler-Koch 2005). European integration with respect to research can be expected to be more challenging to the national systemic control and more based on competition as the means of control. If this is indeed the case than the general picture painted is of a University in search of new pact under very complex conditions.

BEYOND EUROPE

The de- and re-bordering of the European University calls for a comparative baseline, yet in much of the EU studies a *sui generis* approach has implied that little reference has been made to studies of political integration and governance outside Europe as a region. Consequently, these studies largely overlook the comparison with other political systems and other processes of regional integration (Katzenstein 2005; Checkel 2007). Such a position misses the potential for both highlighting European uniqueness and demystifying it by not going beyond Europe, similar to the fruitful analytical angles that are missed in higher education studies by taking the university sector as their *sui generis*.

The need to expand the research agenda beyond Europe also arises from the universal character of the University. The University's basic processes can be seen as inherently transnational and global. In this sense the essential dynamics of academic research and teaching tug at national borders and the means with which these have been upheld. The University can evoke a history of more than 900 years, and it has survived the rise and fall of national states and the fluctuations of national borders. The academic world has a history of common transnational identity that belonged to the medieval roots of the University (Neave 2001). Also the University is one of the European institutions that have been exported successfully on a global scale. Thus the study of European integration and the University offers a case where underneath or parallel to national and local identities a global or European identity can be evoked.

While the University can be seen as a "trustee of the European humanist tradition," its inherent transnational nature "transcends geographical and political frontiers" (cf. The Magna Charta Universitatum, and chapter 2). Consequently it does not follow naturally to resurrect the boundaries of research and higher education around Europe as an "Area." The current emphasis on modernizing the University implies not only the de-bordering of "outdated" national research and higher education systems but also the setting and raising of boundaries around Europe.[150] The idea that "knowledge knows no borders" and the universality of the University contrast, for instance, with saluting the mobility of academic staff and students within Europe while seeing mobility to outside Europe as a question of "brain drain."

In policy documents the dynamics of "Europe's major competitors" is a frequent reference, and a range of untested assumptions of how universities and university systems operate in particularly the US setting are made. The USA has currently the best research universities around that form the benchmark for the rest of the world. The success of US higher education and academic research is assumed to be the result of the marketization of US universities, high private investments in education and research coupled with a weak state. The explanation of the leading US position in higher education globally is sought in the use since the early 1980s of market forces for the governance of higher education (Maassen 2006). As pointed to in chapter 6, the vision of the University as a service enterprise comes closest to being developed as a "mono-culture" in the USA.

On the other hand, the assumptions underlying this vision are not fulfilled by the empirical examples of US universities and other systems, such as Australia, where universities have come a long way in marketization and commercialization of their activities. What the empirical studies of the US universities show is rather a paradox of the marketplace (Geiger 2004: 265):

"The marketplace has brought universities greater resources, better students; a far larger capacity for advancing knowledge; and a more productive role in the US economy. At the same time it has diminished the sovereignty of universities over their own activities; weakened their mission of serving the public; and

---

[150] "The EU has committed itself to building a European Research Area (ERA) that will overcome outdated geographical, institutional, disciplinary and sectoral boundaries. The ERA will extend the single European market to the world of research and technological development, ensuring open and transparent trade in scientific and technological skills, ideas and know-how" (Commission 2004b: 4).

created through growing commercial entanglements at least the potential for undermining their privileged role as disinterested arbiters of knowledge."

The diagnosed gap between the US universities and European universities is also a question of what kind of criteria and objectives that are used to assess performance.

Beyond challenging the dominant diagnosis of the USA – Europe differences, and the apparent "lagging behind" of European universities, the cross-Atlantic reference lends itself to the comparative investigation of governance in multi-levels systems of different kinds. The role of the US state-level as compared to the federal level, indicates that when it comes to marketization the state level has increased the regulative grip on universities and has relied more heavily on the standardization of market information to the customers of the University. Which then leads us to a core comparative question: What is role of the state and federal level for the "USA of Knowledge" as compared to the role of the EU and nation state in the "Europe of Knowledge"? A hypothesis is that with respect to higher education the institutional build-up in Europe is in many respects more federal than in the US. However, with respect to research we can observe the reverse situation. The institutional perspective on regional integration taken as a starting point in this volume could be put to the test in such a comparison. The main items we have put on the research agenda, institutional makeup and history of different levels of governance, and the changes in means of control, will benefit from adding such a comparative light.

Obviously, this part of the research agenda should not be limited to a Europe-USA comparison. Also other non-European higher education systems, inside (e.g. Australia, Canada, Japan, and South Korea), as well as outside the OECD area (e.g. Brazil, China, India, Russia and South Africa), are going through far-reaching processes of institutional reform and change, the study of which might contribute to a better understanding of the specific institutional dynamics of the European University.

CONCLUSION

The perspective on University dynamics and European integration offered in this volume implies a research agenda that directs our attention to shifts in control over knowledge. We have explored the interactions and tensions between, and the shifting importance of, levels of governance, policy areas, institutional spheres, actors, and means of governance. The current transformations have been interpreted to lead the University into a situation where the relationship between state, society and the University is redefined and reorganized. This involves more than the marginal adjustments to changing circumstances. Taken together the ongoing processes amount to a search for a new foundational pact for a key European institution. The University dynamics is part of a higher education and research landscape in Europe of which constitutive identities and systemic borders are in the process of being redefined and possibly transcended. As such the ongoing processes offer a laboratory for studying the dynamics of change within, and in the environment of, a key institution with unique traditions and a history that spans many centuries.

We have argued for the need to study European integration and its impact upon the University against the background of a long-term institutionalization of a European dimension of teaching, learning and scientific research. Over time the European level has become the locus of complex interactions that connect different levels of governance, not primarily as grandstand European integration, but characterized by many smaller, composite and intricate processes of change. This has been the platform where battles over Community programs have been fought; where national governments have grabbed a hold of and accelerated European integration outside EU institutions in the Bologna process; and where leaps have been made inside the established patterns of cooperation and coordination.

There are many different types of processes of European cooperation, coordination and integration that pertain to changes in the parameters of the primary activities of the University, teaching and research. In the current political language these processes are referred to as belonging to a "Europe of Knowledge" and to the efforts to create European areas of higher education and research. These processes are traceable and can be studied empirically down to the level of local practice, in order to see whether European integration initiatives have penetrated the University all the way into its basic activities, that is, the day-to-day teaching and learning activities and research endeavors. It is a potent area for theory-based empirical studies of the multi-level character of the political order of Europe that accommodate the need go beyond the study of European integration as merely involving the two levels of governance – that is, the relationship between the European level and state level – and to adequately address the sub-national, operational level.

While the main ambition has been to shed light upon the dynamics of the European University, the proposed research agenda also offers an encore. The agenda is, for several reasons, likely to contribute to a better understanding of European integration in general.

First, in the EU different policy sectors are differently organized and governed and research on European integration cannot but benefit from broadening the range of sectors and institutional spheres that constitute its basis for analysis.

Second, much of European integration theory has been founded on analyses of economic sectors and objectives, and in particular on studies of the European Community as market building. In comparison, researching the University enables a theoretical understanding based on integration also of the European cultural sphere and the University as an institution standing in the area of tension between economy and culture, and between national political ambition and market adjustment. The four visions elaborated make the case for understanding the University in its different dimensions and suggest that understanding the effects of European integration on the University feeds our insights into the dynamics of European integration that a focus on economic integration alone cannot.

Third, University studies may teach us something about comparative and non-synchronized dynamics and the conditions under which integration is likely to speed up or stagnate. At a time when the European Union in many aspects is at a hold, the European integration efforts aimed directly at the University are intensifying and are representing a period of experimentation and innovation. The level of aspiration has been raised and deliberate efforts of integration and coordination have gained considerable momentum the past five years. This development is in particular surprising on the backdrop of earlier observations of higher education and research as a policy area where European integration has been difficult due to national political sensitivity and systemic diversity.

Finally, exactly because the European University is involved in a search for a new foundational pact, and therefore in inter-institutional processes, studies of University dynamics may help counteract the tendency in integration research to focus on a single institution or policy area.

REFERENCES

Abrahamson, E. 1991, Managerial fads and fashions; the diffusion and rejection of innovation. *Academy of Management Review*, 16: 586–612.

Aho, E. et al. 2006, *Creating an Innovative Europe*. Report of the Independent Expert Group on R&D and Innovation appointed following the Hampton Court Summit. (http://Europe.eu.int/invest-in-research/)

Albæk, E. 1988, *Fra Sannhed til Information*. København: Akademisk Forlag.

Allègre, C. 2002, University autonomy, academic accountability and European integration. In Observatory for Fundamental University Values and Rights: *Autonomy and Responsibility. The University's Obligations for the XXI Century*. Proceedings of the Launch Event for the Magna Charta Observatory 21–22 September 2001. Bologna: Bononia University Press, 17–27.

Altbach, P. 1992, Politics of students and faculty. In B.R. Clark and G. Neave (eds.) *The Encyclopedia of Higher Education*. Vol. 2. New York: Pergamon Press, 1438–1444.

Amaral, A. and A. Magalhães 2004, Epidemology and the Bologna Saga. *Higher Education*, 48: 79–100.

Amaral, A., O. Fulton and I.M. Larsen 2003, A managerial revolution? In A. Amaral, V.L. Meek and I.M. Larsen (eds.) *The Higher Education Managerial Revolution?* Dordrecht: Kluwer Academic Publishers, 275–296.

Amaral, A., V.L. Meek and I.M. Larsen (eds.) 2003, *The Higher Education Managerial Revolution?* Dordrecht: Kluwer Academic Publishers.

Ash, M.G. (ed.) 1999, *Mythos Humboldt: Vergangenheit und Zukunft der deutschen Universitäten*. Vienna: Böhlau verlag.

Ash, M.G. 2005, Bachelor of what, master of whom? The humboldt myth and historical transformations of higher education in German speaking Europe and the United States. In T. Halvorsen and A. Nyhagen (eds.) *The Bologna Process and the Shaping of the Future Knowledge Societies*. Bergen: LOS, 7–21.

Ashby, E. and M. Anderson 1966, *Universities: British, Indian, African. A Study of the Ecology of Higher Education*. London: Weidenfeld and Nicolson.

Askling, B., M. Bauer and S. Marton 1999, *Transforming Universities. Changing Patterns of Governance, Structure and Learning in Swedish Higher Education*. London: Jessica Kingsley.

Association of Governing Boards of Universities and Colleges 1996, *Renewing the Academic Presidency: Stronger Leadership for Tougher Times*. Washington DC: Report of the Commission on the Academic Presidency.

Bache, I. 2006, The Europeanization of higher education: markets, politics or learning? *Journal of Common Market Studies*, 44(2): 231–248.

Baldridge, J.V. 1971, *Power and Conflict in the University. Research in the Sociology of Complex Organizations*. New York: John Wiley and Sons.

Banchoff, T. 2002, Institutions, inertia and European Union research policy. *Journal of Common Market Studies*, 40(1): 1–21.

Banchoff, T. 2003, Political dynamics of the ERA. In J. Edler, S. Kuhlmann and M. Behrens (eds.) *Changing Governance of Research and Technology Policy – The European Research Area*. Cheltenham: Edward Elgar Publishing, 81–97.

Barabba, V., J. Pourdehnad and R.L. Ackoff 2002, On misdirecting management. *Strategy & Leadership*, 30(5): 5–9.

Barroso, J.M. 2005, *Strong Universities for Europe*. Glasgow 2 April 2005. Speech to the European Universities Association Convention.

Barroso, J.M. 2006, *More Europe Where it Matters*. Speech to the European Parliament, Strasbourg, 15th March 2006 (Speech/06/168).

Bartolini, S. 2005, *Restructuring Europe. Centre Formation, System Building and Political Structuring Between the Nation State and the EU.* Oxford: Oxford University Press.

Bartz, O. 2005, Bundesrepublikanische Universitätsleitbilder: Blüte und Zerfall des Humboldtianismus. *die hochschule. journal für wissenschaft und bildung* 3(2): 99–114.

Baumgarten, M. 1997, *Professoren und Universitäten im 19. Jahrhundert. Zur Sozialgeschichte deutscher Geistes- und Naturwissenschaftler.* Göttingen: V& R.

Baumgartner, M. 2001, Professoren- und Universitätsprofile im "Humboldtischen Modell". In R.C. Schwinges, (ed.) *Humboldt International. Der Export des deutschen Universitätsmodells im 19. und 20. Jahrhundert.* Basel: Schwabe, 1810–1914.

Becher, T. 1989, *Academic Tribes and Territories.* Milton Keynes: Open University Press.

Becker, C.H. 1919, *Gedanken zur Hochschulreform.* Leipzig.

Ben-David, J. 1960, Scientific productivity and academic organisation in nineteenth-century medicine. *American Sociological Review,* XXV: 828–843.

Ben-David, J. 1983, Rivalität und kooperation. Wettwerbbedingungen an amerikanischen und deutschen Universitäten. *Hochschulpolitische Information,* 14: 3–6.

Benner, M. and U. Sandström 2000, Institutionalizing the triple helix: Research funding and norms in the academic system. *Research Policy,* 29(2): 291–301.

Benner, M. 2001, *Kontrovers och consensus: Vetenskap och politik i svenskt 1990-tal.* Stockholm: Nya Doxa.

Bennich-Björkman, L. 2004, *Överlever den akademiska friheten? – en intervjuundersökning av svenska forskares villkor i universitetens brytningstid.* Stockholm: HSV.

Berdahl, R. 1990, Academic freedom, autonomy and accountability in British universities. *Studies in Higher Education,* 15: 169–180.

Bergan, S. 2003, Student participation in higher education governance. Paper presented to the *Bologna seminar on student participation in higher education.* SIU, Bergen, June.

Bergan, S., A. Persson, F. Plantan, S. Musteata, and A. Garabagiu 2004, *The university as res publica – Higher education governance, student participation and the university as a site of citizenship.* Strasbourg: Council of Europe higher education series.

Bernal, J.D. 1969 (paperback ed.) [1939], *The Social Function of Science.* Cambridge: The MIT Press.

Bertilsson, T.M. 2002, *Researchers in Europe: A Scarce Resource?* Muscipol Workshop, Athens, 10–11 October.

Beukel, E. 2001, Educational policy: Institutionalization and multi-level governance. In S.S. Andersen and K.A. Eliassen (eds.) *Making Policy in Europe.* London: Sage, 124–125.

Birnbaum, R. 2000, *Management Fads in Higher Education: Where They Come From, What They Do, Why They Fail.* San Francisco: Jossey-Bass.

Björnsson, A., M. Kylhammar and Å. Linderborg (eds.) 2005, *Ord i rättan tid.* Stockholm: Calssons.

Blau, P. 1955, *The Dynamics of Bureaucracy.* Chicago, I: University of Chicago Press.

Bleiklie, I. 2005, Organizing higher education in a knowledge society. *Higher Education,* 49(1–2): 31–59.

Blomquist, G. 1992, *Elfenbenstorn och statsskepp. Stat, universitet och akademisk frihet 1820–1920.* Lund: Lund University Press.

Blomquist, G., H. Jalling and K. Lundequist 1996, The academic profession in Sweden. In P.G. Altbach (ed.) *The Academic Profession. Portraits of Fourteen Countries.* Princeton: The Carnegie Foundation for the Advancement of Teaching, 529–567.

Boer, H. de 2002, On nails, coffins and councils. *European Journal of Education,* 37(1): 7–20.

Boer, H. de 2003, *Institutionele verandering en professionele autonomie. Een empirisch-verklarende studie naar de doorwerking van de wet 'Modernisering Universitaire Bestuursorganisatie' (MUB).* Enschede: Center for Higher Education Policy Studies/University of Twente.

Boer, H. de and B. Denters 1999, Analysis of institutions of university governance: a classification scheme applied to postwar changes in Dutch higher education. In B. Jongbloed, P. Maassen and G. Neave (eds.) *From the Eye of the Storm; Higher Education's Changing Institution.* Dordrecht: Kluwer Academic Publishers, 211–233.

Boer, H. de, B. Denters, and L. Goedegebuure 1998, On boards and councils; shaky balances considered. The governance of Dutch universities. *Higher Education Policy*, 11(2/3), 153–164.

Boer, H. de, P. Maassen, and E. de Weert 1999, The troublesome Dutch university and its route 66 towards a new governance structure. *Higher Education Policy*, 12(4): 329–342.

Bois-Reymond, E. du 1887, *Biographie. Wissenschaft. Ansprachen*. Leipzig: Von Veit.

Bok, D. 2003, *Universities in the Marketplace: The Commercialization of Higher Education*. Princeton, NJ: Princeton University Press.

Borras, S. and K. Jacobsson 2004, The open method of co-ordination and new governance patterns in the EU. *Journal of European Public Policy*, 11(2): 185–208.

Brennan, J. and T. Shah 2000, Quality assessment and institutional change: experiences from 14 countries. *Higher Education*, 40: 331–349.

Brofoss, K.E. and O. Wiig 2000, *Departmentenes FoU engasjement – Utviklingstrekk på 1990-tallet*. Oslo: NIFU Rapport 1/2000.

Bruno, A., S. Jaquot and L. Mandin 2006, Europeanization through its instrumentation: benchmarking, mainstreaming and the open method of co-ordination ... toolbox or pandora's box? *Journal of European Public Policy*, 13(4): 519–536.

Brunsson, N. and B. Jacobsson 2000, The contemporary expansion of standardization. In N. Brunsson, B. Jacobsson and associates *A World of Standards*. Oxford: Oxford University Press, 1–17.

Brunsson, N. and J.P. Olsen 1993, *The Reforming Organization*. London: Routledge. Reprinted 1997, Bergen: Fagbokforlaget.

Brunsson, N. and J.P. Olsen 1998, Organization theory: thirty years of dismantling, and then...? In N. Brunsson and J.P. Olsen (eds.) *Organizing Organizations*. Oslo: Fagbokforlaget, 13–43.

Bulmer, S. and M. Burch 1998, Organizing for Europe: Whitehall, the British State and the European Union. *Public Administration*, 76: 601–628.

Bulmer, S. and S. Padgett 2004, Policy transfer in the European Union: an institutionalist perspective. *British Journal of Political Science*, 35: 103–126.

Burquel, N. 2005, *Conditions for institutional strategies of modernization*. Institutional governance. Report from the conference: "Enabling European Higher education to make its full contribution to the knowledge economy and society." Brussels: DG Education and Culture/EU-Commission.

Bush, V. 1945, *Science – The Endless Frontier: A Report to the President on a Program for Postwar Scientific Research*, July 1945. Reprinted by NSF, Washington, DC, 1990.

Caracostas, P. 2003, Shared Governance Through mutual policy learning – Some implications of the ERA strategy for the open co-ordination of research policies in Europe. In J. Edler, S. Kuhlmann and M. Behrens (eds.) *Changing Governance of Research and Technology Policy – The European Research Area*. Cheltenham: Edward Elgar Publishing, 33–63.

Caswill, C. 2003, Old games, old players – new rules, new results. Influence and agency in the European Research Area (ERA). In J. Edler, S. Kuhlmann and M. Behrens (eds.) *Changing Governance of Research and Technology Policy – The European Research Area*. Cheltenham: Edward Elgar Publishing, 64–80.

Cavallin, M. and S. Lindblad 2006, *Världsmästerskap i vetenskap? En granskning av internationella rankinglistor och deras sätt att hantera kvaliteter hos universitetet*. Göteborg: Göteborgs Universitet Dnr G11 530/06.

Cerych, L. and P. Sabatier 1986, *Great Expectations and Mixed Performance: The Implementation of Higher Education Reforms in Europe*. Stoke-on-Trent: Trentham Books.

Chalmers, D. and M. Lodge 2003, *The Open Method of Co-ordination and the European Welfare State*. London School of Economics: EXRC Centre for Analysis of Risk and Regulation. Discussion paper no. 11, June 2003.

Checkel, S J. 2007, Social mechanisms and regional cooperation: are Europe and the EU really all that different? In A. Acharya and A.I. Johnston (eds.) *Crafting Cooperation: Regional Institutions in Comparative Perspective*. Cambridge, MA: Cambridge University Press (forthcoming).

CHINC 2006, *Changes in University Incomes: Their Impact on University-Based Research and Innovation* (CHINC), Final Report. Sevilla. Joint Research Centre IPTS.

Clark, B.R. 1983, *The Higher Education System. Academic Organization in Cross-National Perspective.* Berkeley, CA: University of California Press.

Clark, B.R. 1995, *Places of Inquiry. Research and Advanced Education in Modern Universities.* Berkeley, CA: University of California Press.

Clark, B.R. 1998, *Creating Entrepreneurial Universities: Organizational Pathways of Transformation.* Oxford: Pergamon.

Clark, B.R. 2004, *Sustaining Change in Universities. Continuities in Case Studies and Concepts.* Maidenhead: SHRE/Open University Press.

Cohen, M.D. and J.G. March 1974, *Leadership and Ambiguity. The American College President.* New York: McGraw Hill. (2nd ed. 1986). Boston, MA: Harvard Business School Press.

Cohen, M.D., J.G. March and J.P. Olsen 1972, A garbage can model of organizational choice. *Administrative Science Quarterly,* 17: 1–25.

Cohen, M.D., J.G. March and J.P. Olsen 1976, People, Problems, Solutions and the Ambiguity of Relevance. In J.G. March and J.P. Olsen (eds.) *Ambiguity and Choice in Organizations.* Bergen, MA: Universitetsforlaget, 24–37.

Cohen, M.D., J.G. March and J.P. Olsen 2007, The Garbage Can Model. To appear in S. Clegg and J.R. Bailey (eds.) *International Encyclopedia of Organization Studies.* London: Sage (forthcoming).

Cole, J.R., E.G. Barber, and St.R. Graubard (eds.) 1994, *The Research University in a Time of Discontent.* Baltimore, MD: Johns Hopkins University Press.

Cole, S. and T.J. Phelan 1999, The scientific productivity of nations. *Minerva,* 37(1): 1–23.

Commissie, P. 1979, *Gewubd en gewogen.* Tweede Kamer der Staten-Generaal, zitting 1978–1979, 15 515. 's-Gravenhage: SDU Uitgeverij.

Commission 1991, *Memorandum on Higher Education in the European Community.* COM (91)349 final.

Commission 1993, *Growth, competitiveness, employment. The challenges and ways forward into the 21st century.* Brussels: European Commission (Delors White Paper).

Commission 1995, *Teaching and Learning. Towards the Learning Society.* Brussels/Luxembourg: White Paper on education and training.

Commission 1995b, *Green Paper on Innovation.* Brussels: European Commission.

Commission 2000a, *Towards a European Research Area.* Brussels: COM (2000) 6.

Commission 2000b, *Making a reality of The European Research Area: Guidelines for EU research activities (2002–2006).* Brussels: COM(2000) 612 final.

Commission 2000c, *Development of an open method of co-ordination for benchmarking national research policies – Objectives, methodology and indicators.* Working document from the Commission services. Brussels, 3 November 2000. SEC (2000) 1842.

Commission 2001, European Governance. *White Paper.* Brussels.

Commission 2002a, *The European Research Area: An Internal Knowledge Market.* Luxembourg: Office for Official Publications of the European Communities. http://ec.europa.eu/research/era/leaflet/pdf/era_en.pdf

Commission 2002b, *More research for Europe. Towards 3% of GDP.* Brussels: COM(2002) 499 final.

Commission 2002c, *The European Research Area: Providing New Momentum. Strengthening-Reorienting-Opening up New Perspectives.* Brussels COM (2002) 565.

Commission 2002d, *European Benchmarks in education and training: follow-up to the Lisbon European Council.* 20.11.2002 COM(2002) 629 final.

Commission 2003a, *The role of the universities in the Europe of knowledge.* Brussels: COM(2003) 58 final.

Commission 2003b, rec recommendation of 11 March 2003; "Putting the Charter and Code into context: Keeping Europe competitive.

Commission 2003c, *"Education & Training 2010" The Success of the Lisbon Strategy hinges on Urgent Reform.* Draft joint interim report on the implementation of the detailed work programme on the follow-up of the objectives of education and training systems in Europe. Communication from the Commission COM (2003) 685 final.

Commission 2003d, *Investing in research – an action plan for Europe*. Communication from the Commission. Brussels 4/6.2003.: COM (2003) 226 final/2.

Commission 2004a, *Outcome of the stakeholders' consultation*. Brussels, European Commission Research Directorate General, 6 April 2004 C1(03) D/568721.

Commission 2004b, *The Europe of knowledge 2020: A vision for university-based research and innovation*. Liège, Belgium 25–28 April 2004, Conference Proceedings edited by G. Blythe, B. Hasewend and B. Laget.

Commission 2005a, *Mobilising the brainpower of Europe: enabling universities to make their full contribution to the Lisbon Strategy*. Brussels: COM(2005) 152 final.

Commission 2005b, *The European Charter for Researchers. The Code of Conduct for the Recruitment of Researchers*. Brussels: Directorate-General for research, Human Resources and Mobility (www.europa.eu.int/eracareers/europeancharter).

Commission 2005c, *More Research and Innovation A Common Approach*. COM(2005) 488.

Commission 2006a, *Implementing the renewed partnership for growth and jobs. Developing a knowledge flagship: the European Institute of Technology*. Brussels: COM(2006) 77 final.

Commission 2006b, *Delivering on the modernization agenda for universities: Education, research and innovation*. Brussels: COM(2006) 208 final.

Commission 2006c, *Frequently asked questions: why European higher education systems must be modernized?* Brussels, 10 May 2006 MEMO/06/190.

Commission 2006d, *Education and Training 2010, diverse systems, shared goals – the education and training contribution to the Lisbon strategy* http://ec.europa.eu/education/policies/2010/et_2010_en.html

Conraths, B. and H. Smidt 2005, *Funding of University-Based Research and Innovation in Europe*. Brussels: European University Association.

Consolazio, W.V. 1965, Dilemma of academic biology in Europe. In N. Kaplan (ed.) *Science and Society* 1965: 322–333. Chicago: Rand McNally. Reprinted from *Science* June 16 1961, Vol. CXXXIII: 1892–1896.

Corbett, A. 2005, *Universities and the Europe of Knowledge: Ideas, Institutions and Policy Entrepreneurship in European Union Higher Education 1955–2005*. Houndmills: Palgrave Macmillan.

Council 2002, *Council Conclusions*. 2467th Council meeting – Competitiveness (Internal Market, Industry, Research) – Brussels, 26 November 2002. 14365/02 (Press 360).

Council 2006, *Contribution of the Competitiveness Council to the Spring European Council 2006*, Brussels 3rd March 2006. 7281/06.

Council and Commission 2004, Education & Training 2010 – The Success of the Lisbon *Strategy Hinges on Urgent Reforms*. Joint interim report of the Council and the Commission on the implementation of the detailed work programme on the follow- up of the objectives of education and training systems in Europe. Adopted by the Council on 26 February 2004 (ec.europa.eu/education/policies/2010/doc/jir_council_final.pdf).

Council of Europe 2004, *European Year of Citizenship Through Education 2005*. Strasbourg: Council of Europe.

Council of Europe 2006, *Academic freedom and university autonomy*. Recommendation 1762 (2006) from the Parliamentary Assembly of the Council of Europe. http://assembly.coe.int/Documents/AdoptedText/ta06/ERec1762.htm

Crawford, E., T. Shinn and S. Sörlin 1993, *Denationalizing Science. The Context of International Scientific Practice*. Dordrecht: Kluwer Academic Publishers.

CREST 1995, *Council Resolution of 28 September 1995 on Crest*. Official Journal, CREST C264, 11/10/1995.

CREST 2003a, *Draft summary conclusions of the 287th meeting of the scientific and technical research committee* (CREST) held in Brussels on 14 January 2003. CREST 1201/03.

CREST 2003b, *Draft summary conclusions of the 288th meeting of the scientific and technical research committee* (CREST) held in Iraklion, Greece, on 27 and 28 March 2003. CREST 1203/03.

CREST 2003c, *Draft summary conclusions of the 290th meeting of the scientific and technical research committee* (CREST) held in Genova, Italy, on 27 and 28 October 2003. CREST 1205/03.

CREST 2004a, *Draft summary conclusions of the 294th meeting of the scientific and technical research committee* (CREST) held in Brussels on 29 June 2004. CREST 1204/04.

CREST 2004b, *On the application of the open method of coordination in favour of the Barcelona research investment objective.* Brussels: European Union, CREST report 1.10.2004. Council doc. CREST 1206/04.

CREST 2004c, *Draft summary conclusions of the 295th meeting of the scientific and technical research committee* (CREST) held in Brussels on 16 July 2004.

CREST 2005, *Report from the Sub-group on the Modus Operandi for the 2nd cycle OMC.* Note to CREST delegations. Brussels 12. January 2005, CREST 1201/05.

CREST 2005a, *Draft summary conclusions 304th meeting of the scientific and technical research committee* (CREST) held in Manchester 19/20 October 2005.

CREST 2006, *Draft summary conclusions of the 307th meeting of the scientific and technical research committee* (CREST) held in Brussels on 19 May 2006. CREST 1204/06.

Crosland, M. (ed.) 1975, *The Emergence of Science in Western Europe.* London: MacMillan.

Currie, J., R. DeAngelis, H. de Boer, J. Huisman and C. Lacotte 2003, *Globalizing Practices and University Responses: European and Anglo-American Differences.* Westport: Praeger.

Cyert, R.M. and J.G. March 1963, *A Behavioral Theory of the Firm.* Englewood Cliffs: Prentice-Hall [2nd edition 1992, Oxford: Basil Blackwell].

Daalder, H. 1982, The sudden revolution and the sluggish aftermath: a retrospect since 1968. In H. Daalder and E. Shils (eds.) *Universities, Politicians and Bureaucrats. Europe and the United States.* Cambridge: University Press, 489–510.

Daalder, H. and E. Shils (eds.) 1982, *Universities, Politicians, and Bureaucrats: Europe and the United States.* Cambridge/New York: Cambridge University Press.

Dahl, R. 1966, *The Political System.* New York: Knopf.

Davies, H. 2004, *Higher Education in the Internal Market.* UACES European Studies Online Essays. No 3. http://www.uaces.org/E53Davies.pdf

De Elera, A. 2006, The European research area: On the way towards a European scientific community? *European Law Journal,* 12(5): 559–574.

Dehousse, R. 2002, "The Open Method of Coordination: A New Policy Paradigm?" Paper presented at the First Pan-European Conference On European Union Policies *"The Politics of European Integration: Academic Acquis and Future Challenges,"* Bordeaux, 26–28 September 2002.

Dill, D.D. 1992, Administration: Academic. In B. Clark and G. Neave. *The Encyclopedia of Higher Education.* Vol. 2. New York: Pergamon Press.

DiMaggio, P.J and Powell, W.W 1991, The iron cage revisited: Institutional isomorphism and collective rationality in organizational fields. In W.W. Powell and P.J. Dimaggio (eds.) *The New Institutionalism in Organizational Analysis.* Chicago, I: Chicago University Press, 63–82.

Douglass, J.A. 2000, *The California Idea and American Higher Education. 1950 to the 1960 Master Plan.* Stanford, CA: Stanford University Press.

Duderstadt, J.J. 2002, *Governing the 21st Century University: A view from the bridge.* Speech to the Association for the Study of Higher Education, Sacramento, California, 23 November 2002. http://milproj.ummu.umich.edu/publications/view_from_bridge/download/view_from_bridge.pdf

Economist, The 2005, *The Brains business.* 8 September.

Edler, J. 2003, Changes in European R&D policy as a complex consensus-building process. In J. Edler, S. Kuhlmann and M. Behrens (eds.) *Changing Governance of Research and Technology Policy – The European Research Area.* Cheltenham: Edward Elgar Publishing, 98–132.

Egeberg, M. 2006a, Europe's executive branch of government in the melting pot – an overview. In M. Egeberg (ed.) *Multilevel Union Administration. On the Transformation of Executive Politics within the European Union.* Houndmills: Palgrave Macmillan, 1–16.

Egeberg, M. 2006b, The commission: Balancing autonomy and accountability. In M. Egeberg (ed.) *Multilevel Union Administration. On the Transformation of Executive Politics within the European Union* Houndmills: Palgrave Macmillan, 31–49.

Egeberg, M. (ed.) 2006c, *The Multi-Level Community Administration: On the Transformation of Executive Politics within the European Union*. Houndmills: Palgrave Macmillan.

Ehrenberg, R.G. 2000, *Tuition rising: Why College Costs so Much*. Cambridge, MA: Harvard University Press.

Eisenstein, E.H. 1980, *The Printing Press as an Agent of Change: Communications and Cultural Transformations in Early-modern Europe Volumes I and II*. Cambridge, MA: Cambridge University Press.

Ellwein, T. 1985, *Die deutsche Universität*. Athenäum: Köningstein.

Elzinga, A. 2004, The new production of reductionism in models relating to research. In K. Grandin, N. Worms and S. Widmalm (eds.) *The Science-Industry Nexus. History, Policy, Implications*. Sagamore Beach: Science History Publications, 277–304.

Enders, J. 2004, Higher education, internationalization, and the nation-state: Recent developments and challenges to governance theory. *Higher Education*, 47: 361–382.

Enders, J., J. File, J. Huisman and D. Westerheijden (eds.) 2005, *The European Higher Education and Research Landscape 2020. Scenarios and Strategic Debates*. Enschede: Center for Higher Education Policy Studies.

Engwall, L. and T. Nybom 2007, The visible vs the invisible hand. Allocation of research resources in Swedish universities. In R. Whitley (ed.) *The Changing Governance of the Sciences. The Advent of Research Evaluation Systems*. Berlin: Springer.

ERT 1995, *Education for Europeans – Towards the Learning Society*. Brussels: The European Roundtable of Industrialists.

Etzkovitz, H. and L. Leydesdorff 1997, *Universities and the Global Knowledge Economy: A Triple Helix of University – Industry – Government Relations*. London: Pinter/Cassel.

European Council 2000, *Presidency conclusions from the Lisbon European Council*. 23–24 March 2000.

European Ministers Responsible for Education 1999, *The Bologna Declaration of 19 June 1999*. Joint Declaration of the European Ministers of Education.

European Ministers Responsible for Education 2001, *Towards the European Higher Education Area*. Communiqué of the meeting of European Ministers in Charge of Higher Education. Prague, May 19th 2001. www.bologna-Berlin2003.de/pdf/Prague_communiquTheta.pdf#search=%22Prague%20communique%22

European Ministers Responsible for Education 2003, *Realizing the European Higher Education Area*. Communiqué of the Conference of Ministers responsible for Higher Education. Berlin, 19th September 2003. www.bmbwk.gv.at/europa/bp/**berlink**omm.xml

European Ministers Responsible for Education 2005, *Bergen Communiqué. The European Higher Education Area – Achieving the Goals*. www.bologna-bergen2005.no/Docs/ 00-Main_doc/050520_Bergen_Communique.pdf

European Parliament and Council 2005, *Directive 2005/36/EC of 7 September 2005 on the recognition of professional qualifications*. L 255/22. Official Journal of the European Union 30/09/2005. (http://www.europarl.europa.eu/oeil/file.jsp?id=220062)

European Science Foundation 2003, *New structures for the support of high-quality research in Europe*. http://www.esf.org/publication/159/ercpositionpaper.pdf

European University Association 2003, *The role of the universities in shaping the future of Europe*. EUA statement to the European Convention, 29 January 2003.

European University Association 2006, *A vision and strategy for Europe's universities and the European University Association*. EUA, 12 March 2006. http://www.eua.be/eua/jsp/en/client/item_view.jsp?type_id=1& item_id=3168

Febvre, L. and H.-J. Martin 1976, *The Coming of the Book: The Impact of Printing 1450–1800*. London: Verso.

Felt, U. 2004, University autonomy in Europe: Shifting paradigms of university research? In: Observatory for Fundamental University Values and Rights, *Managing University Autonomy. Shifting Paradigms in University Research*: 15–99. Proceedings from the seminar of the Magna Charta Observatory, 15 September 2003. Bologna: Bononia University Press.

Figel, J. 2006, *International competitiveness in higher education – A European perspective.* Oxford, 3 April 2006, Association of Heads of University Administration, Annual Conference. http://ec.europa.eu/commission_barroso/figel/speeches/docs/06_04_03_Oxford_en.pdf

Flexner, A. 1930, *Universities American – English – German,* New York: Oxford University Press.

Forman, P. 2002, *In the Era of the Ear-mark: The Post-modern Pejoration of Meritocracy and of Peer-review.* (mim.)

Frängsmyr, T. 2000, *Svensk idéhistoria.* Stockholm: Natur & Kultur.

Frank, R.H. and Ph.J. Cook 1995, *The Winner-Take-All Society.* New York: The Free Press.

Frijhoff, W. 1992, Universities 1500–1900. In B.R. Clark and G. Neave (eds.) *The Encyclopedia of Higher Education.* Oxford: Pergamon Press, 1251–1259.

Fuller, S. 2003, Can universities solve the problem of knowledge in society without succumbing to the knowledge society? *Policy Futures in Education,* 1(1): 106–124.

Fulton, O. 2002, Higher Education Governance in the UK: Change and Continuity. In A. Amaral, G.A. Jones and B. Karseth (eds) *Governing Higher Education: National Perspectives on Institutional Governance.* Dordrecht: Kluwer Academic Publishers, 178–212.

Gardner, J.W. 1962 [1961], *Excellence. Can We Be Equal and Excellent Too?* New York: Harper Colophon Books, Harper and Row.

Geiger, R. 1991, The American University and Research: A historical perspective. In M.A. Trow and T. Nybom (eds.) *University and Society. Essays on the Social Role of Research and Higher Education* London: Jessica Kingsley Press, 200–215.

Geiger, R. 1993, *Research and Relevant Knowledge. American Research Universities since World War II.* Oxford: Oxford University Press.

Geiger, R. 2004, *Knowledge & Money. Research Universities and the Paradox of the Marketplace.* Stanford, CA: Stanford University Press.

Gerbod, P. 2004a, Relations with authority. In W. Rüegg (ed.) *A History of the University in Europe. Vol. III Universities in the Nineteenth and Early Twentieth Centuries (1800–1945).* Cambridge, MA: Cambridge University Press, 83–100.

Gerbod, P. 2004b, Resources and management. In: W. Rüegg (ed.) *A History of the University in Europe. Vol. III Universities in the Nineteenth and Early Twentieth Centuries (1800–1945).* Cambridge, MA: Cambridge University Press, 101–121.

Geurts, P. and P. Maassen 1996, Academics and institutional governance: An international comparative analysis of governance issues in Germany, the Netherlands, Sweden, and the United Kingdom. In P. Maassen and F. van Vught (eds.) *Inside Academia. New Challenges for the Academic Profession.* Utrecht: De Tijdstroom, 69–83.

Geurts, P. and P. Maassen 2005, Academics and institutional governance. In A. Welch (ed.) *The Professoriate. Profile of a Profession.* Dordrecht: Springer, 35–59.

Gibbons, M. et al. 1994, *The New Production of Knowledge.* London: Sage.

Goedegebuure, L. et al. 1993, *Higher Education Policy. An International Comparative Perspective.* Oxford: Pergamon Press.

Godin, B. 2002, The number makers: fifty years of science and technology official statistics. *Minerva,* 40: 375–397.

Godin, B. 2004, The New Economy: what the concept owes to the OECD. *Research Policy,* 33: 679–690.

Godø, H. (ed.) 2004, *Evaluation of Norway's participation in the EU's 5th Framework Programme.* Oslo: NIFU, STEP and Technopolis.

Gornitzka, Å. 2003, *Science, Clients, and the State. A Study of the Scientific Knowledge Production and Use.* Enschede: CHEPS/University of Twente.

Gornitzka, Å. 2006, What is the use of Bologna in national reform? The case of the Norwegian quality reform in higher education. In V. Tomusk (ed.) *Creating the European Area of Higher Education: Voices from Peripheries.* Dordrecht: Springer, 19–41.

Gornitzka, Å., M. Kogan and A. Amaral 2005, Introduction. In Å. Gornitzka, M. Kogan and A. Amaral (eds.) *Reform and Change in Higher Education – Analysing Policy Implementation.* Dordrecht: Springer, 1–14.

Gornitzka, Å., S. Kyvik and B. Stensaker 2005, Implementation analysis in higher education. In Å. Gornitzka, M. Kogan and A. Amaral (eds.) *Reform and Change in Higher Education. Analysing Policy Implementation.* Dordrecht: Springer, 35–57.

Gornitzka, Å. and P. Maassen 2000a, Editorial. The economy, higher education, and European integration: an introduction. *Higher Education Policy*, 13: 217–225.

Gornitzka, Å. and P. Maassen 2000b, Hybrid steering approaches with respect to European higher education. *Higher Education Policy*, 13: 267–285.

Gornitzka, Å. and P. Maassen 2003, Europeiske universiteter mellom marked og myndighet. In I.M. Larsen and B. Stensaker (eds.) *Tradisjon og tilpasning – organisering og styring av universitetene.* Oslo: Cappelen Akademisk Forlag, 35–58.

Gornitzka, Å. and J.P. Olsen 2006, Making sense of change in University governance. *IAU Horizons World Higher Education News* 11.4–12.1: 1–3, 10–11.

Gouldner, A.W. 1957, Cosmopolitans and locals: Toward an analysis of latent social roles. *Administrative Science Quarterly*, 3: 281–292.

Greer, S.L. 2006, Uninvited Europeanization: neofunctionalism and the EU in health policy. *Journal of European Public Policy*, 13(1): 134–152.

Gronbaek, D.J. 2003, A European research council: an idea whose time has come? *Science and Public Policy*, 39(6): 391–404.

Groof, J. de, G. Neave and J. Svec 1998, *Governance and Democracy in Higher Education*, Vol. 2, The Council of Europe series Legislating for higher education in Europe, Dordrecht: Kluwer Academic Publishers.

Gulbrandsen, M. and L. Langfeldt 2004, In search of 'Mode 2': the nature of knowledge production in norway. *Minerva*, 42: 237–250.

Gulbrandsen, M. and J.-C. Smeby 2005, *Forskning ved Universitetene – Rammebetingelser, relevans og resultater.* Oslo: Cappelen Akademisk Forlag.

Gumport, P.J. 2000, Academic restructuring: Organizational change and institutional imperatives. *Higher Education*, 39: 67–91.

Gustavsson, S. 1971, *Debatten om forskningen och samhället. En studie i några teoretiska inlägg under 1900-talet.* Stockholm: Almqvist & Wiksell.

Gustavsson, S. 1997, Forskningens frihet efter det kalla kriget. In C. Öhman (ed.) *Uppsala Universitet inför 2000-talet. Festskrift för Stig Strömholm.* Uppsala: Acta Universitatis Upsalaensis, 39–60.

Guston, D.H. and K. Kenniston 1994, Introduction: the social contract for science. In D.H. Guston and K. Kenniston (eds.) *The Fragile Contract.* Cambridge/London: MIT press, 1–41.

Guzzetti, L. 1995, *A Brief History of European Union Research Policy.* Luxembourg: Office for Official Publications of the European Communities.

Habermas, J. 1967, Universität in der Demokratie – Demokratisierung der Universität. *Merkur*, XXI (5): 416–433.

Habermas, J. 1971, Die deutsche Mandarine. In Habermas, *Philosophisch-politische Profile.* Frankfurt am Main: Suhrkamp, 239–251.

Habermas, J. 1987, The idea of the University: learning processes. *New German Critique*, 41 (Special Issue): 3–22.

Hackl, E. 2001, The intrusion and expansion of community policies in higher education. *Higher Education Management*, 13(3): 99–117.

Hallstein, W. 1969, *Der Unvollendete Bundesstaat. Europäische Erfahrungen und Erkenntnisse.* Düsseldorf & Wien: Econ Verlag.

Hallstein, W. 1972, *Europe in the Making.* London George Allen & Unwin Ltd. [In German: 1969].

Halvorsen, A. 1967, *Et universitet i vekst.* Oslo: Universitetsforlaget.

Hanney, S.R., M.A. Gonzalez-Block, M.J. Buxton, and M. Kogan 2003, The utilization of health research in policy-making: concepts, examples and methods of assessment. *Health Research Policy and Systems*, 1: 2. www.health-policy-systems.com/content/1/1/2.

Haug, G. 1999, *Visions of a European future. Bologna and beyond.* Maastricht: Key note speech to the European Association for International Education. http://.eaie.org/about/speech.html

Hayes, D.A. and J.G. March 1970, *The Normative Problem of University Governance*. Harvard University/Stanford University: Manuscript.

Heller, F. 1998, Influence at work: a 25-year program of research. *Human Relations*, 51(12): 1425–1456.

Hennis, W. 1982, Germany: legislators and the universities. In H. Daalder and E. Shils (eds.) *Universities, Politicians and Bureaucrats. Europe and the United States*. Cambridge, MA: Cambridge University Press, 1–30.

Hobsbawm, E.J. 1987, *The Age of Empire*. London: Weidenfield & Nicholson.

Holm, P. 1995, The dynamics of institutionalisation: transformation processes in Norwegian fisheries. *Administrative Science Quarterly*, 40: 398–422.

Hood, C., O. James, B.G. Peters and C. Scott (eds.) 2004, *Controlling Modern Government. Variety, Commonality and Change*. Cheltenham: Edward Elgar.

Hoxby, C.M. 1997, *How the Changing Market Structure of US Higher Education Explains College Tuition*. National Bureau of Economic Research, Working Paper 6323, December.

Huff, T.E. 1993, *The Rise of Early Modern Science. Islam, China, and the West*. Cambridge, MA: Cambridge University Press.

IAU 2005, *World Higher Education Database 2005/6*, London: Palgrave.

Idenburg, Ph.J. 1960, *Schets van het Nederlandse schoolwezen*. Groningen: J.B. Wolters.

James, E. 1990, Decision processes and priorities in higher education. In S.A. Hoenack and E.I. Collins (eds.) *The Economics of American Universities*. Buffalo, NY: State University of New York Press, 77–106.

James, E. and S. Rose-Ackerman (eds.) 1986, *The Nonprofit Enterprise in Market Economics*. New York: Harwood Academic Publishers.

James, R., G. Baldwin, and C. McInnis 1999, Which University: The factors influences the choices of prospective undergraduates. *Australian Department of Education, Training and Skills (DEST) Evaluation and Investigations Programme document 99/3*. http://www.dest.gov.au/archive/highered/eippubs/99–3/whichuni.pdf

Jaspers, K. 1961, *Die Idee der Universität*. Heidelberg: Springer Verlag.

Jencks, C. and D. Riesman 1969 (2nd edition), *The Academic Revolution*. New York: Doubleday Anchor Book.

Kaiser, R. 2003, Innovation policy in a multi-level governance system. The changing institutional environment for the establishment of science-based Industries. In J. Edler, S. Kuhlmann and M. Behrens (eds.) *Changing Governance of Research and Technology Policy. The European Research Area*. Cheltenham: Edward Elgar, 290–311.

Kaiser, R. and H. Prange 2005, Missing the Lisbon target? Multi-level innovation and EU policy coordination. *Journal of Public Policy*, 25(2): 241–263.

Kalleberg, R. 2000, Universities: complex bundle institutions and the projects of Enlightenment. *Comparative Social Research*, 19: 219–255.

Kallerud, E. 2006, *Akademisk frihet: en oversikt over spørsmål drøftet I internasjonal litteratur*. Oslo: NIFU-STEP arbeidsnotat nr. 18/2006.

Kaplan, N. 1964, Organization: will it choke or promote the growth of science? In K. Hill (ed.) *The Management of Scientists*. Boston, MA: Beacon Press, 103–127.

Kaplan, N. 1965, The Western European scientific establishment in transition. In N. Kaplan (ed.) *Science and Society*, 352–364. Reprinted from *The American Behavioral Scientist*, Chicago: Rand McNally. December 1962: 17–21.

Katzenstein, P.J. 2005, *A World of Regions. Asia and Europe in the American Imperium*. Ithaca: Cornell University Press.

Keller, G. 2001, Governance. The remarkable ambiguity. In P.G. Altbach, P.J. Gumport and D.B. Johnstone (eds.) *In Defense of American Higher Education*. Baltimore: Johns Hopkins Press, 304–322.

Keller, M. and P. Keller 2001, *Making Harvard Modern: The Rise of America's University*. New York: Oxford University Press.

Kelly, P.J. 2005, *As America Becomes More Diverse: The Impact of State Higher Education Inequality*. Boulder: NCHEMS. http://www.higheredinfo.org/raceethnicity/InequalityPaperNov2005.pdf

Kerr, C. 1966 [1964], *The Uses of the University*. New York: Harper Torchbooks.

Kerr, C. 1986, The employment of the university graduates in the United States: the Acropolis and the Agora. In L. Cerych, A. Bienaymé and G. Neave (eds.) *La Professionnalisation de l'Enseignement supérieur*. Paris/Amsterdam: Institut européen d'Education et de Politique sociale, Fondation européenne de la Culture.

Kerr, C. 1991, *The Great Transition in Higher Education, 1960–1980*. New York: SUNY Press.

Kerr, C. 1994, *Troubled Times for American Higher Education. The 1990s and beyond*. New York: SUNY Press.

Kerr, C. 2001, *The Gold and the Blue. A personal Memoir of the University of California 1949–1960*. Berkeley: California University Press.

Kerwer, D. 2005, Rules that many use: Standards and global regulation. *Governance*, 18(4): 611–632.

Kielmansegg, P.G. 1983, The university and democracy. In J.W. Chapman (ed.) *The Western University on Trial*. Berkeley: University of California Press, 46–52.

Kirp, D.L. 2003, *Shakespeare, Einstein and the Bottom Line. The Marketing of Higher Education*. Boston: Harvard University Press.

Knill, C. 2001, *The Europeanisation of National Administrations. Patterns of Institutional Change and Persistence*. Cambridge: Cambridge University Press.

Kogan, M. 2005, Modes of knowledge and patterns of power. *Higher Education*, 49: 9–30.

Kogan, M. 2005, The implementation game. In: Å. Gornitzka, M. Kogan and A. Amaral (eds.) *Reform and Change in Higher Education – Analysing Policy Implementation*. Dordrecht: Springer, 57–66.

Kogan, M. 2007, Modes of Knowledge and Patterns of Power. In S. Sörlin and H. Vessuri (eds.) *Knowledge Society vs. Knowledge Economy. Knowledge, Power, and Politics*. New York: Palgrave.

Kogan, M. 2006, Modes of Knowledge and Patterns of Power. In S. Sörlin and H. Vessuri (eds.) *Knowledge Economy vs. Knowledge Society, Knowledge, Power and Politics*. New York: Palgrave.

Kogan, M. and S. Hanney 2000, *Reforming Higher Education*. London: Jessica Kingsley Publishers.

Kogan, M., M. Henkel and S. Hanney (eds.) 2006, *Government and Research – Thirty Years of Evolution*. Dordrecht: Springer.

Kogan, M., M. Bauer, I. Bleiklie and M. Henkel (eds.) 2000, *Transforming Higher Education. A Comparative Study*. London: Jessica Kingsley.

Kohler-Koch, B. 2005, European governance and system integration. *European Governance Papers* (EUROGOV) No. C-05–01, http://www.connex-network.org/eurogov/pdf/egp-connex-C-05–01.pdf.

Kok, W. (chair) 2004a, *Facing the challenge – The Lisbon strategy for growth and employment*. Report from the High Level Group.

Kok, W. 2004b, Presentation made to the 8th conference of European Ministers of Education, held in Oslo, Norway, June 42 and 25, 2004.

Kuhlmann, S. and J. Edler 2003, Changing governance in European research and technology policy – possible trajectories and the European Research Area. In J. Edler, S. Kuhlmann and M. Behrens (eds.) *Changing Governance of Research and Technology Policy – The European Research Area*. Cheltenham, UK: Edward Elgar Publishing, 3–32.

Kyvik, S. 2004, Structural changes in higher education systems in western Europe. *Higher Education in Europe*, XXIX(3): 393–409.

Kyvik, S. and E. Ødegård 1990, *Universitetene I Norden foran 90-tallet – Endringer i styring og finansiering av forskning*. København: Nordisk ministerråds sekretariat NFR-publikasjon # 13.

Laffan, B. and C. Shaw 2005, *Classifying and Mapping OMC in Different Policy Areas*. NEWGOV reference number: 02/D09. http://www.eu-newgov.org/database/DELIV/D02D09_Classifying_and_Mapping_OMC.pdf.

Larsen, I.M., P. Maassen and B. Stensaker 2005, *Institutional governance in higher education. European trends and perspectives*. Paper presented at the annual EAIR Forum, Riga 28–31 August.

Lay, S. 2004, *The Interpretation of the Magna Charta Universitatum and its Principles*. Observatory for Fundamental University Values and Rights: Carmine A. Romanzi Award. Bologna: Bononia University Press.

Lepenies, W. 1998, *Melancholie und Gesellschaft*. Frankfurt am Main: Suhrkamp.

Lepenies, W. 1999, Alexander von Humboldt – His past and his present, Key-note speech, Jahrestagung der Alexander von Humboldt-Stiftung. 31 May 1999, Berlin.

Lepenies, W. 2006, *The Seduction of Culture*. Princeton: Princeton University Press.

Lepori, B., M. Benninghoff, B. Jongbloed, C. Salerno, and S. Slipersæter 2005, *Changing Pattern of Higher Education Funding: Evidence from CHINC Countries Intermediate report from the CHINC project*. Sevilla: Joint Research Centre Institute for Prospective Technological Studies (IPTS).

Levidov, L., V. Sørgaard and S. Carr 2002, Agricultural public-sector research establishments in Western Europe: research priorities in conflict. *Science and Public Policy*, 29(4): 267–296.

Liedman, S.-E. 1997, *I skuggan av framtiden. Modernitetens idéhistoria*. Stockholm: Bonniers Alba.

Liefner, I. 2003, Funding, resource allocation, and performance in higher education systems. *Higher Education*, 46: 469–489.

Lijphart, A. 1983, University "democracy" in the Netherlands. In J.W. Chapman (ed.) *The western university on trial*. Berkeley: University of California Press, 212–230.

Litt, T. 1955, *Das Bildungsideal der deutschen Klassik und die moderne Arbeitswelt*, Bonn.

Lobkowicz, N. 1983, Man, pursuit of truth, and the university. In J.W. Chapman (ed.) *The western university on trial*. Berkeley: University of California Press, 27–38.

Lundgreen, P. 1999, Mythos Humboldt in der Gegenwart: Lehre-Forschung-Selbstverwaltung. In M.G. Ash (ed.) *Mythos Humboldt: Vergangenheit und Zukunft der deutschen Universitäten*. Vienna: Böhlau verlag, 145–169.

Maassen, P. 1988, Zelfregulering als sturingsmechanisme voor het hoger onderwijs? In: R. Bijleveld and R. Florax (eds.) *Laissez faire in het hoger onderwijs?* Culemborg: LEMMA.

Maassen, P. 2003, Shifts in governance arrangements: An interpretation of the introduction of new management structures in higher education. In A. Amaral, L. Meek and I.M. Larsen (eds.) *The Higher Education Managerial Revolution?* Dordrecht: Kluwer Academic Publishers, 31–55.

Maassen, P. 2006, *The Modernisation of European Higher Education – A multi-level analysis*. Paper presented at the Directors General Meeting for Higher Education, Helsinki, 19–20 October 2006. (http://www.minedu.fi/OPM/Tapahtumakalenteri/2006/10/dg_higher_education.html?lang=en)

Maassen, P. and B. Stensaker 2003, Interpretations of self-regulation: the changing state – higher education relationship in Europe. In R. Begg (ed.) *The Dialogue Between Higher Education Research and Practice*. Dordrecht: Kluwer Academic Publishers, 85–95.

Maassen, P. and F. van Vught (eds.) 1989, *Dutch Higher Education in Transition. Policy Issues in Higher Education in the Netherlands*. Culemborg: LEMMA.

Maddox, J. 1964, Choice and the scientific community. *Minerva*, 2(2): 141–159.

Magna Charta Universitatum 1988, Bologna: Bologna University. (www.magna-charta.org/pdf/mc_pdf/mc_english.pdf).

Mann, T. 1918, *Betrachtungen eines Unpolitischen*, Berlin/Frankfurt am Main.

March, J.G. 1981, Footnotes to organizational change. *Administrative Science Quarterly*, 26: 563–577.

March, J.G. 1999a, A scholars quest. In J.G. March (ed.) *The Pursuit of Organizational Intelligence*. Oxford: Blackwell, 376–378.

March, J.G. 1999b, A learning perspective on the network dynamics of institutional integration. In M. Egeberg and P. Lægreid (eds.) *Organizing Political Institutions – Essays for Johan P. Olsen*. Oslo: Scandinavian University Press, 129–155.

March, J.G. and J.P. Olsen 1976, *Ambiguity and Choice in Organization*. Bergen: Universitetsforlaget.

March, J.G. and J.P. Olsen 1984, The new institutionalism: Organizational factors in political life. *American Political Science Review*, 78: 734–749.

March, J.G. and J.P. Olsen 1986, *Ambiguity and Choice in Organizations*. Oslo: Universitetsforlaget.

March, J.G. and J.P. Olsen 1989, *Rediscovering Institutions. The Organizational Basis of Politics*. New York: The Free Press.

March, J.G. and J.P. Olsen 1995, *Democratic Governance*. New York: Free Press.

March, J.G. and J.P. Olsen 2000, Democracy and schooling: An institutional perspective. In L.M. McDonnell, P.M. Timpane and R. Benjamin (eds.) *Rediscovering the Democratic Purposes of Education*. Lawrence: University Press of Kansas, 148–173.

March, J.G. and J.P. Olsen 2006a, The logic of appropriateness. In M. Rein, M. Moran and R.E. Goodin (eds.) *Handbook of Public Policy*. Oxford: Oxford University Press, 689–708.

March, J.G. and J.P. Olsen 2006b, Elaborating the "New Institutionalism". In R.A.W. Rhodes, S. Binder and B. Rockman (eds.) *The Oxford Handbook of Political Institutions*. Oxford: Oxford University Press, 3–20.

Marginson, S. 2004, Australian higher education: National and global markets. In P. Teixeira, B. Jong-bloed, D. Dill and A. Amaral (eds.) *Markets in Higher Education: rhetoric or reality?* Dordrecht: Kluwer Academic Publishers, 207–241.

Marginson S. and M. Considine 2000, *The Enterprise University: Governance and Reinvention in Australian Higher Education*. Melbourne: Cambridge University Press.

Marton, S. 2005, Implementing the Triple Helix: The Academic Response to Changing University-Industry-Government Relations in Sweden. In Å. Gornitzka, M. Kogan and A. Amaral (eds.) *Reform and Change in Higher Education. Analysing Policy Implementation*. Dordrecht: Springer: 325–342.

Massy, W.F. 1996, *Resource Allocation in Higher Education*. Ann Arbor: The University of Michigan Press.

Massy, W.F. and R. Zemsky 1994, Faculty discretionary time: Departments and the "academic ratchet." *Journal of Higher Education*, 65(1): 1–22.

Mathisen, W.C. 1994, *Universitetsforskeres problemvalg – akademisk autonomi og styring gjennom forskningsprogrammer*. Oslo, Utredningsinstituttet, Rapport 7/94.

Mathisen, W.C. 1996, Research priority areas and research programmes in Norway. *Science and Public Policy*, 4: 251–260.

McClelland, C. 1980, *State, Society, and University in Germany, 1700–1914*. Cambridge: Cambridge University Press.

McClellan III, J.E. 1985, *Science Reorganized: Scientific Societies in the Eighteenth Century*. New York: Columbia University Press.

McDonnell, L.M., P.M. Timpane and R. Benjamin (eds.) 2000, *Rediscovering the Democratic Purposes of Education*. Lawrence: University Press of Kansas.

McMurtry, J. 1991, Education and the market model. *Journal of Philosophy of Education*, 25(2): 209–217.

Meek, V.L. 2002, Changing patterns of coordination. In J. Enders and O. Fulton (eds.) *Higher Education in a Globalising World. – International Trends and Mutual Observations*. Dordrecht: Kluwer Academic Publishers, 53–71.

Meek, L. and F. Wood 1997, *Higher Education Governance and Management: An Australian Study*. Canberra: Australian Govt. Pub. Service.

Merton, R.K. 1937, Science and the social order. Paper read at the American Sociological Society Conference, December 1937. Reprinted in R.K. Merton 1968 (enlarged ed.), *Social Theory and Social Structure*. New York: The Free Press, 591–603.

Merton R.K. 1938/1970, *Science, Technology and Society in Seventeenth Century England*. New York: Howard Fertig Press.

Merton, R.K. 1942, Science and technology in a democratic order. *Journal of Legal and Political Sociology* 1: 115–126. Reprinted as "The normative structure of science". In R.K. Merton (edited and with an introduction by N.W. Storer) 1973, *The Sociology of Science. Theoretical and Empirical Investigations*. Chicago: The University of Chicago Press, 267–278.

Meyer, J.W. 2000, Globalization – Sources and effects on national states and societies. *International Sociology*, 15(2): 233–248.

Meyer, J.W., D.J. Frank, A. Hironaka, E. Shofer, and N.B. Tuma 1997, The structuring of a world environmental regime, 1870–1990. *International Organization*, 51(4): 623–651.

Middlehurst, R. 1993, *Leading Academics*. Buckingham: SRHE & Open University Press.

Mignot-Gerard, S. 2003, Who are the actors in the government of French universities? The paradoxal victory of deliberative leadership. *Higher Education*, (45)1: 71–89.

Mittelstrass, J. 1994, *Die unzeitgemässe Universität*. Frankfurt am Main: Suhrkamp.

Moen, K. 1998, *Fra monopol til konkurranse. EØS, norsk legemiddelpolitikk og Norsk Medisinaldepot*. Oslo: University of Oslo, ARENA Report No 1/98.

Mommsen, W.J. 1994, *Bürgerliche Kultur und künstlerische Avantgarde. Kultur und Politik im deutschen Kaiserreich 1870–1918.* Frankfurt am Main: Suhrkamp.

Moose, M. 1981, *The Post-Land Grant University: The University of Maryland Report.* Adelphi: University of Maryland.

Müller E.H. (ed.) 1990, *Gelegentliche Gedanken über Universitäten. Engel-Erhard-Wolf-Fichte-Schleiermacher-Savigny-v. Humboldt-Hegel.* Leipzig: Reclam.

Muller, S. 1999, Deutsche und amerikanische Universitäten im Zeitalter der Kalkulation. In M.G. Ash (ed) *Mythos Humboldt: Vergangenheit und Zukunft der deutschen Universitäten.* Vienna: Böhlau verlag, 198–200.

Muller, J., P. Maassen and N. Cloete 2006, Modes of governance and the limits of policy. In N. Cloete et al. (eds.) *Transformation in Higher Education: Global Pressures and Local Realities in South Africa.* Dordrecht: Springer, 289–310.

Neave, G. 1987, *La Communidad Europea y la Educacion.* Madrid: Fundación Universidad Empresa.

Neave, G. 2001, The European Dimension in higher education: an excursion into the modern use of Historical Analogues. In J. Huisman, P. Maassen and G. Neave (Eds.) *Higher Education and the Nation State. The International Dimension of Higher Education.*, Oxford: Elsevier Pergamon, 13–73.

Neave, G. 2003, The Bologna Declaration: Some historical dilemmas posed by reconstruction of the Community in Europe's systems of higher education. *Educational Policy*, 17(1): 141–164.

Neave, G. 2004a, Higher education policy as orthodoxy: Being a tale of doxological drift, political intention and changing circumstances. In P. Teixeira, B. Jongbloed, D. Dill and A. Amaral (eds.) *Markets in Higher Education: rhetoric or reality?* Dordrecht: Kluwer Academic Publishers, 127–160.

Neave, G. 2004b, The temple and its guardians: an excursion into the rhetoric of evaluating higher education. *The Journal of Finance and Management in Colleges and Universities*, 1(1): 212–227.

Neave, G. 2005, The Supermarketed University: Reform, Vision and Ambiguity in British Higher Education, *Perspectives: policy and practice in higher education*, vol. 9, No. 1, March: 17–22.

Neave, G. 2006a, *The Bologna Process or, Policy as the Artilleryman's Despair: An Unmoving Tale of Moving Targets.* Unpublished paper presented at Seminar "European Integration and Higher Education", 27/28 April 2006, University of Oslo.

Neave, G. 2006b, Social dimension och social sammanhallning i Bolognaprocessen: Eller, att forlika Adam Smith med Thomas Hobbes. In K. Blückert and E. Österberg (eds.) *Gränslöst i Sverige och i världen.* Stockholm: Natur och Kultur, 382–403.

Neave, G., K. Blückert, and T. Nybom (eds.) 2006, *The European Research University – An Historical Parenthesis?* New York: Palgrave MacMillan.

Nelson, R.R. 2005, Basic scientific research. In R.R. Nelson (ed.) *The Limits of Market Organization.* New York: Russell Sage Foundation, 233–258.

Nevins, A. 1962, *The State Universities and Democracy.* Urbana: University of Illinois Press.

Nielsen, L. 2002, Universitetets grundlov. Speech Københavns Universitets årsfest. 21 November 2002. *Politiken* 22 November 2002. http://politiken.dk/visartikel.asp?TemplateID=679&PageID=243902

Novotny, H., P. Scott and M. Gibbons 2001, *Re-Thinking Science. Knowledge and the Public in an Age of Uncertainty.* Cambridge: Polity Press.

Nuffic 2003, *Dutch national report on the implementation of the Socrates II Programme.* The Hague: Nuffic September 2003.

Nybom, T. 1997, *Kunskap Politik Samhälle. Essäer om kunskapssyn, universitet och forskningspolitikk 1900–2000.* Hargsham: Arete.

Nybom, T. 2001, Europa mellan själatåg och förnyelse, En humanistisk plaidoyer för kontinentens kulturella själ, *Tvärsnitt* 4.

Nybom, T. 2003, The Humboldt legacy: Reflections on the past, present, and future of the European university. *Higher Education Policy*, 16: 141–159.

Nybom, T. and B. Stenlund (eds.) 2004, *"Hinc robur et securitas". Stiftelsen Riksbankens jubileumsfond 1983–2003.* (Evaluation of *The Bank of Sweden Tercentenary Foundation*.). Hedemora: Gidlunds.

Nyborg, P. 2002, *Institutional autonomy. Relations between state authorities and higher education institutions.* Presentation given at the Sarajevo seminar 11–12. November, Sarajevo.

Oakshott, M. 1972, *Hobbes' The Leviathan.* New York: Collier.

Observatory for Fundamental University Values and Rights 2002, *Autonomy and Responsibility. The University's Obligations for the XXI Century.* Proceedings of the Launch Event for the Magna Charta Observatory 21–22 September 2001. Bologna: Bononia University Press.

OECD 1963, *Science, Economic Growth and Government Policy.* Paris: Organisation for Economic co-operation and development.

OECD 1965, *Ministers Talk about Science.* Paris: Organisation for Economic co-operation and development.

OECD 1968, *Problems of Science Policy.* Paris: Organisation for Economic co-operation and development.

OECD 1996, *The Knowledge-Based Economy.* OCDE(96)102. Paris: Organisation for Economic Co-operation and Development.

Olsen, H. 1998, *Europeisering av Universitetet: Fullt og helt eller stykkevis og delt.* Oslo: University of Oslo, ARENA rapport No 2/98.

Olsen, J.P. 1976a, University governance: Non-participation as exclusion or choice. In J.G. March and J.P. Olsen (eds.) *Ambiguity and Choice in Organization.* Bergen: Universitetsforlaget, 277–313.

Olsen, J.P. 1976b, Reorganization as a Garbage Can. In J.G. March and J.P. Olsen (eds.) *Ambiguity and Choice in Organizations.* Bergen: Universitetsforlaget, 314–337.

Olsen, J.P. 1988, Administrative reform and theories of organization. In C. Campbell and B.G. Peters (eds.) *Organizing Governance. Governing Organizations.* Pittsburgh: University of Pittsburgh Press, 233–254.

Olsen, J.P. 1997, Institutional design in democratic contexts. *The Journal of Political Philosophy,* 5: 203–229.

Olsen, J.P. 2000, *Organisering og styring av universiteter. En kommentar til Mjøsutvalgets reformforslag.* Oslo: ARENA Working Paper WP 00/20.

Olsen, J.P. 2001a, Garbage cans, New Institutionalism, and the study of politics. *American Political Science Review,* 95(1): 191–198.

Olsen, J.P. 2001b, Organizing European institutions of governance – A Prelude to an institutional account of political integration. In H. Wallace (ed.) *Interlocking Dimensions of European Integration.* Houndmills: Palgrave, 323–353.

Olsen, J.P. 2002, The many faces of Europeanization. *Journal of Common Market Studies,* 40(5): 921–952.

Olsen, J.P. 2004a, Unity, diversity and democratic institutions: Lessons from the European Union. *The Journal of Political Philosophy,* 12(4): 461–495.

Olsen, J.P. 2004b, *Innovasjon, politikk og institusjonell dynamikk.* Oslo: Arena Working Paper, no. 4, March 2004.

Olsen, J.P. 2006, Maybe it is time to rediscover bureaucracy. *Journal of Public Administration Research and Theory* 16: 1–24. Spanish version: Quizás sea el momento de redescubrir la burocracia. *Revista del CLAD, Reforma y Democracia* (Caracas) 31: 23–62, 2005.

Olsen, J.P. 2007, *Europe in Search of Political Order. An Institutional Perspective on Unity/Diversity, Citizen/their Helpers, Democratic Design/Historical Drift, and the Co-Existence of orders.* Oxford: Oxford University Press. (forthcoming).

Olsen, T. 1966, *Det bevisstløse universitet.* Oslo: Speech in Studentersamfunnet i Bergen 11 March 1966. [A revised version: Universitetets organisasjon og den nye utfordringen was printed in E. Bull et al. 1968: *Universitetet og samfunnet.* Oslo: Det Norske Samlaget, 25–48].

Oosterlinck, A. 2002, *Trade in educational services: A European university perspective.* Washington 23 May 2002 http://www.oecd.org/dataoecd/36/41/2750520.pdf.

Ormala, E. et al. 2004, *Five Year Assessment of the European Union Framework Programmes 1999–2003.* European Commission. http://ec.europe.eu/research/reports/2004/fya_en.html.

Orren, K. and S. Skowronek 2004, *The Search for American Political Development.* Cambridge: Cambridge University Press.

Paletschek, S. 2001, Verbreitete sich "ein Humboldtisches Modell" an den deutschen Universitäten im 19. Jahrhundert? In R.C. Schwinges (ed.) *Humboldt International. Der Export des deutschen Universitätsmodells im 19. und 20. Jahrhundert.* Basel: Schwabe, 75–114.

Pandor, N. 2004, We cannot stand by and watch institutions collapse. *Sunday Independent Dispatches* (Cape Town, South Africa) 24 October 2004.

Parsons, T. and G.M. Platt 1973, *The American University*. Cambridge: Harvard University Press.

Paulsen, F. 1902, *Die deutschen Universitäten und das Universitätsstudium*. Berlin: A. Asher & Co.

Pauly, M. and M. Redisch 1973, The not-for-profit hospital as a physicians' cooperative. *American Economic Review,* 63(1): 87–99.

Pedersen, M.N. 1982, Denmark: state and university – from coexistence to collision. In H. Daalder and E. Shils (eds.) *Universities, Politicians and Bureacrats. Europe and the United States.* Cambridge: Cambridge University Press, 233–274.

Perkins, J.A. 1966, *The University in Transition*. Princeton: Princeton University Press.

Perrow, C. 1984, *Complex Organizations. A Critical Essay*. New York: McGraw-Hill.

Peters, T.J. and R.H. Waterman Jr. 1982, *In Search of Excellence*. New York: Harper and Row.

Petit, I. 2002, *Politique européenne d'éducation et rhétorique économique. Un reflet des contraintes juridico-politique du cadre actionnel de la Commission européenne, Institut d'études européennes*, Montreal: Université de Montréal-McGill. Note de recherche no. 02/02

Pirrie, A, S. Hamilton, S. Kirk and J. Davidson 2003, *Interim Evaluation of the SOCRATES Programme in the UK*. SCRE centre: University of Glasgow/ DfES.

Plantan, F.jr. 2002, *Universities as Sites of Citizenship and Civic Responsibility*. Strasbourg: Council of Europe.

Pochet, P. 2005, The OMC and the Construction of Social Europe. In J. Zeitlin and P. Pochet and L. Magnusson (eds.) *The Open Method of Coordination – The European Employment and Social Inclusion Strategies*. Brussels: P.I.E.- Peter Lang, 37–82.

Polanyi, M. 1962, The republic of science: Its political and economic theory. *Minerva*, 1: 54–74.

Pollitt, C. 1990, *Managerialism and the Public Services: Cuts and Cultural Change in the 1990's*. Oxford: Basil Blackwell.

Potočnik, J. 2005, *Putting the Charter and Code into context: Keeping Europe competitive*. London 8–9 September 2005, Keynote speech UK Presidency Conference on the European Charter and Code for Researchers.

Potočnik, J. 2006a, *Embedding European science into European society*. Vienna, 20 January 2006, Austrian Academy of Sciences.

Potočnik, J. 2006b, *Back to Basics – Putting Excellence at the Heart of European Research*. London, 25 April 2006, London School of Economics & Political Science.

Pressman, J.L. and A. Wildavsky 1973, *Implementation*. Berkeley: University of California Press.

Radaelli, C.M. 2003, *The Open Method of Coordination: A new governance architecture for the European Union?* Stockholm: Sieps (Swedish Institute for European Studies) Report 2003:1.

Radaelli, C.M. 2004, Europeanisation: Solution or Problem? *European Integration online Papers*. 8(16). http://eiop.or.at/eiop/texte/2004–01a.htm.

RCN (Research Council of Norway) 2005, *Report on Science & Technology Indicators for Norway*. Oslo: The Research Council of Norway.

Reagan, M.D. 1969, *Science and the Federal Patron*. New York: Oxford University Press.

Reichert, S. and C. Tauch 2005, *Trends IV: European Universities Implementing Bologna*. Brussels: European University Association (EUA).

Rhoades, G. 1992, Governance: Models. In B. Clark and G. Neave (eds.) *The Encyclopedia of Higher Education*. Vol. 2. New York: Pergamon Press, 1376–1383.

Richardson, K. 2000, *Big Business and the European Agenda*. Sussex: Sussex European Institute Working Paper no.35.

Ridder-Symoens, H. de 1991, *A History of the University in Europe. Vol. 1 Universities in the Middle Ages*. Cambridge: Cambridge University Press.

Ridder-Symoens, H. de 2003, *A History of the University in Europe. Vol. 2 Universities in the Early Modern Europe (1500–1800)*. Cambridge: Cambridge University Press.

Ringer, F.K. 1969, *The Decline of the German Mandarins: The German Academic Community, 1890–1933*. Cambridge: Harvard University Press.

Ringer, F.K. 1978, *Education and Society in Modern Europe*. Bloomington: Indiana University Press.

Ringer, F.K. 1992, *Fields of Knowledge*. Cambridge: Cambridge University Press.

Rip, A. 1988, Contextual transformations in contemporary science. In A. Jamison (ed.) *Keeping Science Straight: A critical look at the Assessment of Science and Technology*. Gothenburg: University of Gothenburg. Department of Theory of Science.

Rip, A. 1993, The Republic of Science in the 1990s. In F.Q. Wood and V.L. Meek (eds.) *Research Grants Management and Funding*. Canberra: Proceedings of an International Symposium – Grant giving and Grant Management Procedures and Processes in Comparative Perspective, 25–26 July 1993, Australian Academy of Science.

Risse, T., M.G. Cowles and J. Caporaso 2001, Europeanization and domestic change: Introduction. In M.G. Cowles, J.A. Caporaso and T. Risse (eds.) *Transforming Europe: Europeanization and Domestic Change*. Ithaca, NY: Cornell University Press, 1–20.

Rodrigues, M.J. (ed.) 2002, *The New Knowledge Economy in Europe – A Strategy for International Competitiveness and Social Cohesion*. Cheltenham: Edward Elgar Publishing.

Roll-Hansen, N. 1985, Myten om elfenbenstårnet. *Nytt Norsk Tidsskrift*, 2(1): 31–46.

Rothblatt, S. (1968) 1981, *The Revolution of the Dons. Cambridge and Society in Victorian England*. Cambridge: Cambridge University Press.

Rothblatt, S. 1997, *The Modern University and its Discontents*. Cambridge: Cambridge University Press.

Rothblatt, S. 2006, *Education's Abiding Moral Dilemma: Merit and Worth in the Cross-Atlantic Democracies, 1800–2006*. Oxford: Symposium Books.

Rothschild, M. and L.J. White 1993, The University in the marketplace: Some insights and some puzzles. In C.T. Clotfelter and M. Rothschild (eds.) *Studies of Supply and Demand in Higher Education*. Chicago: University of Chicago Press.

Rüegg, W. (ed.) 2004, *A History of the University in Europe. Vol. 3 Universities in the Nineteenth and Early Twentieth Centuries (1800–1945)*. Cambridge: Cambridge University Press.

Runciman, G. 1966, *Relative Deprivation and social justice*. Berkeley: University of California Press.

Rupke, N. 2006, The many lives of Humboldt. *Humboldt-kosmos* 87 (25.10.2006). http://www.avh.de/kosmos/kultur/2006_002_en.htm#oben

Salerno, C.S. 2004, Rapid expansion and extensive deregulation: The Development of markets for higher education in the Netherlands. In A. Amaral, D. Dill, B. Jongbloed and P. Teixera (eds.) *Markets in Higher Education: Rhetoric or Reality?* Dordrecht: Kluwer Academic Publishers, 271–291.

Salerno, C.S. 2005, Funding higher education: The economics of options, tradeoffs and dilemmas. In L. Weber and S. Bergan (eds.) *The Public Responsibility for Higher Education and Research*. Strasbourg: Council of Europe Publishing.

Salmon, P. 1982, France: the *loi d'orientation* and its aftermath. In H. Daalder and E. Shils (eds.) *Universities, Politicians and Bureaucrats. Europe and the United States*. Cambridge: Cambridge University Press, 63–102.

Salter, B. and T. Tapper 2000, The Politics of governance in higher education: the case of quality assurance. *Political Studies*, 48: 66–87.

Saunders, M. and J. Machell 2000, Understanding emerging trends in higher education curricula and work connections. *Higher Education Policy*, 13(2000): 287–302.

Scharpf, F. 2001, *European Governance: Common Concerns vs. The Challenge of Diversity*. Working Paper 01/6. Cologne: Max Planck Institute for the Study of Societies.

Schelsky, H. 1963, *Einsamkeit und Freiheit. Idee und Gestalt der deutschen Universität und ihrer Reformer*. Reinbek. Düsseldorf: Bertelsmann.

Schelsky, H. 1969, Die Universitätsidee Wilhelm von Humboldts und die gegenwärtige Universitätsreform. *Abschied von der Hochschulpolitik. Oder: Die Universität im Fadenkreuz des Versagens*. Bielefeld: Bertelsmann.

Schelsky, H. 1971 (2nd ed.), *Einsamkeit und Freiheit. Idee und Gestalt der deutschen Universität und ihrer Reformen.* Düsseldorf: Bertelsmann Universitätsverlag.

Schleicher, A. 2006, The economics of knowledge: Why education is key for Europe's success. *Lisbon Council Policy Brief.* Brussels: The Lisbon Council asbl.

Schnabel, F. 1964, *Deutsche Geschichte im 19.* Jahrhundert. Vol. 2. Freiburg.

Schuster, J. 1989, Governance and the changing faculty condition. In J. Schuster and L. Miller (eds.) *Governing Tomorrow's Campus.* New York: MacMillan/American Council of Education.

Schwarz, S. and D.F. Westerheijden 2004, Accreditation in the framework of evaluation activities: A comparative study in the European Higher Education Area. In S. Schwarz and D.F. Westerheijden (eds.) *Accreditation and Evaluation in the European Higher Education Area.* Dordrecht: Kluwer Academic Publishers, 1–43.

Schwinges, R.C. (ed.) 2001, *Humboldt International. Der Export des deutschen Universitätsmodells im 19. und 20. Jahrhundert.* Basel: Schwabe.

Science 2004, Reinventing Europe's universities. *Science* vol. 304, 14 May 2004 www.sciencemag.org.

Scott, P. 2000, The Impact of the Research Assessment Exercise on the Quality of British Science and Scholarship. *Anglistik,* 1: 129–143.

Searle, J.R. 1972, *The Campus War.* Harmondsworth: Penguin.

Shaw, J. 1999, From Margins to Centre: Education and Training Law and Policy. In P. Craig and G. de Burca (eds.) *The Evolution of EU Law.* Oxford: Oxford University Press: 555–595.

Shils, E. 1997, *The Calling of Education. The Academic Ethic and Other Essays on Higher Education.* Chicago: University of Chicago Press.

Simon, H.A. 1964, On the concept of organizational goal. *Administrative Science Quarterly,* 9: 1–22.

Skoie, H. 2001, *The Research Councils in the Nordic Countries – Developments and Some Challenges.* Oslo: NIFU. Rapport 10/2001.

Slaughter, S. and L.L. Leslie 1997, *Academic Capitalism. Politics, Policies, and the Entrepreneurial University.* Baltimore: The Johns Hopkins University Press.

Slaughter, S. and G. Rhoades 2004, *Academic Capitalism and the New Economy.* Baltimore: Johns Hopkins University Press.

Sloan, D. 1971, *The Scottish Enlightenment and the American College Ideal.* New York: Teachers College Press.

Smeby, J.-C. and Å. Gornitzka 2005, Internasjonalt forskningssamarbeid – globalisering eller europeisering? In M. Gulbrandsen and J.-C. Smeby (eds.) *Forskning ved universitetene. Rammebetingelser, relevans og resultater.* Oslo: Cappelen Akademisk Forlag, 181–197.

Smeby J.-C. and J. Trondal 2005, Globalisation or europeanisation? International contact among university staff. *Higher Education,* 49(4): 449–466.

Soete, L. 2005, *Activating knowledge.* Discussion paper prepared for the UK Presidency October 2005. http://www.fco.gov.uk/Files/kfile/Soete-final.pdf.

Solingen, E. 1994, Domestic structures and the international context: Towards models of the state-scientists interaction. In E. Solingen (ed.) *Scientists and the State – Domestic Structures and the International Context.* Ann Arbor: University of Michigan Press.

Sörlin, S. 1994, *De Lärdas Republik. Om vetenskapens internationella tendenser.* Malmö: Liber Hermods.

Spencer, D. and A. Stevens 2006, Staff and personnel policy in the Commission. In D. Spencer (ed.) with G. Edwards. *The European CommissionCommission.* London: John Harper Publishing, 173–208.

Spranger, E., (ed.) 1910, *Fichte, Schleiermacher, Steffens: über die idee der Universität.* Leipzig: Felix Meiner.

Steinberg, H. 2001, *Wilhelm von Humboldt.* Berlin: Stapp Verlag.

Strang, D. and M.W. Macy 2001, In search of excellence: Fads, success stories, and adaptive emulation. *American Journal of Sociology,* 107(1): 147–182.

Strang, D. and J.W. Meyer 1993, Institutional conditions for diffusion. *Theory and Society* 22: 487–511.

Stephan, P.E. and S.G. Levin 1992, *Striking the Mother Lode in Science: The Importance of Age, Place, and Time.* Oxford: Oxford University Press.

Steunenberg, B. 2002, *Deciding among equals: The sectoral Councils of the European Union and their reform*. Manuscript dated 14 november 2002. Paper prepared for the Conference on European Governance, 10–12 October 2002, Saarbrücken, Germany.

Stone S.A., N. Fliegstein and W. Sandholtz 2001, The institutionalization of European Space. In A.S. Sweet, W. Sandholtz, and N. Fligstein (eds.) *The Institutionalization of Europe*. Oxford: Oxford University Press, 1–28.

Ståhle, B. 1993, *Forskningspolitik i Norden 1992: om forskningsinsatser, prioriteringar och forskningspolitiska huvudlinjer i de nordiska länderna*. NORD 1992:23 København: Nordisk Ministerråd.

Suleiman, E. 2003, *Dismantling Democratic States*. Princeton: Princeton University Press.

Sverdrup, U. 2006, Administering information: Eurostat and statistical integration. In M. Egeberg (ed.) *Multilevel Union Administration. The Transformation of Executive Politics in Europe*. Houndmills: Palgrave Macmillan, 103–123.

Swaan, A. de 1988, *In Care of the State*. Cambridge: Polity Press.

Sykes, C.J. 1989, *Profscam: Professors and the Demise of Higher Education*. New York: St. Martin's Griffin.

Tabatoni, P., J. Davies and A. Barblan 2002, *Strategic Management and Universities' Institutional Development*. Brussels: European University Association.

Teichler, U. 1998, Higher education and changing job requirements: A comparative view. In M. Henkel and B. Little (eds.) *Changing Relationships between Higher Education and the State*. London: Jessica Kingsley, 69–89.

Teichler, U. 2000, The Relationships between higher education research and higher education policy and practice: The researchers' perspective. In U. Teichler and J. Sadlak (eds.) *Higher Education Research. Its Relationship to Policy and Practice*. Oxford: Pergamon, 3–37.

Teixeira, P., B. Jongbloed, D. Dill and A. Amaral (eds.) 2004, *Markets in Higher Education. Rhetoric or Reality?* Dordrecht: Kluwer Academic Publishers.

The National Academy of Sciences 1965, *Basic Research and National Goals*. Washington DC: A Report to the Committee on Science and Astronautics, US House of Representatives.

Tight, M. 1988, *Academic Freedom and Responsibility*. Philadelphia: Open University Press.

Tight, M. 1992, Institutional autonomy. In B. Clark and G. Neave (eds.) *The Encyclopedia of Higher Education*. Vol. 2. New York: Pergamon Press.

Tomusk, V. (ed.) 2006, *Creating the European Area of Higher Education. Voices from the Periphery*. Dordrecht: Springer.

Treue, W. and Gründer, K. (eds) 1987, *Wissenschaftspolitik in Berlin, Minister-Beamte-Ratgeber,* Berlin: Collogium-Verlag.

Trow, M. 1974, Problems in the Transformation from elite to mass Higher Education: Policies for Higher Education. *General Report to the Conference on the future structure of post-secondary education*. Paris : OECD.

Trow, M. 1991, The exceptionalism of American higher education. In M. Trow and T. Nybom (eds.) *University and Society. Essays on the Social Role of Research and Higher Education*. London: Jessica Kingsley Press, 156–172.

Trow, M. 2003, In praise of weakness: Chartering, the university of the United States, and Dartmouth College. *Higher Education Policy*, 16(1): 9–16.

Ugland, T. 2002, *Policy re-categorization and Integration. Europeanization of Nordic Alcohol Control Policies*. Oslo: University of Oslo, ARENA Report No. 3/2002.

Ugland, T. and F. Veggeland 2006, Experiments in food safety policy integration in the European Union. *Journal of Common Market Studies*, 44(3): 607–624.

Vabø, A. and J-C. Smeby 2003, *Norwegian report on the implementation of the second phase of the Socrates programme*. Oslo: NIFU.

Valen-Sendstad, F. 1959, Forhistorien til "Den høiere Landbrugsskole paa Aas": det faglige opplysningsarbeid i norsk landbruk før 1859. In: Norges landbrukshøgskole: *Norges landbrukshøgskole 1859–1959*. Oslo: Grøndal & Søns boktrykkeri.

Veblen, T. 1957 [1918], *The Higher Learning in America*. New York: Hill and Wang.

Veld, R. in 't, H-P. Füssel and G. Neave 1996, *Relations between the State and Higher Education*. Dordrecht: Kluwer Academic Publishers.

Verger, J. 1986, *Histoire des Universités en France*. Toulouse: Privat.

Veysey, L.R. 1970 [1965], *The Emergence of the American University*. Chicago: The University of Chicago Press, Phoenix edition.

Vierhaus, R. 2004, Wilhelm von Humboldt. In W. Treue and K. Gründer (eds.) *Berlinische Lebensbilder. Wissenschaftspolitik in Berlin. Minister, Beamte, Ratgeber.* Berlin: Colloquium Verlag.

Vierhaus, R. and B. von Brocke (eds.) 1990, *Forschung im Spannungsfelt von Politik und Gesellschaft. Geschichte der Kaiser-Wilhelm/Max-Planck-Gesellschaft*. Stuttgart: Deutsche Verlags-Anstalt.

Vijlder, F. de 1996, *Natiestaat en onderwijs. Een essay over de erosie van de relatie tussen westerse natiestaten en hun onderwijssystemen's*. Gravenhage: VUGA Uitgeverij.

von Brocke, B. 1988, Von der Wissenschaftsverwaltung zur Wissenschaftspolitik. Friedrich Althoff (19.2.1839–20.10.1908). *Berichte zur Wissenschaftsgeschichte*, 11: 1–26.

von Bruch, R. 1999, Langsamer Abschied von Humboldt? Etappen deutscher Universitätsgeschichte 1810–1945. In M.G Ash (ed.) *Mythos Humboldt: Vergangenheit und Zukunft der deutschen Universitäten*. Vienna: Böhlau verlag.

Vossensteyn, J.J. 2003, *Fiscal Stress: worldwide trends in higher education finance and in policy responses to the condition of higher education austerity*. Presentation to the Conference 'University Reform and Accessibility in Higher Education, Prague, June 15 – 17th 2003, (mimeo).

Vossensteyn, J.J. 2004, *Portability of student financial support – an inventory in 24 European countries*. Beleidsgerichte studies hoger onderwijs en wetenschappelijk onderzoek. The Hague: Ministry of Education and Science.

Vught, F.A. van (ed.) 1989, *Governmental Strategies and Innovation in Higher Education*. London: Jessica Kingsley Press.

Walther, H.G. 2001, Reform vor der Reform. Die Erfahrungen von Humboldts in Jena 1794 bis 1797. In R.C. Schwinges (ed.) *Humboldt International. Der Export des deutschen Universitätsmodells im 19. und 20. Jahrhundert*. Basel: Schwabe.

Weber, M. 1970, Science as a vocation. In H.H. Gerth and C.W. Mills (eds) *From Max Weber*: 129–156. London: Routledge & Kegan Paul. [speech at Munich University, published in 1919 by Duncker & Humbolt, Munich.]

Weber, M. 1978, *Economy and Society*. Berkeley: University of California Press.

Wehler, H.U. 1987, *Deutsche Gesellschaftsgeschichte. Vol.1: 1700–1815*. München: C.H. Beck, 405–485.

Weick, K.F. 1976, Educational organizations as loosely coupled systems. *Administrative Science Quarterly*, 21: 1–19.

Weisz, G. 1983, *The emergence of modern universities in France, 1863–1914*. Princeton: Princeton University Press.

Wende, M. van der 2003, Bologna is not the only city that matters in European higher education policy. *International Higher Education* 32.

Westerheijden, D.F., L. Goedegebuure, J. Huisman and B. Jongbloed 2006, A tale of three cities: Highlights and problems of Centralia, Octavia and Vitis Vinifera. In J. Enders, J. File, J. Huisman and D. Westerheijden (eds.) *The European Higher Education and Research Landscape 2020. Scenarios and Strategic Debates*. Enschede: Center for Higher Education Policy Studies, 95–101.

Winston, G.C. 1997, Why Can't a College be More Like a Firm? *Discussion Paper* 42. Williams Project on the Economics of Higher Education. http://www.williams.edu/wpehe/DPs/DP-42.pdf

Winston, G.C. 1999, Subsidies, hierarchy and peers: The awkward economics of higher education. *Journal of Economic Perspectives*, 13: 13–36.

Wit, K. de and J. Verhoeven 2001, The higher education policy of the European Union: With or against the member States? In J. Huisman, P. Maassen and G. Neave (eds.) *Higher Education and the Nation State. The International Dimension of Higher Education*. Oxford: Elsevier Pergamon, 175–232.

Witte, J.K. 2006, *Change of Degrees and Degrees of Change: Comparing Adaptations of European Higher Education Systems in the Context of the Bologna Process*. Enschede: University of Twente, Center for Higher Education Policy Studies.

Wittrock, B. 1993, The Modern University: Its three transformations. In S. Rothblatt and B. Wittrock (eds.) *The European and American University since 1800*. Cambridge: Cambridge University Press, 303–362.

Wittrock, B. 2004, Transformations of European universities: Recent literature on universities, disciplines, and professions in England, Germany, and Russia since 1870. *Contemporary European History*, 13(1): 101–116.

Wittrock, B. and P. deLeon 1986, Policy as a Moving target: A call for conceptual realism. *Policy Studies Review*, 6(1): 44–60.

Wolff, R.P. 1969, *The Ideal of the University*. Boston: Beacon Press.

Zängle, M. 2004, The European Union benchmarking experience, From euphoria to fatigue? *European Integration online Papers (EIoP)* Vol. 8 (2004) No 5. hhtp://eiop.or.at/eiop/texte/2004-005a.htm.

Zaunick, R. 1958, *Alexander von Humboldt, Kosmische Naturbetrachtung. Sein Werk im Grundriss*. Stuttgart: Alfred Kröner Verlag.

Zemsky, R., G.R. Wegner, and W.F. Massy 2005, *Remaking the American University: Market-Smart and Mission-Centered*. New Brunswick: Rutgers University Press.

INDEX

HIGHER EDUCATION DYNAMICS

1. J. Enders and O. Fulton (eds.): *Higher Education in a Globalising World.* 2002
   ISBN Hb 1-4020-0863-5; Pb 1-4020-0864-3
2. A. Amaral, G.A. Jones and B. Karseth (eds.): *Governing Higher Education: National Perspectives on Institutional Governance.* 2002
   ISBN 1-4020-1078-8
3. A. Amaral, V.L. Meek and I.M. Larsen (eds.): *The Higher Education Managerial Revolution?* 2003
   ISBN Hb 1-4020-1575-5; Pb 1-4020-1586-0
4. C.W. Barrow, S. Didou-Aupetit and J. Mallea: *Globalisation, Trade Liberalisation, and Higher Education in North America.* 2003
   ISBN 1-4020-1791-X
5. S. Schwarz and D.F. Westerheijden (eds.): *Accreditation and Evaluation in the European Higher Education Area.* 2004
   ISBN 1-4020-2796-6
6. P. Teixeira, B. Jongbloed, D. Dill and A. Amaral (eds.): *Markets in Higher Education: Rhetoric or Reality?* 2004
   ISBN 1-4020-2815-6
7. A. Welch (ed.): *The Professoriate. Profile of a Profession.* 2005
   ISBN 1-4020-3382-6
8. Å. Gornitzka, M. Kogan and A. Amaral (eds.): *Reform and Change in Higher Education. Implementation Policy Analysis.* 2005
   ISBN 1-4020-3402-4
9. I. Bleiklie and M. Henkel (eds.): *Governing Knowledge.* A Study of Continuity and Change in Higher Education – A Festschrift in Honour of Maurice Kogan. 2005
   ISBN 1-4020-3489-X
10. N. Cloete, P. Maassen, R. Fehnel, T. Moja, T. Gibbon and H. Perold (eds.): *Transformation in Higher Educatin.* Global Pressures and Local Realities. 2005
    ISBN 1-4020-4005-9
11. M. Kogan, M. Henkel and S, Hanney: *Government and Research.* Thirty Years of Evolution. 2006
    ISBN 1-4020-4444-5
12. V. Tomusk (ed.): *Creating the European Area of Higher Education.* Voices from the Periphery. 2006
    ISBN 1-4020-4613-8
13. M. Kogan, M. Bauer, I. Bleiklie and M. Henkel (eds.): *Transforming Higher Education.* A Comparative Study. 2006
    ISBN 1-4020-4656-1
14. P.N. Teixeira, D.B. Johnstone, M.J. Rosa and J.J. Vossensteijn (eds.): *Cost-sharing and Accessibility in Higher Education: A Fairer Deal?* 2006
    ISBN 1-4020-4659-6
15. H. Schomburg and U. Teichler: *Higher Education and Graduate Employment in Europe.* Results from Graduates Surveys from Twelve Countries. 2006
    ISBN 1-4020-5153-0
16. S. Parry: *Disciplines and Doctorates.* 2007
    ISBN 1-4020-5311-8
17. U. Teichler (ed.): *Careers of University Graduates.* Views and Experiences in Comparative Perspectives. 2007
    ISBN 1-4020-5925-6
18. M. Herbst: *Financing Public Universities.* The Case of Performance Funding. 2007
    ISBN 978-1-4020-5559-1
19. P. Maassen and Johan P. Olsen: *University Dynamics and European Integration.* 2007
    ISBN 978-1-4020-5970-4

Printed in the United Kingdom
by Lightning Source UK Ltd.
120950UK00008B/1